New ENTERPRISE

Teacher's Book

Jenny Dooley

Express Publishing

Published by Express Publishing

Liberty House, Greenham Business Park, Newbury,
Berkshire RG19 6HW, United Kingdom
Tel.: (0044) 1635 817 363
Fax: (0044) 1635 817 463
email: inquiries@expresspublishing.co.uk
www.expresspublishing.co.uk

First published 2020

Made in EU

ISBN978-4-7647-4138-6

Contents

Introduction to the Teacher

New Enterprise B1+ is a modular course for young adults and adults studying British English at CEFR Level B2. It allows flexibility of approach, which makes it suitable for classes of all kinds, including large or mixed ability classes.

New Enterprise B1+ consists of twelve units. Each unit consists of three lessons plus Culture sections, Reviews & Competences. The corresponding unit in the Workbook provides the option of additional practice.

COURSE COMPONENTS

Student's Book

The **Student's Book** is the main component of the course. Each unit is based on specific themes and the topics covered are of general interest. All units follow the same basic structure (see **Elements of the Coursebook**).

Workbook

The **Workbook** is in full colour and contains units corresponding to those in the Student's Book, with practice in Vocabulary, Grammar, Everyday English & Reading. There is a Revision Section every three units for students to revise the vocabulary and grammar taught. There is also a Skills Practice section for students to get more practice in Listening, Everyday English, Reading and Writing. All the exercises in the Workbook are marked with graded level of difficulty (*, **, ***).

Teacher's Book

The **Teacher's Book** contains step-by-step lesson plans and suggestions on how to present the material. It also includes answers to the exercises in the Student's Book, the audioscripts of all the listening material, suggested speaking and writing models, and evaluation sheets as well as the answers to the exercises in the Workbook and Grammar Book.

Class Audio CDs

The **Class Audio CDs** contain all the recorded material which accompanies the course. This includes the monologues/dialogues and texts in the Listening and Reading sections, Values, Presentation Skills, Public Speaking Skills & CLIL sections as well as the Pronunciation/Intonation sections in the Student's Book, and the material for all listening tasks in the Workbook.

IWB

The **IWB** contains all the material in the Student's Book, Teacher's Book, Workbook, Grammar Book and Audio CDs and aims to facilitate lessons in the classroom. It also contains grammar presentations of all the grammar structures in the Student's Book as well as **videos** closely linked to the texts in the course and activities for Ss to further practise their English and expand their knowledge, as well as **games** for students to revise the vocabulary and grammar taught.

Digibook applications

The **Digi apps** contain all the material in the Student's Book, Workbook and Grammar Book and help students monitor their progress and improve their stats which are stored so that they can be accessed at any time.

Grammar Book

The **Grammar Book** contains clear presentations of all grammar structures that appear in the course with a variety of graded exercises.

ELEMENTS OF THE COURSEBOOK

Each unit begins with a brief overview of what will be covered in the unit.

Each unit contains the following sections:

Vocabulary

Vocabulary is introduced in a functional and meaningful context. It is practised through a variety of exercises, such as picture-word association and completing set phrases in order to help students use everyday English correctly.

Reading

Each unit contains reading texts, such as: articles, blog entries, articles, emails, tweets, forum entries, adverts, etc. These allow skills, such as reading for gist, for specific information, for cohesion & coherence etc to be systematically practised.

Grammar

The grammar items taught in each unit are first presented in context, then highlighted and clarified by means of clear, concise theory boxes. Specific exercises and activities methodically reinforce learners' understanding and mastery of each item. Detailed explanations of all grammar points and exercises are in the Grammar Reference. The Workbook contains practice on each grammar structure presented within each unit.

Listening

Learners develop their listening skills through a variety of tasks which employ the vocabulary and grammar practised in the unit in realistic contexts. This reinforces learners' understanding of the language taught in the unit.

Speaking

Controlled speaking activities have been carefully designed to allow learners' guided practice before leading them to less structured speaking activities.

Everyday English

Functional dialogues set in everyday contexts familiarise students with natural language. The dialogues are followed by language boxes to help learners practise.

Pronunciation/Intonation

Pronunciation/Intonation activities help learners to recognise the various sounds of the English language, distinguish between them and reproduce them correctly.

Writing

There are writing activities throughout the units, based on realistic types and styles of writing, such as emails, letters, blogs, online forms, reviews, stories, articles, essays, news reports, etc. These progress from short paragraphs to full texts, allowing learners to gradually build up their writing skills.

Culture

Each unit is accompanied by a *Culture* section.

In each *Culture* section, learners are provided with cultural information about aspects of English-speaking countries that are thematically linked to the unit. Learners are given the chance to process the information they have learnt and compare it to the culture of their own country.

Study Skills/Writing Tips

Brief tips, explanations and reminders at various points throughout each unit help learners to develop strategies which improve holistic learning skills and enable them to become autonomous learners of the English language.

Review

This section appears at the end of each unit, and reinforces students' understanding of the topics, vocabulary and structures that have been presented in the unit. A Competences marking scheme at the end of every *Review* section allows learners to evaluate their own progress and identify their strengths and weaknesses.

Values

This section aims to develop moral values learners need to have in our globalised world.

Public Speaking Skills

This section aims to help learners develop their public speaking skills, giving them guidance on how to become competent public speakers.

CLIL

The *CLIL* sections enable learners to link the themes of the units to an academic subject, thus helping them contextualise the language they have learnt by relating it to their own personal frame of reference. Lively and creative tasks stimulate learners and allow them to consolidate the language they have learnt throughout the units.

Each *CLIL* section is aimed to be taught after the corresponding *Values & Public Speaking Skills* sections.

Irregular Verbs

This provides students with a quick reference list for verb forms they might be unsure of at times.

SUGGESTED TEACHING TECHNIQUES

A Presenting new vocabulary

The new vocabulary in *New Enterprise B1* is frequently presented through pictures. *(See Student's Book, Unit 1, p. 4, Ex. 1.)*

Further techniques that you may use to introduce new vocabulary include:

- **Miming.** Mime the word you want to introduce. For instance, to present the verb sing, pretend you are singing and ask learners to guess the meaning of the word.
- **Synonyms, antonyms, paraphrasing and giving definitions.** Examples:
  - present the word **strong** by giving a synonym: 'powerful'.
  - present the word **strong** by giving its opposite: 'weak'.
  - present the word **weekend** by paraphrasing it: 'Saturday and Sunday'.
  - present the word **famous** by giving its definition: 'very well-known (person or thing)'.
- **Example.** Use of examples places vocabulary into context and consequently makes understanding easier. For instance, introduce the words **city** and **town** by referring to a city and a town in the learners' country: 'Rome is a city, but Parma is a town.'
- **Sketching.** Draw a simple sketch of the word or words you want to explain on the board. For instance:

- **Use of L1.** In a monolingual class, you may explain vocabulary in the learners' native language. This method, though, should be employed in moderation.
- **Use of a dictionary.** In a multilingual class, learners may refer to a bilingual dictionary.

The choice of technique depends on the type of word or expression. For example, you may find it easier to describe an action verb through miming than through a synonym or a definition.

> **Note:** ✓ ***Check these words*** sections can be treated as follows: Go through the list of words after Ss have read the text and ask Ss to explain the words using the context they appear in. Ss can give examples, mime/draw the meaning, or look up the meaning in their dictionaries.

B Choral & individual repetition

Repetition will ensure that learners are thoroughly familiar with the sound and pronunciation of the lexical items and structures being taught and confident in their ability to reproduce them.

Always ask learners to repeat chorally before you ask them to repeat individually. Repeating chorally will help learners feel confident enough to then perform the task on their own.

C Reading & Listening

You may ask learners to read and listen for a variety of purposes:

- **Reading for detail.** Ask learners to read for specific information. *(See Student's Book, Unit 1, p. 4, Ex. 3. Ss will have to read the text in order to do the task. They are looking for specific details in the text and not for general information.)*
- **Listening for detail.** Learners listen for specific information. *(See Student's Book, Unit 1, p. 8, Ex. 2.)*
- **Listening and reading for gist.** Ask learners to read and/or listen to get the gist of the dialogue or text being dealt with. *(See Student's Book, Unit 1, p. 8, Ex. 3a. Tell Ss that in order to complete this task successfully, they do not need to understand every single detail in the text.)*

> **Note:** VIDEO
> Main texts in the Student's Book are accompanied by videos that are included in the digi applications and the IWB. The videos can be watched after learners have read the texts. Activities that accompany the videos can be done in class or assigned as HW.

D Speaking

- Speaking activities are initially controlled, allowing for guided practice in language/structures that have just been learnt. *(See Student's Book, Unit 2, p. 16, Ex. 1a.)*.
- Ss are led to free speaking activities. *(See Student's Book, Unit 1, p. 8, Ex. 4, where Ss are provided with the necessary lexical items and structures and are asked to act out their dialogues.)*

E Writing

All writing tasks in *New Enterprise B1+* have been carefully designed to closely guide learners to produce a successful piece of writing. They are fully analysed in the *Skills in Action* sections in the Student's Book with model texts and exercises that aim to help learners improve their writing skills.

- Make sure that Ss understand that they are writing for a purpose. Go through the writing task so that Ss are fully aware of why they are writing and who they are writing for. *(See Student's Book, Unit 2, p. 17, Ex. 9. Ss are asked to write a story.)*
- It would be well advised to actually complete the task orally in class before assigning it as written homework. Ss will then feel more confident with producing a complete piece of writing on their own.

F Assigning homework

When assigning homework, prepare learners as well as possible in advance. This will help them avoid errors and get maximum benefit from the task.

Commonly assigned tasks include:

Dictation – learners learn the spelling of particular words without memorising the text in which they appear;

Vocabulary – learners memorise the meaning of words and phrases or use the new words in sentences of their own;

Reading Aloud – assisted by the digi apps, learners practise at home in preparation for reading aloud in class;

Writing – after thorough preparation in class, learners are asked to produce a complete piece of writing.

G Correcting learners' work

All learners make errors – it is part of the learning process. The way you deal with errors depends on what the learners are doing.

- **Oral accuracy work:**
  Correct learners on the spot, either by providing the correct answer and allowing them to repeat, or by indicating the error but allowing learners to correct it. Alternatively, indicate the error and ask other Ss to provide the answer.
- **Oral fluency work:**
  Allow learners to finish the task without interrupting, but make a note of the errors made and correct them afterwards.

- **Written work:**
  Do not over-correct; focus on errors that are directly relevant to the point of the exercise. When giving feedback, you may write the most common errors on the board and get the class to attempt to correct them.

Remember that rewarding work and praising learners is of great importance. Praise effort as well as success.

H Class organisation

- **Open pairs**
  The class focuses its attention on two learners doing the set task together. Use this technique when you want your learners to offer an example of how a task is done. *(See Student's Book, Unit 3, p. 22, Ex. 4.)*
- **Closed pairs**
  Pairs of learners work together on a task or activity while you move around offering assistance and suggestions. Explain the task clearly before beginning closed pairwork. *(See Student's Book, Unit 1, p. 8, Ex. 4.)*
- **Stages of pairwork**
  - Put Ss in pairs.
  - Explain the task and set a time limit.
  - Rehearse the task in open pairs.
  - In closed pairs, get Ss to do the task.
  - Go around the class and help Ss.
  - Open pairs report back to the class.
- **Group work**
  Groups of three or more Ss work together on a task or activity. Class projects or role-play are most easily done in groups. Again, give Ss a solid understanding of the task in advance.
- **Rolling questions**
  Ask Ss one after the other to ask and answer questions based on the texts.

I Using L1 in class

Use L1 in moderation and only when necessary.

ABBREVIATIONS

Abbreviations used in the Student's and Teacher's Books.

T	teacher	p(p).	page(s)
S(s)	student(s)	e.g.	for example
HW	homework	i.e.	that is
L1	students' native language	etc	et cetera
		sb	somebody
Ex(s).	exercise(s)	sth	something

Key to symbols used in the Student's/Teacher's Books

 audio

 pairwork

 groupwork

 videos related to the themes of the texts

 words to be explained using the context each appears in

ICT tasks to help learners develop research skills

Study Skills suggestions to help learners become autonomous

Writing Tip suggestions to help learners develop their writing skills

THINK sections to develop Ss' critical thinking skills

Culture texts to familiarise Ss with the culture of English-speaking countries and develop cross-cultural awareness

VALUES sections to help Ss develop critical thinking skills and values

CLIL sections that link the themes of the units to a subject from the core curriculum

On the map

Topic	
In this unit, Ss will explore the topics of geographical features, map symbols and road signs.	
1a Reading & Vocabulary	**4-5**
Lesson objectives: To introduce vocabulary for map symbols, to scan a text, to read for key information (multiple choice), to learn collocations relating to hiking and map reading, to learn prepositional phrases, to practise words easily confused, to learn phrasal verbs with *dry*, to talk about a hiking trail, to prepare and present a podcast about a hiking trail **Vocabulary:** Map symbols (*mountain, peak, hills, lake or pond, river or stream, canal, bridge, forest or woods, footpath or hiking trail, railway line with station, main road, youth or other hostel, campsite)*; Nouns *(mountain range, majority, equivalent, moose, encounter, sunbeam, route, record, exhaustion, achievement)*; Verbs *(complete, soar, capture)*; Phrasal verbs *(catch on)*; Adjectives *(humid, entire, worn-out, troublesome, spectacular, epic)*; Adverbs *(roughly, mainly)*, Phrase *(on average)*	
1b Grammar in Use	**6-7**
Lesson objectives: To revise/learn the present simple, the present continuous and stative verbs, to revise/practise adverbs of frequency, to revise/learn the present perfect and the present perfect continuous, to talk about a hike, to write a message	
1c Skills in Action	**8-9**
Lesson objectives: To learn vocabulary for road signs, to listen for specific information (T/F statements), to read for specific information, to listen and read for lexical cohesion (open cloze), to act out a dialogue and practise everyday English for asking for and giving directions, to practise discourse markers, to read for lexical cohesion (word formation), to write a flyer, to discuss the value of direction **Vocabulary:** Road signs *(30-mph speed limit, stop and give way, crossroads, junction, pedestrian crossing, traffic lights, cycle lane, roundabout, dead end)*	
Culture 1	**10**
Lesson objectives: To listen and read for key information, to read for specific information (multiple matching), to talk about tours and express preference, to write a section for a webpage **Vocabulary:** Nouns *(crawl, kingfisher, route, outing, commentary, cityscape)*; Verb *(splash)*; Adjectives *(gentle, splendid, choosy, thrilling, amphibious)*; Adverb *(steadily)*; Phrase *(on board)*	
Review 1	**11**
Lesson objectives: To test/consolidate vocabulary and grammar learnt throughout the unit; to practise everyday English	

Go through the objectives box and tell Ss that these are the topics, skills and activities this unit will cover.

1a

Vocabulary

1 **Aim To present vocabulary related to map symbols**

- Ask Ss to read the words in the list.
- Explain/Elicit the meanings of any unknown words and then ask Ss to do the task in closed pairs.
- Monitor the activity around the class and then ask some Ss to share their answers with the rest of the class.

Answer Key

1	*peak*	*5*	*canal*	*9*	*station*
2	*hills*	*6*	*bridge*	*10*	*main*
3	*pond*	*7*	*woods*	*11*	*hostel*
4	*stream*	*8*	*footpath*	*12*	*campsite*

Reading

2 **Aim To scan a text**

- Have Ss scan the text quickly to look for the vocabulary items in Ex. 1.
- Elicit which ones they find and how many.

Answer Key

hiking trail, forest, hostel, campsite, woods, peak (6)

3 **Aim To read for key information (multiple choice)**

- Ask Ss to read the text again and then read the questions and answer choices carefully and do the task.
- Ss can work in closed pairs or on their own and then compare their answers.
- Check Ss' answers.
- Then, give Ss time to look up the meanings of the words in bold in the Word List or in their dictionaries and elicit definitions from Ss around the class.

Answer Key

1 C (it is not an extremely difficult walk ... covered in thick forests)
2 D (People have been doing ... at this moment)
3 A (The only large animals ... avoid people)
4 C (whole text – mostly last paragraph)

Suggested Answer Key

roughly (adv): *approximately*
route (n): *a way from a starting point to a destination*
entire (adj): *whole*
catching on (phr v): *becoming popular*

mainly (adv): *mostly*
record (n): *the best performance*
exhaustion (n): *a state of being very tired; tiredness*
complete (v): *to finish*
equivalent (n): *a matching amount/number*
worn-out (adj): *no longer usable due to damage/wear*
troublesome (adj): *causing problems*
spectacular (adj): *amazing*
soar (v): *to fly high*
achievement (n): *sth done successfully and with skill; accomplishment*
epic (adj): *impressive*
capture (v): *to show; record accurately*

- Give Ss time to look up the meanings of the words in the ***Check these words*** box in the Word List.
- Play the video for Ss and elicit their comments.

4 Aim To consolidate new vocabulary & practise collocations

- Ask Ss to look through the text and find the words that pair with the words in the list to make collocations.
- Check Ss' answers.

Answer Key

1 mountain	*4 hiking*	*7 personal*
2 thick	*5 worn-out*	*8 epic*
3 final	*6 poisonous*	

Suggested Answer Key

The Appalachians are a ***mountain range****.*
There are ***thick forests*** *on the Appalachian Trail.*
Winter snow can make the ***final stage*** *impossible.*
You need good ***hiking boots*** *to walk the Appalachian Trail.*
Hikers spend a lot of money to replace ***worn-out equipment****.*
You may come across ***poisonous snakes*** *on the trail.*
Hikers who finish the trail have a great sense of ***personal satisfaction****.*
Through-hiking the Appalachian Trail is an ***epic journey****.*

5 Aim To consolidate prepositional phrases from a text

- Give Ss time to read the sentences and choose the correct prepositions. Ss can use their dictionaries if they want to, either printed or online.
- Check Ss' answers.
- Ask Ss to create a prepositions section in their notebooks and list prepositional phrases they come across in alphabetical order. Ss should do that throughout the year. Ask Ss to revise regularly and try to memorise these phrases. Encourage Ss to use them in sentences of their own.

Answer Key

1 on 2 in 3 to 4 in 5 of

6 Aim To understand words easily confused

- Explain the task and give Ss time to use their dictionaries to help them complete it.
- Check Ss' answers.

Answer Key

1 hold	*3 catch*
2 grab	*4 capture*

7 Aim To learn phrasal verbs with *dry*

- Ask Ss to read the phrasal verbs box and make sure that Ss understand the definitions.
- Then give Ss time to complete the task and check their answers.
- Tell Ss to create a phrasal verbs list in their notebooks and list the phrasal verbs they come across in alphabetical order together with a definition and an example sentence. Tell Ss to revise this list from time to time and to add to it every time they come across a new phrasal verb.

Answer Key

1 off 2 up 3 out

Speaking & Writing

8 Aim THINK To consolidate information in a text; to develop critical thinking skills

- Play the recording and ask Ss to listen to and read the text.
- Have Ss discuss the question in closed pairs and then ask some pairs to share their answers with the class.

Suggested Answer Key

A: I think through-hiking the Appalachian Trail is an epic journey because hikers travel a really long distance that takes a long time.
B: That's right. It's 3,500 km and it can take at least 41 days. That's epic!
A: Absolutely. Also, they see all sorts of different geographical features.
B: Yeah. They also get to be in nature and see all sorts of animals.

9 Aim ICT To develop research skills; to prepare & present a podcast

- In groups, Ss research online for information about a hiking trail in their country and make notes for each of the points listed.

- Give Ss time to prepare a podcast (digital audio file) about it.
- Ask various groups to play their podcasts to the class. This task can be assigned as HW.

Suggested Answer Key

Name: *the Inca Trail*
Route: *from Piscacucho to Machu Picchu; tropical jungle, cloud forests and alpine tundra*
Geography: *Vilcanota River, Andes Mountain Range, Veronika Mountain, Cusichaca River, Dead Woman's Pass*
Wildlife: *alpaca, deer, spectacled bear, condor and many other species of birds*
Places of interest along the route: *ancient ruins at Llactapata and Huillca Raccay, Inca paving stones, ancient tunnels, 'gringo killer' stairs*

Hey everyone and welcome back to the podcast. Today we're discussing a famous hiking trail in Peru – the Inca Trail! It starts in Piscacucho and ends at Machu Picchu. It is only 43 km long but it takes you through amazing mountain scenery including cloud forests, tropical jungle and alpine tundra. At the highest point it is 4,200 m above sea level.
The Inca Trail is the best-known part of the Inca road system, which is a UNESCO World Heritage site. On your journey, you will pass ancient ruins and walk over Inca paving stones and through ancient tunnels.
People usually hike the trail over 4 days and 3 nights, but there are shorter routes.
The Classic Inca Trail starts when you cross the bridge over the Vilcanota River. Then, after a couple of hours you will see the Andes Mountain Range and the snow-capped Veronika Mountain. Next on the trail is Llactapata and Huillca Raccay. Here you can stop and explore the ancient ruins. Later, you follow the left bank of the Cusichaca River and then camp for the night at 3,000 m above sea level.
Along the way, you might see some unusual animals called alpacas roaming around, or some deer. If you are very lucky, you may see a beautiful condor or a very rare spectacled bear!
On the second day, you start the hard trek up and down the trail's highest mountain pass. It is a steep and difficult climb to Dead Woman's Pass and you might feel the effects of altitude sickness. The breathtaking views are worth the effort, though.
On the third day, you will go down ancient Inca steps and go through an Inca tunnel. You pass through tropical jungle and cloud forests. Here, there are colourful plants and lots of birds. The cloud forests get their name because of the clouds of fog there.
Then on the final day, you arrive at Machu Picchu. Just before you get there, there are the 'gringo killer' stairs which take you to the Sun Gate and the entrance to one of the most famous ancient sites in the world. This marks the end of your epic journey along the Inca Trail.

1b Grammar in Use

1 a) Aim To revise the present simple and the present continuous

- Ask Ss to read the blog entry and identify the verb tenses in bold. Have students read the list of uses and then match them to the tenses in bold.
- Check Ss' answers and refer Ss to the ***Grammar Reference*** section for more information or to check any points they are unsure of.

Answer Key

I'm lying – present continuous – an action happening now
is growing – present continuous – a changing situation
I'm climbing – present continuous – a fixed future arrangement
leaves – present simple – a timetable (future meaning)
live – present simple – a permanent state
drive – present simple – a repeated action
is coming – present continuous – an annoyance

b) Aim To identify stative forms

- Ask Ss to read the blog entry again and find the stative forms. Elicit answers from Ss around the class and elicit how the meaning changes in the continuous form.
- Refer Ss to the ***Grammar Reference*** section for more information or to check any points they are unsure of.

Answer Key

think – have the opinion
thinking – considering
look – seem
looking – to see with the eyes

2 Aim To practise the present simple, the present continuous and stative verbs

Give Ss time to complete the exercise and then check their answers around the class.

Answer Key

1 is working
2 have (stative)
3 doesn't smell (stative)
4 are you looking
5 doesn't leave
6 do you go

3 **Aim To practise the present simple and the present continuous**

- Give Ss time to complete the sentences.
- Elicit answers from Ss around the class with reasons.

Answer Key

1 *doesn't open (a repeated action)*
2 *are enjoying (a changing situation)*
3 *Does the train depart (a timetable)*
4 *rains (a general truth)*
5 *are rising (a changing situation)*
6 *is sunbathing (an action happening now)*
7 *Does it often snow (a general truth)*
8 *are flying (an action happening now)*
9 *Are you going (a fixed future arrangement)*
10 *is always taking (an annoyance)*

4 **Aim To practise stative verbs**

Explain the task and give Ss time to complete it and then check their answers. Elicit reasons from Ss and ask various Ss to explain what each verb means.

Answer Key

1 a *looks (present simple to describe a state) (seems)*
b *is looking (present continuous for an action happening now) (seeing with the eyes)*
2 a *think (present simple to describe a state) (have the opinion)*
b *is thinking (present continuous for an action happening now) (is considering)*
3 a *see (present simple to describe a state) (understand)*
b *am seeing (present continuous for a fixed future arrangement) (am meeting)*
4 a *tastes (present simple to describe a state) (has the flavour of)*
b *is tasting (present continuous to describe an action happening now) (is trying)*

Speaking

5 **Aim To revise the present simple and the present continuous using personal examples**

Ask Ss to work in closed pairs and complete the task. Monitor the activity around the class and then ask some Ss to share their answers with the rest of the class.

Suggested Answer Key

I brush my teeth and have breakfast in the morning. I don't walk to work. I take the bus. Right now, I am having an English lesson and I am writing in my notebook. This weekend I am meeting my friends. I'm not getting up early.

Speaking

6 **Aim To revise adverbs of frequency**

- Ask Ss to read the adverbs of frequency and read the phrases in the list.
- Read out the example and ask various Ss around the class to say what they do when they visit a new place, following the example.

Suggested Answer Key

I always research the place on the Internet. I sometimes upload photos on social media. I often buy souvenirs. I never talk to locals or keep a travel diary. I usually sample local food. I occasionally check in online. I rarely take a selfie. I seldom send postcards.

7 **Aim To revise the present perfect and the present perfect continuous**

- Ask Ss to read the blog entry and identify the underlined tenses. Have Ss read the list of uses and then match them to the underlined tenses.
- Check Ss' answers and refer Ss to the ***Grammar Reference*** section for more information or to check any points they are unsure of.

Answer Key

I've been walking – an action that started in the past and continues up to the present with emphasis on duration
has hit – a recently completed action
have changed – an experience or change

8 **Aim To practise the present perfect and the present perfect continuous and adverbs used with these tenses**

- Give Ss time to complete the task.
- Check Ss' answers around the class.

Answer Key

1 *has been raining since*
2 *has just called*
3 *Have you visited, yet*
4 *Have been swimming, all morning*
5 *haven't started, yet*
6 *have been hiking, all day*
7 *have been planning, for*
8 *Has, already booked*
9 *has never travelled*
10 *Have you seen, yet*

9 **Aim To practise *have been/have gone***

- Explain the task and give Ss time to complete the sentences.
- Check Ss' answers around the class.

Answer Key

1 *has gone to*
2 *have been to*
3 *have ... been in*
4 *have gone to*
5 *have ... been to*

Speaking

10 Aim To practise the present perfect and the present perfect continuous

- Explain the task and read out the example.
- Ask Ss to work in closed pairs and complete the task using the phrases and following the example.
- Monitor the activity around the class and then ask some Ss to share their answers with the class.

Suggested Answer Key

Dan has been complaining for an hour.
Sue has eaten three energy bars since morning.
Peta's feet have been hurting for days.
Mandy has taken 30 photos so far.

11 Aim To practise present tenses

Give Ss time to complete the task and then elicit answers from Ss around the class.

Answer Key

1 *Are you enjoying*
2 *are having*
3 *hasn't rained*
4 *hike*
5 *haven't visited*
6 *are going*
7 *have read*
8 *stretch*
9 *haven't seen*
10 *Are you doing*

Writing

12 Aim To write a message

- Explain the task and give Ss time to write a message in reply to the one in Ex. 11.
- Ask various Ss to read out their messages to the class.
- This task can be assigned as HW.

Suggested Answer Key

Hi! It sounds like you're having a great time. I'm having a nice holiday, too. We're in the South of France. We're staying on a campsite and we've been driving around the French countryside all day, every day. It's very beautiful. We've visited a chateau and a vineyard so far. The weather is great, too, so I've got a bit of a tan. Tomorrow, we're going to go to the beach. Not very exciting, but very relaxing.

1c Skills in Action

Vocabulary

1 a) Aim To present vocabulary related to road signs

- Ask Ss to read the words in the list. Explain/Elicit the meanings of any unknown words or ask Ss to look them up in the Word List or in their dictionaries.
- Then ask Ss to look at the road signs and complete the gaps.
- Elicit answers from Ss around the class.

Answer Key

1 *speed*
2 *way*
3 *crossroads*
4 *junction*
5 *pedestrian*
6 *lights*
7 *lane*
8 *roundabout*
9 *end*

b) Aim THINK To talk about road signs

- Ask Ss to work in closed pairs and look at the map and talk about where they might see the roads signs following the example.
- Monitor the activity around the class and then ask various pairs to share their answers with the class.

Suggested Answer Key

A: *You might see a 30-mph speed limit sign on Hill Street. It's probably a quiet street.*
B: *Yeah. I think you might see a stop and give way sign on Mill Road. There's probably a lot of cars that come down Elm Street.*
A: *You'll probably see roundabout signs at the end of Elm Street, Holly Avenue and Riverside Avenue.*
B: *Hillside Close, Valley Close and Birch Close are dead ends so you might see dead end signs there.*
A: *You might see a junction sign on Elm Street and a crossroads sign on Holly Avenue.*
B: *I agree. You might see a pedestrian crossing sign and a traffic lights sign on Holly Avenue, too, because it seems like a busy road.*

Listening

2 Aim To listen for key information (T/F statements)

- Ask Ss to read the sentences (1-6) and then play the recording and have Ss mark the statements as true or false according to what they hear.
- Check Ss' answers.
- Play the recording again with pauses for Ss to check their answers.

Answer Key

1 T 2 F 3 T 4 F 5 T 6 F

Everyday English

3 a) Aim To read for specific information

Ask Ss to read the dialogue and then elicit answers to the questions.

Answer Key

The driver is on the other side of the river before the bridge. She is going to Potter's Pond.

b) Aim To listen and read for lexical cohesion (open cloze)

- Give Ss time to read the dialogue again and complete the gaps with an appropriate word.
- Play the recording for Ss to listen and read and check their answers.

Answer Key

1 from 3 on 5 on
2 across 4 onto 6 at

4 Aim To act out dialogues and practise everyday English for asking for and giving directions

- Explain the task and ask Ss to act out dialogues similar to the one in Ex. 3 in pairs using the prompts.
- Write this diagram on the board for Ss to follow.

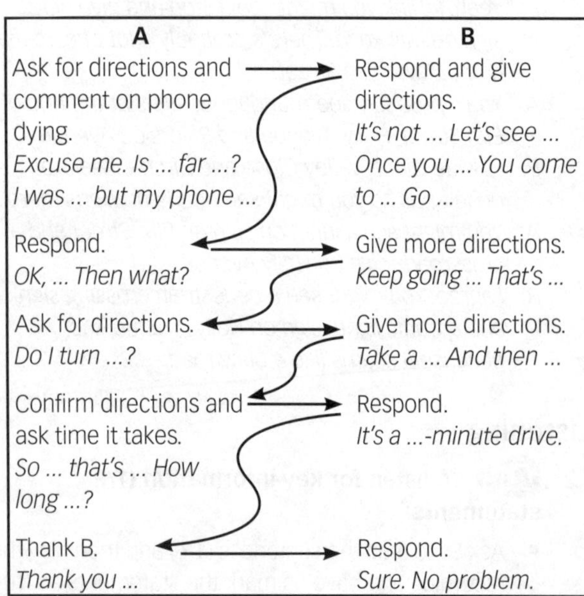

A
B
Ask for directions and comment on phone dying.
Excuse me. Is ... far ...?
I was ... but my phone ...
Respond and give directions.
It's not ... Let's see ...
Once you ... You come to ... Go ...
Respond.
OK, ... Then what?
Give more directions.
Keep going ... That's ...
Ask for directions.
Do I turn ...?
Give more directions.
Take a ... And then ...
Confirm directions and ask time it takes.
So ... that's ... How long ...?
Respond.
It's a ...-minute drive.
Thank B.
Thank you ...
Respond.
Sure. No problem.

- Monitor the activity around the class and offer assistance as necessary.
- Then ask some pairs to act out their dialogues in front of the class.
- Ask Ss to evaluate pairs' performances.

Suggested Answer Key

A: Excuse me. Is Valley Close far from here? I was following the map on my phone, but my phone died.
B: It's not very far. Let's see ... Once you cross the bridge here in front of you, you come to a roundabout. Go straight across onto Ivy Road.
A: OK, got it. Then what?
B: Keep going straight on until you reach a junction. That's Beech Street.
A: And do I turn left or right there?
B: Take a right onto Beech Street and then take the first left into Hill Street. And then Valley Close is the first street on your right.
A: So ... that's straight on at the first roundabout, right at the junction, first left and first right. How long does that take?
B: It's a two-minute drive. Maybe a little more.
A: Thank you so much for your help!
B: Sure, no problem!

A: Excuse me. Is Mill Road far from here? I was following the map on my phone, but my phone died.
B: It's not very far. Let's see ... Once you cross the bridge here in front of you, you come to a roundabout. Take the first exit onto Riverside Avenue.
A: OK, got it. Then what?
B: Keep going straight on until you reach a crossroads.
A: And do I turn left or right there?
B: Go straight on onto Elm Street and then Mill Road is the first street on your left.
A: So ... that's the first exit at the roundabout, straight on at the crossroads and first left. How long does that take?
B: It's a two-minute drive. Maybe a little less.
A: Thank you so much for your help!
B: Sure, no problem!

Intonation

5 a) Aim To present discourse markers

- Play the recording with pauses for Ss to repeat chorally and/or individually. Check Ss' intonation and correct where necessary.
- Then elicit which sentences express which of the options in the list.
- Check Ss' answers.

Answer Key

1 determination 3 uncertainty
2 arrangement 4 confirmation

b) **Aim** **To practise discourse markers**

- Explain to Ss what discourse markers are (words or phrases like *right*, *OK*, etc. we use them to connect, organise and manage what we say/ write).
- Give Ss time to think of their own sentences using the discourse markers and then elicit answers from Ss around the class. Ask Ss to use appropriate intonation.

Suggested Answer Key

Right! Let's go for a hike on Sunday.
So, pick me up at 6.
Well, maybe the weather will be nice.
OK, I'll call you later.

Reading & Writing

6 **Aim** **To read for lexical cohesion (word formation)**

- Give Ss time to read the flyer and complete the gaps with a word formed from the word in brackets.
- Check Ss' answers on the board.

Answer Key

1 *sights*	3 *cooker*	5 *separately*
2 *beautiful*	4 *spacious*	6 *impressive*

7 **Aim** **To prepare for a writing task**

- Read out the ***Writing Tip*** and tell Ss that this advice will help them to complete the writing task successfully.
- Have Ss read the flyer in Ex. 6 again and identify all the underlined features from the ***Writing Tip*** in the flyer.
- Elicit answers from Ss around the class.

Answer Key

Directions: *We're only a leisurely five-minute walk ... red building on the left.*
Description: *There's a shared kitchen ... no cooking facilities.*
Special offer: *50% off your first night with this flyer!*

8 **Aim** **To identify descriptive language**

- Explain the task and give Ss time to scan the flyer again and find the descriptive words or phrases the flyer uses.
- Check Ss' answers around the class.

Answer Key

1 *impressive*	4 *the most beautiful*
2 *leisurely*	5 *cosy*
3 *spacious*	6 *a short stroll from*

9 **Aim** **To prepare for a writing task**

- Ask Ss to copy the table into their notebooks and complete it with the prompts in the list.
- Check Ss' answers on the board.

Answer Key

location	• *in the town centre* • *near the river* • *at the junction*
facilities	• *gym* • *restaurant* • *rooftop swimming pool*
rooms	• *single rooms with a view* • *double rooms with large balconies* • *twin rooms*

Writing

10 **Aim** **To write a flyer**

- Tell Ss to use their notes from Ex. 9 and the plan to help them write their flyer.
- Give Ss time to complete the task and then ask various Ss to read their flyers to the class.
- This task may be assigned as HW.

Suggested Answer Key

The Park Hotel
Location
We're right in the heart of the town near the junction with Park Road and just a short stroll from one of the most beautiful rivers in the country.
Facilities
We offer a wide range of facilities including a fully-equipped modern gym, a top-class restaurant and a delightful rooftop swimming pool.
Rooms
We have a wide range of comfortable rooms available. There are single rooms with a view, double rooms with large balconies and twin rooms.
Directions
We are just five minutes' walk from the railway station. Take a right coming out of the main entrance and walk along Long Street for about 100 metres. At the crossroads, turn left onto Bridge Road and cross the bridge. That takes you straight into Station Road. Follow the road round without making any turns and in a couple of minutes you will find us, the grand stone building on the left. We're looking forward to having you as our guest!
Special offer
25% off your stay with this flyer!

VALUES

Ask Ss to read the quotation, then initiate a class discussion about its meaning. Encourage all Ss to participate.

Suggested Answer Key

A: *I think the quotation means that it doesn't matter how fast or slow you go as long as you are heading towards something worthwhile.*

B: *I totally agree. I also think it refers to having a goal in life that may take some time to reach, but it will be worth it when you do. For example, studying for a profession takes years but it offers more rewards than an unskilled job you can get straight out of high school. etc.*

Culture 1

Listening & Reading

1 Aim To introduce the topic; to listen and read for specific information

- Play the recording. Ss listen to and read the text and answer the question.
- Elicit answers from Ss.

Answer Key

B, C

2 Aim To read for key information (multiple matching)

- Give Ss time to read the text again and then answer the questions.
- Elicit answers from Ss around the class.

Answer Key

1 D (a bit expensive)
2 B (ducks…kingfisher)
3 A (steadily growing)
4 C (commentary)
5 A (passengers past ... in the other)
6 B (Starting ... countryside)
7 D (bus tour route)
8 C (five-course meal)

- Then give Ss time to explain the words in bold using their dictionaries or the Word List to help them.

Suggested Answer Key

choosy (adj): *taking extra care when making a choice*
thrilling (adj): *very exciting*
outing (n): *a pleasure trip*
commentary (n): *a description of an event as it happens*
cityscape (n): *a city landscape*
amphibious (adj): *able to travel on land and on water*
splash (v): *to enter the water noisily*

- Give Ss time to look up the meanings of the words in the ***Check these words*** box in the Word List.
- Play the video for Ss and elicit their comments.

Speaking & Writing

3 Aim THINK To develop critical thinking skills; to express an opinion

- Have Ss work in closed pairs and discuss the question in the rubric.
- Monitor the activity around the class and then ask some pairs to share their answers with the class.

Suggested Answer Key

A: *I'd like to go on the amphibious tour because it is something unusual and I have never done anything like that before. I think it would be very memorable.*

B: *I know what you mean, but I'd like to go on the night tour and have a five-course meal. I think it would be like a luxury cruise.*

4 Aim ICT To develop research skills; to write a webpage about city tours

- Ask Ss to work in small groups and give them time to research online and find out information about ways to see the capital city in their country or another country and use this information to write a webpage with a shared introduction and separate sections. Each student in the group should write a section.
- Ask various groups of Ss to present their webpages to the class.
- This task may be assigned as HW. Remind Ss to add pictures.

Suggested Answer Key

Top Paris Tours

Paris is one of the most famous cities in the world and a top destination for tourists and travellers. There are lots of options for exploring this city, so here's a list of our top ways to see the sights.

Lunch Cruise

Why not book a ticket on one of the long lazy afternoon cruises that head west along the Seine? Starting at Notre Dame, these gentle outings take you past the Musée d'Orsay and the National Assembly towards the Eiffel Tower and then back again. There's a delicious lunch offered on board.

Dinner Cruise
Every city looks magical at night and Paris is no exception. There are a large number of night-time tours that sail up and down the river, offering a five-course meal and a guide giving a running commentary in 14 languages. All of them offer the unbeatable cityscape of Paris, lit up for your pleasure. The boats are called Bateaux Parisiens and they are all glass to protect you from the night air. They also have live music to create a romantic atmosphere.

Enchanted Cruise
This cruise is a magical experience for children and adults. Two actors host the experience and provide a magical show with musical entertainment, songs, riddles, stories and other surprises. Guests enjoy a 360° view of the sights along the river during their hour-long tour and they can get a CD of the experience to keep.

Review 1

Vocabulary

1 **Aim To consolidate vocabulary from the unit**

- Explain the task.
- Give Ss time to complete it.
- Check Ss' answers.

Answer Key

1 trail 2 lights 3 peak 4 campsite 5 limit 6 mountain 7 railway 8 final 9 hiking 10 routes

2. **Aim To consolidate vocabulary from the unit**

- Explain the task.
- Give Ss time to complete it.
- Check Ss' answers.

Answer Key

1 thick 2 crossing 3 grab 4 pond 5 way

3 **Aim To practise prepositional phrases and phrasal verbs**

- Explain the task.
- Give Ss time to complete it.
- Check Ss' answers.

Answer Key

- 1 up 2 to 3 in 4 off 5 on

Grammar

4 **Aim To practise the present simple, the present continuous**

- Explain the task.
- Give Ss time to complete it.
- Check Ss' answers.

Answer Key

1 are you tasting 2 doesn't like 3 is always making 4 isn't working 5 researches

5 **Aim To practise present tenses**

- Explain the task.
- Give Ss time to complete it.
- Check Ss' answers.

Answer Key

1 has already uploaded 2 has been walking 3 has gone 4 Have you seen 5 has been doing

Everyday English

6 **Aim To match exchanges**

- Explain the task.
- Give Ss time to complete it.
- Check Ss' answers.

Answer Key

- 1 b 2 a 3 e 4 c 5 d

Competences

Ask Ss to assess their own performance in the unit by ticking the items according to how competent they feel for each of the listed activities.

Legends & Festivals

Topic	
In this unit, Ss will explore the topics of festivities, celebrations & customs.	
2a Reading & Vocabulary	**12-13**
Lesson objectives: To introduce key vocabulary, to read for gist, to read for cohesion and coherence (gapped text), to learn collocations relating to legends and festivals, to learn phrasal verbs with *blow*, to learn prepositional phrases, to practise words easily confused, to prepare and present a podcast about a legend and a celebration, to write an article about a legend **Vocabulary:** Festivities *(Polish dishes, street food stalls, street performers, jugglers, fireworks, balloon, parade, costumes)*; Nouns *(legend, flames, cave, residents, cattle, sulphur, juggling, highlight, sculpture, contest)*; Verbs *(burst, soar, march, celebrate)*; Phrasal verbs *(set off, come up with)*; Idiom *(roar into life)*; Phrase *(bring to life)*	
2b Grammar in Use	**14-15**
Lesson objectives: To revise/learn the past simple and past continuous, to revise/practise the past simple vs the present perfect, to learn *used to/would – be/get used to*, to talk about celebrations/cultural events, to listen for order of events, to write a summary of a legend	
2c Skills in Action	**16-17**
Lesson objectives: To learn vocabulary for types of holidays (UK celebrations & customs), to listen for general gist, opinion, attitude, etc (multiple matching), to listen and read for specific information, to act out a dialogue describing an event, to practise stress-shift, to read for lexical cohesion (word formation), to practise giving recommendations, to listen for ideas/specific information (gap fill), to write an email about a celebration you attended, to discuss the value of traditionalism **Vocabulary:** Types of holidays *(Burns Night, Mother's Day, Mothering Sunday, May Day, Bonfire Night, Remembrance Day, New Year's Eve)*, Nouns: *(fireworks, midnight, bonfire, toffee apples, procession, bagpipes, haggis, poppies, silence)*; Verbs *(let off, light, gather, prepare)*	
Culture 2	**18**
Lesson objectives: To listen and read for gist, to read for specific information (comprehension questions), to talk about sayings about good/bad luck, to present information on superstitions and sayings about good/bad luck **Vocabulary:** Nouns *(penny, saying, path, playwright)*, Verbs *(admit, recite, spin around, store)*; Adjectives *(interesting, unique, common, cautious, occasional)*	
Review 2	**19**
Lesson objectives: To test/consolidate vocabulary and grammar in the unit; to practise everyday English	

Go through the objectives box and tell Ss that these are the topics, skills and activities this unit will cover.

2a

Vocabulary

1 Aim To present vocabulary related to festivities

- Ask Ss to read the words in the list.
- Explain/Elicit the meanings of any unknown words/ phrases and then ask Ss to do the task in closed pairs.
- Monitor the activity around the class and then ask some Ss to share their answers with the rest of the class.

Answer Key

1 *dishes*	4 *jugglers*	7 *parade*
2 *stalls*	5 *fireworks*	8 *costumes*
3 *performers*	6 *balloon*	

Reading

2 Aim To read for gist

- Elicit Ss' guesses as to what the text is about.
- Ask Ss to quickly go through the text to check if their guesses were correct.

Suggested Answer Key

The text is about the Dragon Parade in Krakow, Poland. The legend behind it is about how a clever man kills a dragon and marries a princess.

3 Aim To read for text structure, cohesion & coherence (gapped text)

- Go through the ***Study Skills*** box with Ss.
- Ask Ss to read the text, then read the sentences carefully and look for hints that can help them do the task.
- Ss can work in closed pairs or on their own and then compare their answers.
- Check Ss' answers. Ss should justify their choices.
- Then, give Ss time to look up the meanings of the words in bold in the Word List or in their dictionaries and elicit definitions from Ss around the class.

Answer Key

1 G (scared me to death!; I couldn't believe my eyes!)
2 A (The brave men set off ...; But ... had each of them for dinner.)
3 F (... extremely thirsty.; ... was so thirsty that ...; drank so much)

4 B (The fireworks display began, ...; It was the start ...)
5 D (There was dancing and juggling ...; Also, the streets were packed with people ...; Many of them were ...)
6 C (... street stalls selling pierogi.; It's a traditional dish... .)

Suggested Answer Key

brought to life (phr): *made something lively*
sculpture (n): *a 3D representation of sth in stone, wood or other material*
set off (phr v): *began a journey*
came up with (phr v): *thought of*
celebrating (v): *acknowledging a special day or an event with enjoyable activities*
contest (n): *competition*

- Give Ss time to look up the meanings of the words in the ***Check these words*** box in the Word List.
- Play the video for Ss and elicit their comments.

4 Aim To consolidate new vocabulary & practise collocations

- Ask Ss to look through the text and find the words that pair with the words in the list to make collocations.
- Check Ss' answers

Answer Key

1 hold 3 roar 5 offer
2 take 4 believe 6 win

Suggested Answer Key

*Krakow **holds** the Dragon Parade every summer.*
*I always **take photos** on holiday.*
*The huge dragon **roared into life**.*
*I **couldn't believe my eyes** when I saw the huge dragon.*
*The king **offered his daughter in marriage**.*
*People tried to **win** the best **dragon contest**.*

5 Aim To learn phrasal verbs with *blow*

- Ask Ss to read the phrasal verbs box and make sure that Ss understand the definitions.
- Then give Ss time to complete the task and check their answers.

Answer Key

1 out, up 2 into 3 away, off

6 Aim To consolidate prepositional phrases from a text

- Give Ss time to read the gapped text and fill in the gaps with the correct prepositions.
- Then check Ss' answers.

Answer Key

1 to 3 with 5 in 7 of
2 by 4 in 6 into

7 Aim To understand words easily confused

- Explain the task and give Ss time to use their dictionaries to help them complete it.
- Check Ss' answers.

Answer Key

1 culture 2 custom 3 tradition

Speaking & Writing

8 Aim ICT To consolidate information in a text; to develop research skills; to prepare & present a podcast

- Play the recording. Ask Ss to listen to and read the text.
- In groups, have Ss research online for more information on the topic, then prepare a podcast (digital audio file) about it.
- Ask various groups to play their podcasts to the class. This task can be assigned as homework.

Suggested Answer Key

Hey everyone. Last week I visited Krakow and was lucky enough to be there for the Dragon Parade. So, in this podcast I'm going to tell you all about the legend of the Wawel Dragon.
The legend goes back to the time Krakow was Poland's main city and was ruled by King Krakus, the city's founder. The king had a daughter called Wanda. A terrible dragon was living nearby, at the foot of Wawel Hill on the Vistula River. It used to attack the residents, even eating their young daughters! King Krakus decided something had to be done. He offered his daughter in marriage to anyone brave enough to kill the dragon.
Lots of brave men set off hoping to win the hand of the princess but the dragon had them all for dinner! Then one day a shoemaker by the name of Skuba came forward. He wasn't brave but he had a clever plan. He took the skin of a sheep and filled it with sulphur and mustard seeds. He left it outside the dragon's cave at the bottom of the hill and the greedy dragon came out and ate it hungrily. Of course, the sulphur and the mustard seeds made it dreadfully thirsty! It went down to the river and drank and drank. In fact, it drank so much that it burst into a million pieces, as the legend says! With the dragon dead, Skuba was free to marry the princess. In the oldest version of the legend in the 12th century, the dragon was killed by two princes, sons of a King Krak.

So that's the legend that the city celebrates today every late May or early June. It's a weekend-long event. On Saturday night, there's the light and sound spectacle. I was there to see the amazing fireworks display, followed by huge dragon-shaped balloons soaring into the sky surrounded by smoke and colourful lasers. There were dragon boats on the river, too, and I visited the Groteska Theater, where actors re-enacted the story.
Sunday is the Kid's Parade held in the Main Square of the Old Town. There was dancing, juggling, folk music, you name it. People taking part in the parade were dressed up in medieval costumes and some were holding handmade dragon puppets, hoping to win the best dragon contest. The whole weekend families have picnics by the river - that's where I first tried the delicious Polish dumplings called pierogi.
So ... if you get the chance to go to the City of Dragons - grab it!

9 **Aim** **ICT** **To develop research skills; to write an article about a legend**

- Ask Ss to research a legend in their country that is celebrated today and make notes on it under the headings provided. Then they use their notes to write an article about it.
- Ask various Ss to read their articles to the class. This task can be assigned as homework.

Suggested Answer Key

legend: *Robin Hood, lived in Sherwood Forest as an outlaw after the Sheriff of Nottingham stole his castle and his land, stole from the rich and gave to the poor*
name of event: *Robin Hood Festival*
when/where: *August 5th-11th, Sherwood Forest Visitor Centre, Nottinghamshire, England*
activities: *watch live shows with Robin Hood and his Merry Men, watch jousting tournaments with horse stunts, archery and staff fighting, watch comedy performances, see magic tricks, listen to medieval music, see a falconry show, try archery, watch performers and entertainers, buy souvenirs, art and handmade crafts from stalls, try festive food and drinks*

The Robin Hood Festival

According to legend, there was an Englishman who went by the name of Robin Hood. He lived in Sherwood Forest as an outlaw after the Sheriff of Nottingham stole his castle and his land. He stole from the rich and gave to the poor and became a folk hero.
These days every year from August 5th-11th the Robin Hood Festival takes place in Sherwood Forest Visitor Centre, Nottinghamshire, England. The festival celebrates the man and the legend and offers people plenty of things to see and do. Visitors can watch live shows with Robin Hood and his Merry Men. This includes jousting tournaments with horse stunts, archery and staff fighting. They can also watch comedy performances, see magic tricks and listen to medieval music. That's not all!
Other activities include seeing a falconry show, trying archery, watching performers and entertainers, buying souvenirs such as art and handmade crafts from stalls and also trying festive food and drinks. There is so much to see and do at this fantastic festival. If you ever get the chance to go, don't miss it!

2b Grammar in Use

1 a) **Aim** **To revise the past simple and the past continuous**

- Ask Ss to read the blog entry and identify the verb tenses in bold. Have students read the list of uses (1-8) and then match them to the tenses in bold.
- Check Ss' answers and refer Ss to the ***Grammar Reference*** section for more information or to check any points they are unsure of.

Answer Key

Past Simple: *saw-2, went-6, burnt-8, opened/rushed-3, noticed-5*
Past Continuous: *was blowing-1, were standing/were chatting-4, was walking-5, were enjoying-7*

b) **Aim** **To identify time expressions used with the past simple and the past continuous**

- Ask Ss to read the blog entry again and find time expressions used with the past simple and the past continuous. Elicit answers from Ss around the class.
- As an extension, ask Ss to make sentences using the time expressions.

Answer Key

Past simple: *last summer, as a child, in the late 16th and early 17th century, in 1997, at 7:45, after about an hour*
Past continuous: *as, on the evening of, soon*

2 **Aim** **To practise the past simple and the past continuous**

Give Ss time to complete the exercise and then check their answers around the class.

Answer Key

1 *was watching, started*
2 *didn't go, didn't feel/weren't feeling*
3 *crowned*
4 *Were people singing, was playing*
5 *wasn't chatting, was rehearsing*
6 *was blowing, was pouring*
7 *did the event first take*

3 a) Aim To practise the past simple and the past continuous

- Give Ss time to complete the sentences with the past simple and the past continuous using their own ideas.
- Elicit answers from Ss around the class.

Suggested Answer Key

1 *... the birds were singing.*
2 *... bought a new dress.*
3 *... a car went through a puddle and splashed him.*
4 *... she didn't get wet because she had an umbrella.*
5 *... a bird came and sat beside her.*

b) Aim To practise the past simple and the past continuous through storytelling

- Ask various Ss around the class to choose one of the sentences in Ex. 3a and continue the story using the past simple and the past continuous tenses.
- Elicit answers from various Ss.
- The class can vote for the best story.

Suggested Answer Key

She was sitting on a bench when a bird came and sat beside her. It was a small blue bird. It wasn't scared and it came closer to her. She thought it might be someone's pet. She held out her hand and it hopped up onto it. She opened the large pocket of her coat and moved her hand slowly towards it. To her surprise, the bird hopped inside. She went to the local police station and reported finding the bird. A young boy came in while she was telling the officer behind the desk about the bird. It was his lost bird. The boy was so happy to get him back.

4 Aim To revise the past simple vs the present perfect

- Refer Ss to the blog entry in Ex. 1 again and tell them to look at the underlined verb forms. Elicit how the present perfect differs from the past simple and when we use it.
- Refer Ss to the ***Grammar Reference*** section for more information or to check any points they are unsure of.

Suggested Answer Key

The present perfect is different from the past simple in the way it is formed.
We form the present perfect with the auxiliary verb 'have' and the past participle.
We use the present perfect for an action which started at an unstated time in the past and for an action which started in the past and is still continuing in the present.

5 Aim To practise the past simple and the present perfect tenses

Give Ss time to complete the task and check Ss' answers. Ask Ss to give reasons for their answers.

Answer Key

1 *didn't attend (an action which happened at a stated time in the past)*
2 *has started (an action which happened at a stated time in the past)*
3 *Have you taken (an action which started in the past and is still continuing in the present)*
4 *did they let off (an action which happened at a stated time in the past)*
5 *I have never flown (an action which happened at a stated time in the past)*
6 *was (an action which started and finished in the past)*

6 Aim To practise the past simple, the past continuous and the present perfect tenses

- Give Ss time to complete the gaps in the email with the correct forms of the verbs in brackets.
- Check Ss' answers. Ss should justify the tenses they have used.

Answer Key

1 *Have any of you ever been (experience – ever)*
2 *arrived (action at specific time in the past – last night)*
3 *was taking (past action in progress)*
4 *showed (past action – time implied)*
5 *told (past action – time implied)*
6 *have taken (period of time that is not finished at the time of the speaking)*
7 *attracted (action at specific time in the past – in the 1930s)*
8 *haven't been (period of time that is not finished at the time of the speaking)*
9 *has raised (period of time that is not finished at the time of the speaking)*
10 *began (past action – time implied)*

7 **Aim** **To present *used to/would – be/get used to***

- Go through the theory box with Ss and refer them to the ***Grammar Reference*** section for more information and to clarify any points they are unsure of.
- Alternatively, you can write the examples in the theory box on the board and elicit uses.
- Then give Ss time to complete the task in closed pairs.
- Check Ss' answers around the class.

Answer Key

1 was going	*3 didn't use to*
2 wouldn't	*4 Would you go*

Speaking

8 **Aim** **To practise *used to/would – be/get used to* with personal examples**

- Explain the task and read out the prompts and the example.
- Ask Ss to work in closed pairs and complete the task. Then ask various Ss to share some of their answers with the rest of the class.

Suggested Answer Key

*My mum used to **prepare a special meal** on New Year's Eve.*
*The whole family used to **take part in the town procession** on Gala day.*
*On New Year's Day, my family used to **watch special TV programmes** together.*
*We used to **light bonfires** on November 5th.*
*We used to **exchange gifts** on new Year's Day.*
*I used to **watch a fireworks display** on New Year's Eve.*

9 **Aim** **To practise the past simple, the past continuous, the present perfect and *used to/would – be/get used to* through sentence transformations**

Explain the task and give Ss time to complete it and then check Ss' answers.

Answer Key

1 was wrapping gifts
2 were eating dinner
3 haven't/have not watched a parade
4 didn't use to like
5 has got used to eating

Listening & Writing

10 **Aim** **To listen for order of events**

- Explain the task and play the recording. Ss listen and order the events according to what they hear.
- Check Ss' answers.

Answer Key

A 3	*C 4*	*E 2*	*G 5*
B 8	*D 6*	*F 7*	*H 1*

11 **Aim** **To write a summary of a legend**

- Give Ss time to use their answers in Ex. 10 to write a summary of a legend. Play the recording again if necessary. Ask various Ss to read out the summaries to the class.
- This task can be assigned as HW.
- As an extension, you can ask Ss to research another legend and narrate it to the class.

Suggested Answer Key

A strange man walked into a blacksmith's shop. The stranger asked him to make a gold horseshoe. The two men went to a secret cave. In the cave, there were sleeping knights and horses. The blacksmith replaced a horse's shoe with the gold one. The stranger said the knights were a secret army and they would wake up one day to fight in a great battle for Poland. The blacksmith promised not to tell anyone what he saw. The stranger gave the blacksmith a bag of gold. The blacksmith didn't keep the secret and told everyone. The bag of gold turned into sand and he never found the cave again.

2c Skills in Action

Vocabulary

1 a) **Aim** **To present vocabulary related to types of holidays (UK celebrations & Customs)**

- Ask Ss to read the list of UK celebrations (1-6) and the customs (a-f) and give them time to match them.
- Explain/Elicit the meanings of any unknown words or phrases or ask Ss to look them up in the Word List.
- Read out the example sentences and then give Ss time to make sentences of their own.
- Elicit answers from Ss around the class.

Answer Key

1 e   2 d   3 c   4 b   5 f   6 a

2

Suggested Answer Key

On Burns' Night, people in the UK read Burns' poems aloud, listen to traditional music on the bagpipes and eat haggis.
On Mother's Day, people in the UK buy flowers or prepare breakfast for their mothers.
On May Day, people in the UK gather flowers and follow a procession led by the May Queen.
On Bonfire Night, people in the UK light a huge bonfire, let off fireworks and eat toffee apples.
On Remembrance Day, people in the UK wear poppies and hold a two-minute silence.

b) Aim To talk about important celebrations in one's country

- Ask Ss to work in closed pairs. Ss think of two important celebrations in their country and tell their partner how celebrate them.
- Ask various students to tell the class.

Suggested Answer Key

On New Year's Day we exchange gifts and eat a special meal. We sometimes visit relatives and have lunch together.
On birthdays, we celebrate with our family and friends. We blow out candles on a special cake, play games and have fun with family and friends.

Listening

2 Aim To listen for general gist, opinion, attitude, etc (multiple matching)

- Ask Ss to read the sentences (A-E) and find the key words. Play the recording twice. Ss match the speakers to the sentences. Remind Ss there is one extra sentence.
- Check Ss' answers. You can play the recording again with pauses for Ss to check their answers.

Answer Key

1 E 2 C 3 A 4 B

Everyday English

3 Aim To listen and read for specific information

- Ask Ss to read the first two exchanges in the dialogue. Elicit what event Steve attended.
- Play the recording for Ss to listen and read and find out if their guesses were correct.

Answer Key

Steve attended Burns' Night.

4 Aim To act out a dialogue and practise everyday English for describing an event

- Explain the task and ask Ss to act out a dialogue similar to the one in Ex. 3 in pairs.
- Write this diagram on the board for Ss to follow.

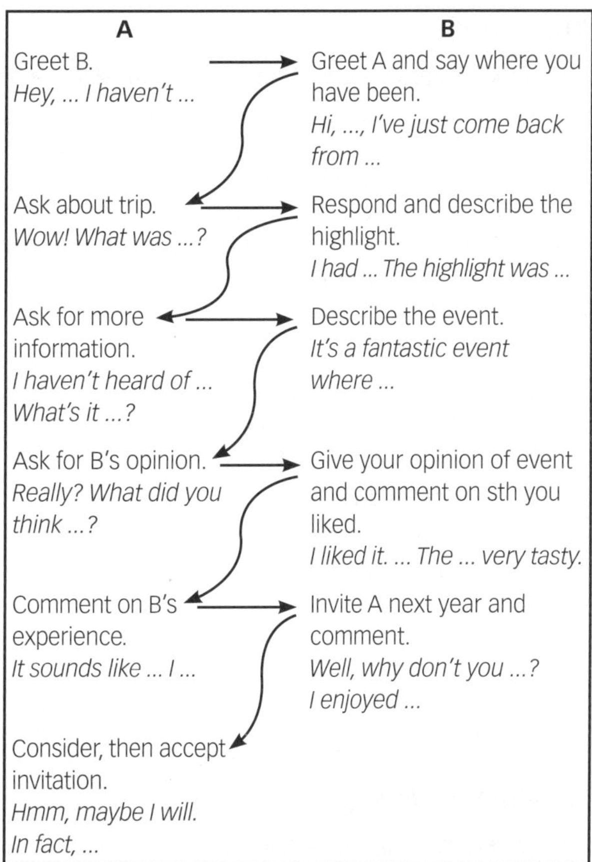

A
B
Greet B.
Hey, … I haven't …
Greet A and say where you have been.
Hi, …, I've just come back from …
Ask about trip.
Wow! What was …?
Respond and describe the highlight.
I had … The highlight was …
Ask for more information.
I haven't heard of …
What's it …?
Describe the event.
It's a fantastic event where …
Ask for B's opinion.
Really? What did you think …?
Give your opinion of event and comment on sth you liked.
I liked it. … The … very tasty.
Comment on B's experience.
It sounds like … I …
Invite A next year and comment.
Well, why don't you …?
I enjoyed …
Consider, then accept invitation.
Hmm, maybe I will.
In fact, …

- Monitor the activity around the class and offer assistance as necessary.
- Then ask some pairs to act out their dialogues in front of the class.

Suggested Answer Key

A: Hey Ann. I haven't seen you in a while.
B: Hi, Sue. I've just come back from the UK. I was there for five days.
A: Wow! What was it like?
B: I had the time of my life. The highlight was on my last day when I celebrated Bonfire Night with an English friend in London.
A: I haven't heard of that. What's it about?
B: It's a fantastic event where people light a huge bonfire and let off fireworks. I also tried a toffee apple!
A: Really? What did you think of it?
B: I liked it. Toffee apples are very tasty.

A: It sounds like you had a wonderful time. I haven't experienced anything like that.
B: Well, why don't you come with me next year? I enjoyed it so much that I'm definitely going back.
A: Hmm, maybe I will. In fact, count me in!

Intonation

5 **Aim Learning about and practicing stress-shift**

- Read out the theory box and explain the task. Have Ss identify the forms and check their answers.
- Then, play the recording with pauses for Ss to repeat chorally and/or individually. Check Ss' intonation.
- Then elicit sentences from Ss around the class using the words in bold. Correct intonation where necessary.

Answer Key

1 a noun b verb
2 a verb b noun
3 a verb b noun

Suggested Answer key

I got a refund on a faulty phone.
They refunded me straight away.
I updated my software on my computer.
I downloaded the updates online.
My school presented me with a certificate.
I always buy presents for my family when I go on holiday.

Reading & Writing

6 **Aim To read for lexical cohesion (word formation)**

- Give Ss time to read the email and complete the gaps with a word formed from the word in brackets.
- Check Ss' answers on the board and then elicit what each paragraph is about.

Answer Key

1 celebration 5 magicians
2 heroic 6 performances
3 wealthy 7 tasty
4 happily 8 fascinated

A name and place of festival
B the legend behind the festival
C festival activities
D final comments

7 **Aim To identify tenses**

- Read out the ***Writing Tip*** and tell Ss that this advice will help them to complete the writing task successfully.
- Have Ss read the email in Ex. 6 again and identify all the present and past tenses.
- Elicit answers from Ss around the class.

Answer Key

Present tenses *– takes place, is, come*
Past tenses *– went, was, hated, decided, stole, tried, escaped, lived, was, entered, were doing, were giving, were, was, missed*

Recommending

8 a) **Aim To practise recommending**

- Explain the task and give Ss time to complete the expressions usually used for recommending with the words/phrases in the list.
- Check Ss' answers.

Answer Key

1 must 4 disaster
2 miss 5 well worth
3 waste of time

b) **Aim To identify language for recommending in a model**

Elicit how the writer in Ex. 6 has recommended the celebration.

Answer Key

The Robin Hood Festival is a must for anyone who's fascinated by history.

Writing

9 **Aim To prepare for a writing task; to analyse a rubric**

- Give Ss time to read the rubric and underline the key words.
- Then elicit answers to the questions from Ss around the class.

Suggested Answer Key

Key words: *email, pen friend, cultural celebrations based on a legend, have you attended one recently? What legend is it based on? How did people celebrate it? Would you recommend it? email, 120-180 words*

I am going to write an email. It is for Ben, my penfriend. It should be about a cultural celebration based on a legend. I should use informal style.

Listening for ideas

10 Aim To listen for ideas/specific information (gap fill)

Ask Ss to read the gapped text and think of what information may be missing. Then play the recording twice if neccessary. Ss listen and complete the gaps. Check Ss' answers.

Answer Key

1 *Sussex*
2 *80,000*
3 *huge parade*
4 *7/seven*
5 *baked*

11 Aim To develop writing skills; to write an email about a celebration you attended

- Tell Ss to use their notes from Ex. 10 and the plan to help them write their email.
- Give Ss time to complete the task and then ask various Ss to read their emails to the class.
- This task may be assigned as homework.

Suggested Answer Key

Hi Ben,
Thanks for your email. Last week I went to the Lewes Bonfire Night in Sussex. Perhaps you can write about this for your teacher. It's a celebration of Bonfire Night. It takes place every year on 5th November.
According to history, some people wanted to kill the king back in the early 17th century and planned to blow up the Houses of Parliament while he was giving a speech there. The king's men caught them before they blew everything up.
The celebration was fantastic! The evening began with a parade of locals wearing costumes and carrying torches through Lewes High Street. Marching bands were playing traditional music, too. Then they split into seven groups and let off fireworks and lit their bonfires. There were also food stalls with tasty bonfire night food. I had a delicious toffee apple.
I had the time of my life. The Lewes Bonfire Night is a must for anyone who likes parades and fireworks. Why not come with me next year?
Lucy

VALUES

Ask Ss to read the quotation, then initiate a class discussion about its meanings. Encourage all Ss to participate.

Suggested Answer Key

A: *I think the quotation means that a people's history and culture is what connects them to their community.*
B: *I totally agree. I also think it refers to how a shared history is what links people in a society and a place and with it they are stronger. etc.*

Culture 2

Listening & Reading

1 Aim To introduce the topic; to listen and read for specific information

- Ask Ss to read through the list of actions and explain/elicit the meanings of any unknown words. Then elicit which ones Ss think people say bring bad luck in the UK.
- Play the recording. Have Ss listen and read the text to find out.

Answer Key

People say that a building having a 13th floor and saying the title of a play all bring bad luck in the UK.

2 Aim To read for specific information (comprehension questions)

- Give Ss time to read the text again and then answer the questions.
- Elicit answers from Ss around the class.

Answer Key

1 *Over half of the people in the UK believe in superstitions.*
2 *They should recite a line from another of Shakespeare's plays.*
3 *They miss it out and just have floors 12 and 14.*
4 *Tourists can see the Crown Jewels and seven ravens at the Tower of London.*
5 *It marks the end of the UK.*

3 Aim To consolidate new vocabulary through synonyms

Give Ss time to complete the task using their dictionaries to help them if necessary and then check their answers.

Answer Key

interesting = *fascinating*
unique = *one of a kind*
common = *ordinary*
cautious = *careful*
stored = *kept*
occasional = *infrequent*

4 Aim To consolidate new vocabulary through antonyms

Give Ss time to complete the task and then check their answers.

Answer Key

admitting *≠ denying*
accidentally *≠ on purpose*
exit *≠ enter*
strange *≠ normal*
miss out *≠ add*
content *≠ depressed*

Speaking & Writing

5 **Aim** THINK **To discuss sayings about luck**

- Have Ss work in closed pairs and discuss the sayings about luck answering the questions in the rubric.
- Monitor the activity around the class and then ask some pairs to share their answers with the class.

Suggested Answer Key

A: I think the first saying means that if you are born lucky you will be more successful than if you are born rich.
B: I think you're right and I agree with it, do you?
A: Yes, I think I do.
B: I think the second saying means that you can be successful by making the most of opportunities.
A: Yeah. I think it also means that your decisions affect your life more than something called 'luck'. I think that is true.
B: Me too. The last saying means that negative experiences happen in threes. I don't think that is true.
A: I don't think it is either, but I think sometimes you can have more than one bad thing happen to you. etc

6 **Aim** ICT **To develop research skills; to write about superstitions and/or sayings about good/bad luck**

- Give Ss time to research online and find out information about superstitions or sayings in their country or various countries and use this information to write a short text about them.
- Ask various Ss to present their information to the class.
- This task may be assigned as homework.

Suggested Answer Key

In the UK, one superstition is that if you walk under a ladder you will have bad luck. Another says that if you open an umbrella indoors, it is bad luck. Another superstition says that you will have seven years bad luck if you break a mirror.

One saying that is used a lot in the UK is 'Lucky at cards, unlucky in love.' This means that if you win at card games you will not be happy in your romantic relationships. Another saying is 'knock on wood' or 'touch wood'. This relates to the superstition that knocking on wood will ward off bad luck.

Review 2

Vocabulary

1 **Aim** **To consolidate vocabulary from the unit**

- Explain the task.
- Give Ss time to complete it.
- Check Ss' answers.

Answer Key

1 dishes
2 costumes
3 parades
4 stalls
5 performers

2 **Aim** **To consolidate vocabulary from the unit**

- Explain the task.
- Give Ss time to complete it.
- Check Ss' answers.

Answer Key

1 highlight
2 local
3 hold
4 display
5 puppets
6 procession
7 offered
8 custom
9 brings
10 believe

3 **Aim** **To practise prepositional phrases and phrasal verbs**

- Explain the task.
- Give Ss time to complete it.
- Check Ss' answers.

Answer Key

1 in
2 up
3 up
4 with
5 out

Grammar

4 **Aim** **To practise the past simple, the past continuous or the present perfect**

- Explain the task.
- Give Ss time to complete it.
- Check Ss' answers.

Answer Key

1 went out
2 Have they arrived
3 learnt
4 hasn't eaten
5 Were you driving
6 were walking
7 started
8 entered
9 were watching
10 haven't attended

5 **Aim To practise *used to/would – be/get used to***

- Explain the task.
- Give Ss time to complete it.
- Check Ss' answers.

Answer Key

1 used to
2 is
3 use
4 get
5 didn't use to

Everyday English

6 **Aim To match exchanges**

- Explain the task.
- Give Ss time to complete it.
- Check Ss' answers.

Answer Key

1 d 2 a 3 e 4 c 5 b

Competences

Ask Ss to assess their own performance in the unit by ticking the items according to how competent they feel for each of the listed activities.

Adventures

Topic	
In this unit, Ss will explore the topics of travel, adventure activities and travel problems.	
3a Reading & Vocabulary	**20-21**
Lesson objectives: To listen and read for specific information, to read for key information (multiple matching), to learn collocations relating to adventures, to learn prepositional phrases, to practise words easily confused, to learn vocabulary relating to adventure activities, to learn phrasal verbs with *look*, to write an article for a travel magazine **Vocabulary:** Adventure activities *(hire a helicopter, come face to face with animals, interact with another culture, explore a cave, snap pictures, track rhinos)*; Nouns *(lifetime, slide, pool, abseiling, dizziness, surface)*; Verbs *(descend, admit, appreciate)*; Adjectives *(ferocious, fully-trained, leafless, leading, thrilling, extraordinary, exhausted, incredible, breathtaking)*; Adverbs *(beforehand, apparently, downstream)*	
3b Grammar in Use	**22-23**
Lesson objectives: To revise/learn the past perfect and past perfect continuous, to revise/practise the past simple vs the past perfect, to revise past tenses, to revise *a/an, the*, to continue a chain story	
3c Skills in Action	**24-25**
Lesson objectives: To learn vocabulary for types of holidays & travel disasters, to listen for key information (multiple choice), to listen and read for specific information, to act out a dialogue and practise everyday English for describing an experience and expressing interest & shock, to learn about sentence stress, to read for lexical cohesion (word formation), to listen for ideas (order of events), to write a short story, to discuss the value of boldness **Vocabulary:** Types of holidays *(agritourism holiday, diving holiday, hiking trip, camping trip, safari holiday, cruise, city break, ecotourism holiday)*; Travel disasters *(got seasick, nearly drowned, poisonous snake bit me, bee sting, burnt hand, got an infection, broke my arm, twisted my ankle)*	
Culture 3	**26**
Lesson objectives: To listen and read for specific information, to read for specific information (T/F/DS statements), to rank activities, to write a review for an online magazine **Vocabulary:** Nouns *(gust, access)*, Verbs *(whizz, tailor, squeeze, crawl, range, purchase)*; Phrasal verb *(stick to sth)*; Adjectives *(adrenaline-filled, action-packed)*; Phrases *(on your doorstep, tip of the iceberg, the basics)*	
Review 3	**27**
Lesson objectives: To test/consolidate vocabulary and grammar learnt throughout the unit; to practise everyday English	

Go through the objectives box and tell Ss that these are the topics, skills and activities this unit will cover.

3a

Listening & Reading

1 Aim To listen and read for gist

- Ask Ss to look at the pictures and elicit which countries Ss think Daniel has visited.
- Play the recording. Ss listen to and read the text to find out.

Answer Key

Daniel has visited Belize in Central America, Lake Kaindy in Kazakhstan, Forest Canyon in Nametoko Valley in Japan and Mount Nyiragongo in Congo, Africa.

Reading

2 Aim To read for specific information (multiple matching)

- Ask Ss to read the text then read the questions carefully and complete the task.
- Check Ss' answers. Ss should justify their answers.
- Then, give Ss time to look up the meanings of the words in bold in the Word List or in their dictionaries and elicit definitions from Ss around the class.

Answer Key

1 A (lionfish)
2 D (we spent the night in cabins next to the lake)
3 A (they cause problems ... reefs)
4 B (earthquake – flooding)
5 C (I'd never heard of it ... I went there)
6 B (the low temperature of the water)
7 D (gorilla tracking)
8 A (make a delicious meal)

- Give Ss time to look up the meanings of the words in the ***Check these words*** box in the Word List.

Suggested Answer Key

fully-trained (adj): *skilled*
admit (v): *to agree that sth is true*
leafless (adj): *without leaves*
appreciate (v): *to recognise how good sth is*
surface (n): *the top part of sth*
leading (adj): *the most important*
thrilling (adj): *very exciting*
extraordinary (adj): *very unusual*
exhausted (adj): *very tired*
incredible (adj): *amazing*
breathtaking (adj): *very beautiful*

- Play the video for Ss and elicit their comments.

3 **Aim** THINK **To develop critical thinking skills; to express an opinion**

Ask Ss to consider the questions on their own or with a partner and then ask various Ss to share their answers with the class.

Suggested Answer key

Daniel is an adventurous person because he travels to exotic, faraway or dangerous places and he tries new, unusual and interesting activities.
I think Lake Kaindy in Kazakhstan is the most interesting because it shows how amazing nature can be. The parts of the trees above the water have lost their leaves but those below have kept them. I think it is an amazing experience to see an underwater forest like that.

Background Information

Belize is a Central American country. English is the official language. Its capital city is Belmopan. Belize City is the largest city in Belize.
The **Republic of Kazakhstan** is located in Central Asia with the most western parts of it located in Eastern Europe. Kazakh is the official language. Its capital city is Nur-Sultan. Other major cities are Almaty and Karaganda.
Japan is an island country off the eastern coast of Asia. Japanese is the official language. Its capital city is Tokyo. Other major cities are Yokohama, Osaka, Sapporo and Kyoto.
The **Democratic Republic of Congo** is a country in Central Africa. Its official language is French. Its capital city is Kinshasa located on the southern banks of the Congo River. Other major cities are Lubumbashi and Mbuji-Mayi.

4 **Aim To consolidate new vocabulary & practise collocations**

- Ask Ss to look through the text and find the words that pair with the words in the list to make collocations.
- Check Ss' answers.

Answer Key

1 coral	*3 low*	*5 active*
2 sea	*4 high*	*6 absolutely*

Suggested Answer Key

I would love to go diving over a ***coral reef*** *and see the fish living there.*
Lake Kaindy is 2,000 metres above ***sea level****.*
The water in the lake has a ***low temperature*** *so the water is very cold.*
Canyoning involves floating downstream at ***high speed****; it's one of the best adrenaline activities.*
Mount Nyiragongo is an ***active volcano****; it has erupted at least 34 times since 1882.*
Climbing it left Daniel ***absolutely exhausted*** *so he decided to take a rest.*

5 **Aim To consolidate prepositional phrases from a text**

- Give Ss time to read the gapped text and fill in the gaps with the correct prepositions.
- Then check Ss' answers.

Answer Key

1 In	*3 over*	*5 for*
2 in	*4 for*	

6 **Aim To understand words easily confused**

- Explain the task and give Ss time to use their dictionaries to help them complete it. Ss can work in closed pairs.
- Check Ss' answers.
- As an extension, ask Ss to make sentences using the other options.
- Answer Key

1 site	*3 experienced*
2 anxious	*4 trained*

Vocabulary

7 **Aim To present vocabulary related to adventure activities**

- Give Ss time to read the six short ads and complete the gaps with the words in the list.
- Explain/Elicit the meanings of any unknown words and then check Ss' answers.

Answer Key

1 Hire	*3 interact*	*5 Snap*
2 Come	*4 Explore*	*6 track*

Background Information

Hawaii is a state of the USA located in the Pacific Ocean. Its official languages are English and Hawaiian. Its capital city is Honolulu. Other cities are Pearl City and Hilo.
The **Republic of Kenya** is a country in East Africa. Its official languages are English and Swahili. Its capital city is Nairobi. Other major cities are Mombasa and Kisumu.
The **Republic of Tanzania** is a country in East Africa. Its official languages are Swahili, English and Arabic. Its capital city is Dodoma. Other cities are Dar es Salaam and Mwanza.

8 **Aim** **To learn phrasal verbs with *look***

- Ask Ss to read the phrasal verbs box and make sure that Ss understand the definitions.
- Then give Ss time to complete the task in closed pairs and check their answers.
- Answer Key

1 *through*	3 *over*	5 *back*
2 *out for*	4 *around*	

Speaking & Writing

9 **Aim** **ICT** **To develop research skills; to write about an imaginary adventurous experience; to present an experience**

- Have Ss research online for information about adventure activities in their country or in another country and make notes under the headings provided. Tell Ss they may choose one from the experiences in Ex. 7 if they wish.
- Then give Ss time to use their notes to write a text using their notes as if they experienced the activity.
- Ask various Ss to present their experiences to the class. This task can be assigned as HW.

Suggested Answer Key

name: *Daintree Rainforest*
place: *Queensland, Australia*
what to do there: *trek through jungle, see wildlife from viewing platforms, go zip lining, stay in a lodge, cruise the river looking for saltwater crocodiles*
special skills/experience required: *none*
who appropriate for: *anyone fit*

One of the most amazing places I have ever visited is Daintree Rainforest in Queensland, Australia. It's an amazing place full of natural beauty and offers the chance to try lots of adventurous activities. I trekked through the jungle and saw lots of wildlife in their natural habitat both on the ground and from special viewing platforms hidden in the trees. The most exciting thing, though, was when I went zip lining through the canopy. What a thrill that was! You don't need to have any experience or special skills to do it, but you have to be fit. I stayed overnight in a lodge and then got up early the next day for a cruise down the river to spot saltwater crocodiles. The whole trip was an amazing experience!

3b Grammar in Use

1 **Aim** **To revise the past perfect and the past perfect continuous**

- Ask Ss to read the dialogue and find examples of the past perfect and the past perfect continuous tenses. Elicit forms.
- Have students read the list of uses (1-4) and then match them to the tenses.
- Check Ss' answers and refer Ss to the ***Grammar Reference*** section for more information or to check any points they are unsure of.

Answer Key

Past perfect: *I had always thought, the water had flooded, I had finally seen*

Past perfect continuous: *It had been raining, the guide had been working*

1 – past perfect (had flooded)
2 – past perfect (had always thought, had finally seen)
3 – past perfect continuous (had been working)
4 – past perfect continuous (had been raining)

2 **Aim** **To practise the past perfect and the past perfect continuous**

Give Ss time to complete the exercise and then check their answers around the class.

Answer Key

1 *had travelled*	6 *had been hiking*
2 *Had you been waiting*	7 *hadn't packed*
3 *hadn't woken up*	8 *Had the storm passed*
4 *had you been saving*	
5 *had booked*	

3 **Aim** **To practise the past perfect and the past perfect continuous**

- Explain the task and read out the example.
- Give Ss time to complete the task following the example.
- Elicit answers from Ss around the class.

Suggested Answer Key

2 *had seen lots of wild animals on the safari*
3 *hadn't been feeling well all morning*
4 *had been looking for a hotel for hours*
5 *hadn't taken a map*

Speaking

4 **Aim** **To practise the past perfect and the past perfect continuous using a visual prompt**

- Explain the task and ask two Ss to read out the example exchange.
- Ask Ss to ask and answer questions based on the picture following the example exchange and using the past perfect and the past perfect continuous.
- Monitor the activity around the class and then ask some pairs of Ss to ask and answer in front of the class.

Suggested Answer Key

A: Had any of the group been there before?
B: Yes, my cousin had visited the previous year.
A: How long had they been riding the elephant in this photo?
B: They had been riding the elephant for an hour.
A: Had you been riding an elephant, too?
B: Yes, I had been riding an elephant, too.
A: How long had you been riding before you reached your destination?
B: We had been riding for three hours.. etc

5 **Aim To revise the past simple vs the past perfect**

- Explain the task and give Ss time to complete it. Check Ss' answers and elicit which action happened first.
- Refer Ss to the ***Grammar Reference*** section for more information or to check any points they are unsure of.

Answer Key

1 *booked, decided, had recommended (her cousin recommended the diving holiday first)*
2 *Did you set off, left, had finished (they finished their breakfast first)*
3 *got, drove, went, hadn't done (her not going mountain climbing before came first)*
4 *Did you see, realised, hadn't brought (not bringing the camera came first)*

6 **Aim To revise/practise past tenses**

Give Ss time to read the text and complete the task and then check Ss' answers.

Answer Key

1	*Did you go*	7	*hadn't heard*
2	*caught*	8	*spoke*
3	*had been travelling*	9	*had visited*
4	*reached*	10	*went*
5	*were driving*	11	*hadn't been flying*
6	*was wondering*	12	*had been waiting*

Background Information

The **Republic of Peru** is a country in South America. Its official language is Spanish. Its capital city is Lima. Other major cities are Cusco and Arequipa.

7 **Aim To practise past tenses with personal examples**

Give Ss time to complete the sentences and then elicit answers from Ss around the class.

Suggested Answer Key

1 *... I got stuck in traffic.*
2 *... I went on a skiing holiday in France.*
3 *... I watched some TV.*
4 *... the phone rang.*
5 *... I felt confident enough to speak to a native speaker.*
6 *... I was thrilled to find out we would go next May.*

8 **Aim To revise/practise *A/An – The***

- Refer Ss to the ***Grammar Reference*** section to revise the usage of *a/an* and *the* if necessary.
- Then explain the task and give Ss time to complete it.
- Have Ss check their answers online. Alternatively, check Ss' answers in class..

Answer Key

1	*a*	9	*a*	17	*–*	25	*–*
2	*–*	10	*the*	18	*a*	26	*the*
3	*–*	11	*the*	19	*an*	27	*the*
4	*the*	12	*the*	20	*The*	28	*–*
5	*–*	13	*the*	21	*–*	29	*a*
6	*the*	14	*an*	22	*the*	30	*–*
7	*an*	15	*–*	23	*the*	31	*–*
8	*–*	16	*–*	24	*the*	32	*–*

1	*A*	3	*A*	5	*A*	7	*B*	9	*A*
2	*B*	4	*B*	6	*A*	8	*B*	10	*A*

Speaking

9 **Aim To narrate a story; to practise past tenses and definite/indefinite articles**

- Explain the task and read out the prompts and the example sentence.
- Ask Ss to work in small groups and complete the task. Then, ask various Ss to share some of their answers with the rest of the class.

Suggested Answer Key

He had already seen Big Ben and been on a river cruise down the River Thames. Tony wanted to see Tower Bridge and so they went together. Later, they went shopping in Oxford Street and bought lots of souvenirs for their friends and family. While they were walking down Oxford Street carrying all their bags, Max stepped out into the road and had an accident. He was hit by a cyclist. He hadn't seen him. The cyclist was alright but Max had been knocked to the ground and hit his head. Tony called an ambulance and Max went to hospital.

Luckily, the cyclist hadn't been going very fast and Max wasn't seriously injured. He was allowed to leave after a couple of hours. It certainly was a trip to remember.

3c Skills in Action

Vocabulary

1 a) Aim To present vocabulary related to types of holidays and travel disasters

- Ask Ss to read the list of travel disasters and the list of types of holidays.
- Explain/Elicit the meanings of any unknown words or phrases or ask Ss to look them up in the Word List and give Ss time to match the lists. Ss work in closed pairs.
- Elicit answers from Ss around the class.

Answer Key

1 f　　3 h　　5 d　　7 a
2 b　　4 g　　6 c　　8 e

b) Aim To talk about travel disasters

- Ask Ss to work in closed pairs and talk about any travel disasters like the ones in Ex. 1a that may have happened to them.
- Ask various pairs to tell the class.

Suggested Answer Key

A: *Once on a camping holiday, I fell over and twisted my ankle.*
B: *Really? On a hiking trip one time, I cut myself on a branch. etc*

Listening

2 Aim To listen for key information (multiple choice)

- Ask Ss to read questions 1-4 and the answer choices and find the key words.
- Play the recording twice. Ss listen and choose their answers.
- Check Ss' answers. You can play the recording again with pauses for Ss to check their answers.

Answer Key

1 A　　2 C　　3 B　　4 B

Everyday English

3 Aim To listen and read for specific information

- Read out the question and elicit Ss' guesses in answer to it.
- Play the recording for Ss to listen and read and find out if their guesses were correct.

Answer Key

Joan experienced a snake bite.

4 Aim To act out a dialogue and practise everyday English for describing an experience – expressing interest & shock

- Explain the task and ask Ss to act out a dialogue similar to the one in Ex. 3 in pairs using the language box and their own ideas.
- Write this diagram on the board for Ss to follow.

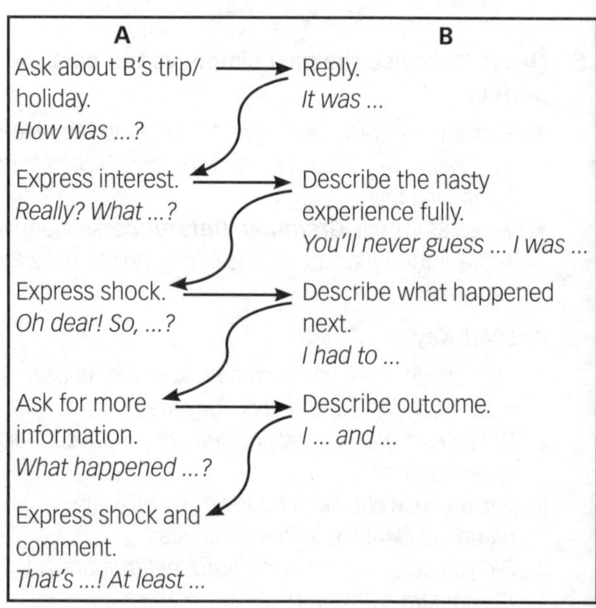

- Monitor the activity around the class and offer assistance as necessary.
- Then ask some pairs to act out their dialogues in front of the class. Ss can videotape their dialogue and evaluate it.

Suggested Answer Key

A: *How was your hiking trip in the mountains, Jane?*
B: *It was awful.*
A: *Really? What went wrong?*
B: *You'll never guess what happened. I was walking through a forest when I tripped and fell onto a dead tree and a branch cut my arm.*
A: *Oh dear! So, what did you do?*
B: *I had to make my way back to the nearest town and go to the hospital.*
A: *And what happened next?*
B: *I got some stitches and had to stay in hospital overnight.*
A: *That's awful. At least you're OK now.*

Intonation

5 **Aim** **To learn about sentence stress**

Play the recording and then elicit answers to the questions in the rubric.

Answer Key

1 *The emphasis is on the person making the request. (I) It answers the question 'Who asked?'*
2 *The emphasis is on the person required to do the action. (you) It answers the question 'Who was asked?'*
3 *The emphasis is on the object to be given. (the keys) It answers the question 'What was to be given?'*
4 *The emphasis is on the place. (to the reception) It answers the question 'Where were the keys to be given?'*

Reading & Writing

6 **Aim** **To read for lexical cohesion (word formation)**

- Give Ss time to read the story and complete the gaps with a word formed from the word in brackets.
- Check Ss' answers on the board and then elicit what type of narrative it is.

Answer Key

1 *sunny*	4 *Immediately*
2 *themselves*	5 *safety*
3 *tired*	6 *exhausted*

It is a third-person narrative.

7 **Aim** **To learn how to expand sentences**

- Read out the ***Writing Tip*** and tell Ss that this advice will help them to complete the writing task successfully.
- Have Ss read the story in Ex. 6 again and elicit an example of an expanded sentence in the story.

Answer Key

Jack and his friends, Anna, Joe and Dean, were at the local lake where they had all gone paddle boarding.

8 **Aim** **To practise expanding sentences**

- Explain the task and give Ss time to expand the sentences following the advice in the ***Writing Tip***.
- Elicit answers from Ss around the class.

Suggested Answer Key

1 *Kevin travelled by plane to Kenya last Saturday to go on a safari holiday.*
2 *Last summer, Ann went to a resort in Canada with her family to go skiing.*
3 *Last week, Jack and his sisters Kelly and Sarah were stuck in their hotel in the Alps because of an avalanche.*
4 *Yesterday, on my safari holiday in Kenya I saw an elephant.*
5 *On Sunday, Carl was hiking in the mountains with his friend Tom when he fell and injured his leg.*

Writing

9 **Aim** **To prepare for a writing task; to analyse a rubric**

- Give Ss time to read the rubric and underline the key words.
- Then elicit answers to the questions from Ss around the class.

Suggested Answer Key

Key words: *short story competition, English-language magazine for young people, must begin with 'It was a beautiful January day, and Emma and her guide, Oliver, were out husky sledding.' 120-180 words*

1 *I am going to write a short story.*
2 *The readers of an English-language magazine are going to read it.*
3 *I must start my piece of writing with 'It was a beautiful January day, and Emma and her guide, Oliver, were out husky sledding.'*
4 *I should use a third-person narrative.*
5 *I should use past tenses.*

Listening for ideas

10 **Aim** **To listen for ideas; to order events**

Ask Ss to read the sentences (A-H) and think of what order the events may have happened in. Then play the recording twice. Ss listen and order the events. Check Ss' answers.

Answer Key

1 *D*	3 *A*	5 *C*	7 *E*
2 *F*	4 *G*	6 *H*	8 *B*

11 **Aim** **To write a short story**

- Tell Ss to use the events in Ex. 10 and the plan to help them write their short story.
- Give Ss time to complete the task and then ask various Ss to read their stories to the class. Tell Ss to give their story a title.
- This task may be assigned as HW.

Suggested Answer Key

A Perfect Storm

It was a beautiful January day, and Emma and her guide, Oliver, were out husky sledding. The sky was cloudy and grey, but Emma had a big smile on her face.
They had been sledding for almost two hours when they decided to take a break. Suddenly, snow started falling heavily. Before long, they couldn't see a thing, and when they tried to move the sled, Emma slipped and hurt her ankle. Emma started to panic, but Oliver had an idea to make a shelter in the snow. They quickly dug a hole and climbed in.
They could hear the storm raging around them, but the shelter kept them safe and warm. Once the storm finally stopped, Oliver took Emma to the nearest hospital and the doctors checked her ankle. Thankfully, she hadn't broken it – just twisted it.
Emma felt relieved that she had been with Oliver. He had stayed calm and kept them both safe in the storm.

VALUES

Ask Ss to read the proverb, then initiate a class discussion about its meaning. Encourage all Ss to participate.

Suggested Answer Key

A: *I think the proverb means good luck often happens to brave people.*
B: *I think you're right. I also think it refers to how if you take a chance on something you are more likely to have a good outcome as in another saying, 'He who dares, wins.'*

Culture 3

Reading & Listening

1 **Aim To introduce the topic; to generate topic-related vocabulary**

- Set a one-minute time limit and have Ss think of as many outdoor activities as they can and write them down in their notebooks.
- At the end of the minute elicit answers from Ss around the class.

Suggested Answer Key

jogging, hiking, mountain/rock climbing, running, cycling, skateboarding, roller skating, wind-surfing, sailing, water-skiing, skiing, snowboarding, etc

2 **Aim To listen and read for specific information**

- Ask Ss to look at the headings and the pictures in the text and elicit Ss' guesses as to which of the activities people have to pay for.
- Play the recording. Ss listen to and read the text to find out if their guesses were correct.

Answer Key

You have to pay for kite-buggying in East Sussex, gorge walking on the Isle of Skye and coasteering in County Antrim. Rock climbing in Snowdonia National Park is free.

Background Information

Sussex is a county in **southeast** England.
The Isle of Skye is situated off the West Coast of Scotland. It is the largest island in the Inner Hebrides archipelago. Its main town is Portree.
Snowdonia is a region in northwestern Wales.
County Antrim is one of six counties that form Northern Ireland. Two of its main towns are Antrim and Ballymena.

3 a) **Aim To read for specific information (T/F/DS statements)**

- Give Ss time to read the statements (1-8) and to read the text again and then mark the statements according to what they read.
- Check Ss' answers around the class. Ss should justify their answers.

Answer Key

1 F (quick lesson to learn the basics)
2 T (whizzing ... sandy beach)
3 DS
4 T (guides tailor ... needs)
5 F (first-time climbers)
6 F (we had to ... hands)
7 F (adrenaline-filled)
8 DS

- Give Ss time to look up the meanings of the words in the ***Check these words*** box in the Word List.
- Play the video for Ss and elicit their comments.

b) **Aim To consolidate new vocabulary**

Give Ss time to explain the words in bold using their dictionaries to help them if necessary and then check their answers.

Suggested Answer Key

the basics (phr): *the most important parts*
squeezed (v): *managed to get through a small space*
crawled (v): *moved slowly with your body stretched out on the ground*

***range* (v):** *to vary*
***purchase* (v):** *to buy*
***adrenaline-filled* (adj):** *being full of excitement; exciting*
***action-packed* (adj):** *thrilling; being full of activity*

Suggested Answer Key

It's a good idea to learn ***the basics*** *before you try kite-buggying for the first time.*
Some canyons are so narrow that it's really difficult to ***squeeze*** *through them.*
When you go gorge walking, you sometimes have to ***crawl*** *up streams.*
There is a ***range*** *of different routes for rock climbers in Snowdonia.*
You can ***purchase*** *climbing equipment near the National Park if you haven't got your own.*
Coasteering sounds like a really ***adrenaline-filled*** *experience.*
An ***action-packed*** *day at the Giant's Causeway includes climbing, diving off cliffs and swimming.*

Speaking & Writing

4 **Aim** THINK **To develop critical thinking skills; to consolidate information in a text**

Give Ss time to complete the task and then ask various Ss to share their answers with the class.

Suggested Answer Key

1 D 2 C 3 B 4 A

I think coasteering would be too extreme for me because I am not very fit and I am not a strong swimmer.

5 **Aim** ICT **To write a review of outdoor activity breaks**

- Give Ss time to research online and find out information about outdoor activity breaks in their country and use this information to write a review about them including all the points in the rubric.
- Ask various Ss to present their reviews to the class.
- This task may be assigned as homework.

Suggested Answer Key

A Camel Safari, Uluru
Have you ever ridden a camel or been to Uluru before? This camel safari lets you do both as you roam the Australian desert on a slow-paced tour with an expert guide. It's not suitable for children or people weighing more than 100 kg. $47 for 2 hours

B Sandboarding, Stockton Bight
Visit Stockton Bight Sand Dunes, the largest sand dune system in Australia, stretching for 32 kilometres, for an adrenaline-filled sandboarding experience. As first-time sandboarders we stuck to the easier dunes but if you are more daring, you can try the enormous dunes for a bigger thrill at high speed. $28 for 1.5 hours.

C Sydney Bridge Climb, Sydney
Sydney Harbour Bridge is a tourist attraction, but it is also popular with climbers. After a full safety briefing, we put on our climbing gear and followed our guide to the top of the bridge. The view was amazing. You have to be reasonably fit to do this because by the end we had worked every muscle in our bodies. $103 for 2.5 hours.

D Kayaking, Moreton Island
We were particularly excited by this one because we had never been to Moreton Island before. We went on a tour of the Tangalooma Wrecks in a transparent kayak. We saw all the marine life swimming underneath and witnessed first-hand the beauty of the colourful corals and tropical fish below. $25 for 1 hour or $40 for 3 hours.

Review 3

Vocabulary

1 **Aim To consolidate vocabulary from the unit**

- Explain the task.
- Give Ss time to complete it.
- Check Ss' answers.

Answer Key

1 coral 3 twisted 5 explored
2 anxious 4 perfect

2 **Aim To consolidate vocabulary from the unit**

- Explain the task.
- Give Ss time to complete it.
- Check Ss' answers.

Answer Key

1 infection 3 break 5 spot
2 cruise 4 snap

3 **Aim To practise prepositional phrases and phrasal verbs**

- Explain the task.
- Give Ss time to complete it.
- Check Ss' answers.

Answer Key

1 in	*3 over*	*5 for*
2 over	*4 back on*	

Grammar

4 Aim To practise the past perfect and the past perfect continuous

- Explain the task.
- Give Ss time to complete it.
- Check Ss' answers.

Answer Key

1 *had left*
2 *hadn't been searching*
3 *hadn't brought*
4 *had reached*
5 *had been hoping*

5 Aim To practise past tenses

- Explain the task.
- Give Ss time to complete it.
- Check Ss' answers.

Answer Key

1 *Had Janet been hiking*
2 *had you been dreaming*
3 *visited*
4 *hadn't charged*
5 *had been working*

Everyday English

6 Aim To match exchanges

- Explain the task.
- Give Ss time to complete it.
- Check Ss' answers.

Answer Key

1 d   2 c   3 e   4 b   5 a

Competences

Ask Ss to assess their own performance in the unit by ticking the items according to how competent they feel for each of the listed activities.

Values: Curiosity

1 **Aim To introduce the topic: to listen and read for gist**

- Read out the questions and elicit answers from Ss around the class.
- Play the recording. Ss listen and read the text to find out if their answers were correct.

Suggested Answer Key

Curiosity makes us more intelligent, makes our lives more exciting, makes us better people, and makes us more successful. We can develop our curiosity by using technology, listening more and getting inspired by culture.

2 **Aim To read for key information (multiple matching)**

- Ask Ss to read the statements (A-F) and give them time to read the text again and match them to the benefits (1-4) in the text.
- Check Ss' answers.

Answer Key

A 2 B 1 C 3 D 4 E 3 F 2

3 **Aim To consolidate new vocabulary**

- Give Ss time to look up the meanings of the words/ phrases in bold in the text in the Word List or in their dictionaries.
- Elicit explanations from Ss around the class.

Suggested Answer Key

passionately (adv): *in a way that shows you have very strong feelings*
admire (v): *to like and respect one*
social lives (n): *the activities one does for pleasure*
wonder (n): *a feeling of admiration from seeing or experiencing sth new*
satisfied (adj): *content because you have what you want*
empathy (n): *the ability to share sb else's feelings by putting yourself in their situation*
likeable (adj): *easy to like*
on the go (phr): *while you are moving around*
daily routine (phr): *the usual activities you do every day*

4 **Aim THINK To personalise the topic**

Give Ss time to consider their answers and have Ss discuss the questions in pairs. Then ask some Ss to share their answers with the class.

Suggested Answer Key

The last time I felt curious about something was when I saw a war film and I wanted to know if the story was true. I looked on the Internet for more information and there was a lot. I also watched a lot of documentary films. I found out a lot of terrible and sad things but I also learnt about a lot of brave men and women. It really made me think about humanity and history.

5 **Aim ICT THINK To encourage curiosity; to develop research skills; to use prior knowledge; to write about a research project**

- Have Ss read the statements and tick the ones they know and research one of the ones they don't know and write a short text.
- Give Ss time to complete the task or assign as homework.
- Ask various Ss to read their text to the class.

Suggested Answer Key

I was curious to find out what the most popular first name in the world is because I hadn't really thought about it before. I did a simple Internet search and the result was Mohammed. This was surprising to me because I expected to see a Chinese name because China has the largest population in the world. Then I considered that Mohammed is traditionally a Muslim name and therefore there must be a large population of Muslims in the world so I looked that up and found out that there are 1.8 billion Muslims in the world. Then I wondered what the most popular girl's name in the world is. It is Sophia. This was also surprising because I guess I thought it would be a Muslim name. Sophia is originally a Greek name and today it is the most popular name in Mexico, Russia, Argentina, Italy, Switzerland, Estonia, Chile and Slovakia.
This one question made me curious to find out more about names and where they come from. I was surprised by what I found out and I was amazed by how one answer leads to another question.

Public Speaking Skills

1 **Aim** To analyse a rubric

Read the rubric aloud and elicit answers to the questions from Ss around the class.

Answer Key

1 *I am going to speak to secondary school students.*
2 *The talk is going to be about the benefits of going on a gap year abroad.*
3 *The purpose of the talk is to give information and advice.*

2 **Aim** To analyse a model talk

- Read out the ***Study Skills*** box and tell Ss that this tip will help them to complete the speaking skills task successfully.
- Play the recording. Ss listen to and read the model.
- Elicit answers to the questions from Ss around the class.

Answer Key

The speaker includes a personal anecdote about the first day of their gap year in Thailand.

Suggested Answer Key

I think the effect on the audience was to amuse them and make them more interested in what the speaker had to say.

3 **Aim** ICT To give a talk about going on a gap year

- Read out the rubric and explain the situation. Give Ss time to research online, consider what they will say and prepare a talk. Remind Ss to include a personal anecdote.
- Ask various Ss to give their talk to the class.

Suggested Answer Key

Good morning everyone. Congratulations! You've decided to go on a gap year. There are many options to choose from and I'm sure you'll choose what's best for you. Today I want to give you some advice to make sure you have a safe and enjoyable year.
First of all, it's a good idea to make sure you learn about the customs and manners in the country you are travelling to. For example, in Thailand, you shouldn't touch someone on the head. I found this out the hard way when I patted a small child on the head and his mother screamed at me. I didn't do it again.
Learning about the customs shows you respect the culture of the country you are visiting and will make people friendlier towards you. You should also try to learn as much of the language as you can. This will take some time, but you can learn a few phrases before you go, such as 'please' and 'thank you' and 'hello' and 'goodbye.'
Another thing you should do before you go is arrange for full travel insurance in case you become ill or have an accident abroad. You should give a copy of this and your passport and other important documents to your parents or a friend in case you lose them.
Another safety tip is to leave all your expensive gadgets at home. You won't need them and it makes you a target for crime. Plus you will see more of a country if you are not staring at a screen. You should buy a cheap phone and a local SIM card. A cheap phone will not be a target for thieves and you will not have to pay roaming charges.
Similarly, do not display any valuables when you are travelling. Leave jewellery and watches at home and keep your wallet or purse under your clothes and not in your pockets. One really good tip I learnt abroad is to have a fake wallet on you with an expired card and a small amount of money to hand over if you get robbed.
Finally, try to make friends with the locals and not just the other gap year students. This way you will get to see the place in a different light and you will really get the most out of your time in another country.
Well, that's about it from me. If anyone has any concerns they want to talk about, just find me in my office after school.

There's no place like home!

Topic	
In this unit, Ss will explore the topic of accommodation.	
4a Reading & Vocabulary	**30-31**
Lesson objectives: To introduce vocabulary for types of houses, to listen and read for gist, to read for key information (multiple matching), to learn prepositional phrases, to learn collocations related to houses, to practise words easily confused, to learn phrasal verbs with *move*, to learn idioms with *house & home*, to talk and write about an unusual home **Vocabulary:** Types of houses *(bungalow, mobile home, townhouse, cottage, terraced house, farmhouse, villa, detached house, flat, houseboat, castle, semi-detached house)*; Idioms: house & home *(get on like a house on fire, make yourself at home, nothing to write home about, put your own house in order)*; Nouns *(hook, swing, pole, concrete cube, complex, fate, resident, lack of, comfort, facility)*; Verbs *(hang, avoid, express, stretch, remind)*; Adjectives *(bumpy, level, functional, uninviting, soundproof, dull, odd, located, stunning, enormous)*; Phrases *(physical challenge, convenient access)*	
4b Grammar in Use	**32-33**
Lesson objectives: To revise/learn comparisons/types of comparisons, to learn about impersonal sentences	
4c Skills in Action	**34-35**
Lesson objectives: To learn vocabulary for accommodation, to listen for specific information (text completion), to listen and read for specific information, to act out a dialogue and practise everyday English for expressing satisfaction/dissatisfaction, to read for lexical cohesion (word formation), to learn/practise rising/falling intonation, to practise advertising language, to write an advert for a home exchange **Vocabulary:** Accommodation *(studio flat, train station, en-suite bathroom, roof garden, heated towel rail, air conditioning, central heating, basement flat, private entrance, open-plan kitchen, open fireplace, king-size bed, solar water heater, clothes dryer)*	
Culture 4	**36**
Lesson objectives: To listen and read for gist, to read for specific information (text completion), to talk about two neighbourhoods and express preference, to prepare a video/digital presentation about two neighbourhoods **Vocabulary:** Nouns *(gourmet bistro, vegan kiosk, designer boutique, barbershop, graffiti, celebrity, share, hotspot)*; Verb *(feature)*; Adjectives *(ornate, unique, well-developed, trendiest)*; Phrases *(be going strong, in the heart of)*	
Review 4	**37**
Lesson objectives: To test/consolidate vocabulary and grammar learnt throughout the unit; to practise everyday English	

Go through the objectives box and tell Ss that these are the topics, skills and activities this unit will cover.

4a

Vocabulary

1 **Aim To present vocabulary related to types of houses**

- Go through the types of houses in the list and explain/elicit the meanings of any that are unknown words Then ask Ss to do the task in closed pairs.
- Monitor the activity around the class and then ask some Ss to share their answers with the rest of the class.

Suggested Answer Key

In my country, townhouses, cottages, detached houses and flats are the most common types of houses. I live in a flat.

Reading & Listening

2 **Aim To listen and read for gist**

- Ask Ss to read the title and look at the pictures. Elicit what Ss think makes these houses unusual and what they are like on the inside.
- Play the recording. Ss listen to and read the text and find out

Suggested Answer Key

I think the size and shape of the houses makes them unique. I think on the inside they have all the usual rooms as well as some unusual features.

3 **Aim To read for key information (multiple matching)**

- Ask Ss to read the text again and then read the questions carefully and do the task.
- Ss can work in closed pairs or on their own and then compare their answers.
- Check Ss' answers.
- Then give Ss time to look up the meanings of the words in bold in the Word List or in their dictionaries and elicit definitions from Ss around the class.

Answer Key

1 A (metal poles ... accident)
2 C (Habitat 67 ... country cottage)
3 B (remind you ... trees)
4 A (The whole point ... luxury)
5 B (Next to ... 6 people)
6 C (Looking ... uninviting)

Suggested Answer Key

fate (n): *a power that some people believe controls our lives; destiny*
express (v): *to show what you feel or think*
residents (n): *people who live in a place or house; inhabitants*
stretch (v): *to make yourself/sth longer*
dull (adj): *boring*
remind (v): *to make sb think of sth they may have forgotten*
odd (adj): *unusual*
located (adj): *being in a place*
stunning (adj): *amazing*
lack of (n): *the fact that there is not enough of sth*
enormous (adj): *very big*
comfort (n): *relaxation*
convenient access (phr): *easy to be reached*
facilities (n): *buildings, equipment and services*

- Give Ss time to look up the meanings of the words in the ***Check these words*** box in the Word List.
- Play the video for Ss and elicit their comments.

Background Information

Japan is an island country off the eastern coast of the Asian continent. Its official language is Japanese and its currency is the Japanese yen. Its capital city is Tokyo. Other major cities are Yokohama and Osaka.
The Netherlands, or Holland, is a country in Western Europe along the North Sea coast. Its official language is Dutch and its currency is the euro. Its capital city is Amsterdam. It's second-largest city, Rotterdam, is a major port.
Canada is a country in the northern part of North America, Its official languages are French and English, and its currency is the Canadian dollar. Its capital city is Ottawa. Other major cities are Quebec City, Toronto, Vancouver and Montreal.

4 Aim THINK **To consolidate comprehension of a text**

Read out the questions and ask Ss to work in closed pairs and discuss them. Ask various Ss to share their answers with the class.

Suggested Answer Key

A: *I think a flat in Habitat 67 would be the most expensive to buy because it is a luxury complex and each flat has designer furniture in it.*
B: *Perhaps, but I think one of the Cube Houses in Rotterdam would be the most expensive to buy because they have 3 floors and they are in the city centre. Also, they have all the kitchen appliances as well the furniture including a TV in them. Some of them have roof gardens, too.*
A: *You have a point. It's difficult to say for sure.*

5 Aim To consolidate prepositional phrases from a text

- Give Ss time to read the sentences and choose the correct prepositions.
- Then check Ss' answers and elicit which house from Ex. 2 the advert is about.

Answer Key

1 in	*3 with*	*5 above*
2 On	*4 On*	*6 of*

The advert is for the Cube Houses in Rotterdam.

6 Aim To consolidate new vocabulary & practise collocations

- Ask Ss to look through the text and find the words that pair with the words in the list to make collocations.
- Check Ss' answers

Answer Key

1 physical	*4 narrow*	*7 natural*
2 dull	*5 fresh*	*8 luxury*
3 busy	*6 private*	

Suggested Answer Key

Climbing lots of stairs is a ***physical challenge*** *for elderly people.*
You can never have a ***dull moment*** *in New York; there is always something to do.*
I wouldn't like to live on a ***busy road****; I can't stand the noise.*
The ***narrow stairs*** *make it difficult for people to pass each other.*
I'm going outside to get some ***fresh air****.*
Each flat in the block over the road has a ***private balcony*** *with a great view of the sea.*
Big windows allow lots of ***natural light*** *to come into the house.*
Tom lives in a ***luxury complex*** *of large flats with seaside views.*

7 Aim To understand words easily confused

- Explain the task and give Ss time to use their dictionaries to help them complete it.
- Check Ss' answers.

Answer Key

1 *home*
2 *staying*
3 *study*
4 *convenient*

8 **Aim To learn phrasal verbs with *move***

- Ask Ss to read the phrasal verbs box and make sure that Ss understand the definitions.
- Then give Ss time to complete the task and check their answers.

Answer Key

1 *in*
2 *on*
3 *away*
4 *into*
5 *up*

Idioms: *house & home*

9 **Aim To learn idioms with *house* & *home***

- Give Ss time to complete the idiomatic sentences using their dictionaries if they wish.
- Elicit answers from Ss around the class.

Answer Key

1 *house* 2 *home* 3 *home* 4 *house*

Suggested Answer Key

get on like a house on fire: *get on really well*
make yourself at home: *make yourself comfortable*
nothing to write home about: *nothing special*
put your own house in order: *solve your own problems*

Speaking & Writing

10 **Aim THINK To design and present an unusual home**

- Present the situation and have Ss design an unusual home in groups and answer all the questions in the rubric.
- Then ask various groups to present their home to the rest of the class.
- After each group has presented their homes, have the class vote for the most creative design.

Suggested Answer Key

Our home is located on the outskirts of the city. It is unique because it is made of old shipping containers. The containers are joined together and stacked on top of each other. Each container is a room. Each home has two floors. There are three bedrooms so a family of 4-6 people can live there. If they want more space, they can easily add another floor of containers. The home has a modern kitchen with a cooker, a fridge and a dishwasher. It also has a comfortable lounge with a large sofa and a TV.

4b Grammar in Use

1 **Aim To revise/learn comparisons**

- Ask Ss to read the reviews and identify the comparative and superlative forms. Then elicit how we form and use them.
- Refer Ss to the ***Grammar Reference*** section for more information or to check any points they are unsure of. Focus Ss' attention on spelling rules that apply while forming the comparative/superlative degree of some adjectives/adverbs as well as irregular forms.
- Drill Ss. You can use these adjectives: *happy, good, dry, little, cosy, bad, well, lazy, nice, far.*

Answer Key

Comparative forms: *nearer, more quickly, more relaxing, quieter, harder*
Superlative forms: *the most enjoyable, the best, the noisiest, the biggest*
*We form the comparative with one-syllable adverbs and one and two-syllable adjectives by adding **-er** (nice – nicer). With adverbs of two syllables and adjectives of more than two syllables, we form the comparative with **more** (expensive – more expensive). With some two-syllable adjectives, we form the comparative either with **-er** or with **more** (quiet – more quiet/quieter).*
*We form the superlative with one-syllable and two-syllable adjectives, by adding **-est** (nice – nicer – the nicest). With adverbs and adjectives of more than two syllables, we form the superlative with **the most** (expensive – more expensive – the most expensive). With some two-syllable adjectives, we form the superlative either with **-est** or with **the most** (quiet – more quiet/quieter – the most quiet/the quietest).*

2 **Aim To practise comparative forms**

- Give Ss time to complete the task.
- Elicit answers from Ss around the class with reasons.

Answer Key

1 *the most fashionable – superlative*
2 *less modern – comparative*
3 *the earliest – superlative*
4 *hotter – comparative*
5 *more eco-friendly – comparative*
6 *the most frequently – superlative*
7 *simpler – comparative*
8 *the busiest – superlative*

3 **Aim To practise comparative/superlative forms**

Give Ss time to complete the exercise and then check their answers on the board.

Answer Key

1 *well, more professional*
2 *quieter/more quiet, the most stressful*
3 *big, cosier*
4 *faster, more sensible*
5 *the happiest, better*
6 *more efficiently, more expensive*

4 **Aim To learn about/practise types of comparisons**

- Ask Ss to read the theory box and explain any points Ss are unsure about. Refer them to the ***Grammar Reference*** section for more information if necessary.
- Then, explain the task and give Ss time to complete it. Ss can do the task is closed pairs.
- Check Ss' answers and elicit examples from the reviews in Ex. 1

Answer Key

1 *by far*	5 *to live*	9 *enough*
2 *even*	6 *too*	10 *by far*
3 *as*	7 *as*	
4 *very*	8 *very*	

Examples: *close enough, very charming, by far the biggest*

Speaking

5 **Aim To practise making comparisons**

- Explain the task and ask two Ss to read out the examples.
- Ask Ss to work in closed pairs and complete the task.
- Monitor the activity around the class and then ask some Ss to share their answers with the rest of the class.

Suggested Answer Key

...
A: *The flat isn't in an area that is as quiet as the semi-detached house.*
B: *True, but the villa is in the quietest area of all.*
A: *The semi-detached isn't as modern as the villa.*
B: *No, but the flat is the most modern of all.*
A: *The most reasonably priced accommodation is the flat.*
B: *That's true. The semi detached house is more reasonably priced than the villa.*
A: *The villa is the least economical to run.*
B: *That's true. The flat is the most economical to run.*

6 **Aim To practise comparisons through sentence transformations**

- Explain the task and give Ss time to complete it.
- Check Ss' answers around the class.

Answer Key

1 *the most beautiful house*
2 *is not as expensive as*
3 *the most attractive of*
4 *as much as*
5 *more comfortable than*
6 *by far the biggest*
7 *isn't big enough*
8 *best thing about the house*

7 **Aim To learn about impersonal sentences (*there – it*)**

- Go through the theory box with Ss. Refer Ss to the ***Grammar Reference*** section for more information or to check any points they are unsure of.
- Elicit examples from the reviews in Ex. 1.

Answer Key

There are lots of flowers ..., it's amazing how ...

8 **Aim To practise impersonal sentences**

- Give Ss time to complete the task.
- Check Ss' answers around the class.

Answer Key

1 *it, there*	5 *there, there, It*
2 *there, It*	6 *There, it*
3 *It, There, it*	7 *It, there*
4 *it, There*	

9 **Aim THINK To practise impersonal sentences in a chain story**

- Explain the task and ask Ss to take turns to say sentences using *there/it* to continue the story around the class.
- Continue until the story comes to a natural end or until you feel Ss have had enough practice.

Suggested Answer Key

There was no traffic on the roads. It was dark and rainy. It was past 10 o'clock when he arrived home. When he pulled up in his drive, there was a light on in his house. It was strange because the house was empty. There was no reason for there to be a light on. etc.

4c Skills in Action

Vocabulary

1 Aim To present vocabulary related to accommodation

- Ask Ss to read the words in the lists. Explain/Elicit the meanings of any that are unknown or ask Ss to look them up in the Word List or in their dictionaries.
- Then ask Ss to look at the adverts and complete the gaps.
- Elicit answers from Ss around the class.

Answer Key

A 1 *studio* 2 *train* 3 *en-suite* 4 *roof* 5 *heated* 6 *conditioning* 7 *central*

B 1 *basement* 2 *entrance* 3 *open-plan* 4 *fireplace* 5 *king-size* 6 *solar* 7 *dryer*

2 Aim THINK To talk about accommodation and reach a decision

- Ask Ss to work in closed pairs and discuss the questions.
- Monitor the activity around the class and then ask various pairs to share their answers with the class.

Suggested Answer Key

A: *I think the studio flat would be good for a family of three for a weekend because it is near the train station and the shops. Also, it sleeps four people.*
B: *Yes, but I think the basement flat would be the best because it is convenient for sightseeing and it has two king-size beds which are enough for a family of three. Also, it has private parking.*
A: *Yes, I suppose they are both suitable.*
B: *I think what makes the basement flat the best is that it has 5 stars from 42 reviews and the studio flat doesn't seem to have any.*
A: *OK. I can't argue with that.*

Listening

3 Aim To listen for specific information (gap fill)

- Ask Ss to read the gapped text and then play the recording twice and have Ss fill the gaps according to what they hear.
- Check Ss' answers. You can play the recording again with pauses for Ss to check their answers.

Answer Key

1 *34* 2 *walk* 3 *bus* 4 *living room* 5 *central heating* 6 *garden(s)*

Background Information

Bristol is a city and county in southwest England. It is located 120 miles west of London and is the largest city in the southwest of England. It is is situated on the River Frome and River Avon. It is a green city with 400 parks and gardens.

Everyday English

4 Aim To listen and read for specific information

Play the recording. Ss listen to and read the dialogue. Then, elicit answers to the question.

Answer Key

Mr Davies does not like the colour scheme and the fact that there is no bath.

5 Aim To act out a dialogue and practise everyday English for expressing satisfaction/dissatisfaction

- Explain the task and ask Ss to act out a dialogue similar to the one in Ex. 4 in pairs using the prompts.
- Write this diagram on the board for Ss to follow.

A
B
Welcome B and show them the first room.
So glad ... Please step ... Just through here is ...
Express satisfaction and comment.
Fantastic! It's ...
Agree and describe other features of the house/flat.
Indeed! There is ...
Express satisfaction/ dissatisfaction.
I like that. I don't really like ..., though.
Respond and show B another feature.
That's easy ... Here's the ... Look at ...!
Express satisfaction/ dissatisfaction.
That's ..., but I'd prefer ...
Respond and say a feature.
There isn't ... but there is ...
Express satisfaction and ask about price.
Perfect! What's ...?
Say price.
... pounds
Respond and comment.
Right, well, ...
Respond.
Very good. ... I'll ...

- Monitor the activity around the class and offer assistance as necessary.
- Then ask some pairs to act out their dialogues in front of the class.

Suggested Answer Key

A: *So glad you could make it for the viewing, Miss Brown. Please step this way. Just through here is the modern hall and living room.*
B: *Fantastic! It's bright and airy in here.*
A: *Indeed! There is a double bedroom with built-in wardrobes so there's lot of storage space.*
B: *I like that. I don't really like the light fittings, though.*
A: *That's easy to fix. Here's the bathroom. Look at that big bath!*
B: *That's lovely, but I'd prefer to have a shower.*
A: *There isn't a shower, but there is a heated towel rail.*
B: *Perfect! What's the price again?*
A: *One hundred and twenty thousand pounds.*
B: *Right, well, I'll think about it and let you know.*
A: *Very good, I'll look forward to that.*

Intonation

6 a) **Aim To present/identify rising/falling intonation**

- Play the recording. Elicit how each speaker feels and which sentences have rising intonation.
- Then play the recording again with pauses for Ss to repeat chorally and/or individually. Check Ss' intonation and correct where necessary.

Answer Key

1 *pleased* 3 *anxious*
2 *dissatisfied* 4 *sarcastic*

b) **Aim To practise rising/falling intonation**

Give Ss time to think of their own sentences expressing the same feelings as in Ex. 6a. Then have Ss work in open pairs with one S saying their sentence using the correct intonation and the other S guessing the emotion.

Suggested Answer Key

A: *This house ↘ is charming.*
B: *You are being sarcastic. I ↗ really like it.*
A: *You are pleased. etc*

Reading & Writing

7 **Aim To read for lexical cohesion (word formation)**

- Give Ss time to read the advert and complete the gaps with a word formed from the word in brackets.
- Check Ss' answers.

Answer Key

1 *Located* 6 *Spacious*
2 *walking* 7 *equipped*
3 *comfortable* 8 *central*
4 *recently* 9 *different*
5 *visitors* 10 *gardening*

Background Information

Edinburgh is Scotland's capital city. It is the seat of the Scottish Government, the Scottish Parliament and the supreme courts of Scotland. The city's Palace of Holyroodhouse is the official residence of the monarch in Scotland.

8 **Aim To prepare for a writing task**

- Read out the ***Writing Tip*** and tell Ss that this advice will help them to complete the writing task successfully.
- Have Ss read the advert in Ex. 7 again and find examples of all the advertising language features in the list.
- Elicit answers from Ss around the class.

Answer Key

a) *15-minute bus ride ..., House consists of ..., Second bathroom ..., Kitchen fully-equipped ...*
b) *Modern, greatest, official, comfortable, bigger, smaller, redecorated, convenient, fully-equipped, highest*

9 **Aim To practise advertising language**

- Explain the task and read out the example.
- Give Ss time to complete the task and check Ss' answers around the class.

Answer Key

2 *Cool, shady garden on roof.*
3 *Spare bedroom in basement.*
4 *Ten-minute train ride to centre.*
5 *Full English breakfast provided.*
6 *Situated by the river.*

Writing

10 a) **Aim To prepare for a writing task**

Ask Ss to copy the headings into their notebooks and make notes about their home.

Suggested Answer Key

Type of house: *flat*
Location: *city centre, close to public transport*

Description: *first floor flat, two double bedrooms, fully equipped kitchen, open-plan lounge & dining area, large balconies*
Features: *central heating, air conditioning, private parking, Wi-Fi, cable TV*
More about you: *my sister and I love travelling, I like going to concerts and plays, sister likes walking and hiking*

b) **Aim To write an advert for a home exchange**

- Tell Ss to use their notes from Ex. 10a and the plan to help them write their advert.
- Give Ss time to complete the task and then ask various Ss to read their adverts to the class.
- This task may be assigned as homework.

Suggested Answer Key

HolidayHomeExchange
Great Flat in central Athens
2 bedrooms ***Sleeps 4*** ***1 bathroom***
About our home
Located in the heart of Athens city centre, this modern flat offers the greatest opportunity to see the city sights. The Acropolis and the old town of Plaka are both within walking distance.
Flat consists of two comfortable double bedrooms and a modern fully equipped kitchen. Open-plan lounge and dining area as well as large balconies with great views.
Features
central heating *air conditioning*
private parking *Wi-Fi*
cable TV
More about us
My sister and I love travelling and seeing new places and meeting new people. We like exploring cities and we also love the countryside. In my free time, I like going to concerts and plays and my sister likes walking and hiking.

VALUES

Ask Ss to read the quotation, then initiate a class discussion about its meanings. Encourage all Ss to participate.

Suggested Answer Key

A: *I think the quotation means that if you can be content at home then you are happier than most people.*
B: *I agree. I also think it refers to being able to be satisfied with what you have in life. Like, for example, whether your home is a small flat or a big house as long as you are comfortable and relaxed there, it doesn't matter what luxuries you may or may not have. etc.*

Culture 4

Listening & Reading

1 **Aim To introduce the topic; to listen and read for gist**

- Ask Ss to look at the map and read the title of the text. Explain that the two areas are in New York. Read out the question. Play the recording. Ss listen to and read the text and answer the question.
- Elicit answers from Ss.

Answer Key

Both of these neighbourhoods are in the district of Manhattan in New York City. They both have brownstone houses and they are both related to the arts.

2 **Aim To read for key information (text completion)**

- Give Ss time to read the text again and then complete the email extract with one-word answers.
- Elicit answers from Ss around the class.

Answer Key

1 neighbourhoods	*4 organised*
2 artists	*5 graffiti*
3 townhouses	*6 African*

- Then give Ss time to explain the words in bold using their dictionaries or the Word List to help them.

Suggested Answer Key

in the heart of (phr): *in the centre of*
well developed (adj): *having grown in a positive way*
celebrities (n): *famous people*
trendiest (adj): *the most fashionable*
has got its share of (phr): *has got a reasonable amount of sth*
hotpsot (n): *a popular place*
featured (v): *included sth/sb as an important part*

- Give Ss time to look up the meanings of the words in the ***Check these words*** box in the Word List.
- Play the video for Ss and elicit their comments.

Speaking & Writing

3 **Aim THINK To compare two neighbourhoods; to express a preference**

- Have Ss work in closed pairs and compare the two neighbourhoods and discuss which one they prefer and why.
- Monitor the activity around the class and then ask some pairs to share their answers with the class.

Suggested Answer Key

A: *Greenwich Village is downtown but Harlem is uptown.*
B: *That's right, but both neighbourhoods are related to the arts.*
A: *Yes, though Greenwich Village is a bit more cultured because it attracted artists and writers and Harlem attracted street artists.*
B: *Yeah. Greenwich Village is trendy and expensive whereas Harlem is less trendy and less expensive.*
A: *That's right but Harlem has deep roots in African American culture and helped to make jazz and R&B more popular especially through the Apollo Theater.*
B: *I think I would like to live in Harlem because it has a rich history and there are still family-owned businesses and cafés there that have been there for 40 years. I think it would have a good community atmosphere.*
A: *OK, well, I think I would like to live in Greenwich Village because it is a trendy and rich area with lots of designer boutiques. I think it would be cool to live there.*

4 **Aim** ICT **To present two neighbourhoods via video or a digital presentation**

- Ask Ss to work in small groups and give them time to research online and find out information about two neighbourhoods in their town/city or their capital city and make notes under the headings provided. Then tell Ss to use this information to prepare a video or a digital presentation.
- Ask various groups of Ss to make their presentations to the class.
- This task may be assigned as homework.

Suggested Answer Key

Neighbourhoods of London

Soho

The West End neighbourhood of Soho in the City of Westminster has always been a fashionable area popular with the upper class. It became well known up to the 19th century as the home of the aristocracy. Later, it became a major entertainment area with music clubs, theatres and publishing houses. These days, Soho is an extremely well developed and rich area. Along with the theatres and music clubs there are lots of gourmet restaurants and media offices and it is home to the independent British film industry. Families, celebrities and business people live there making it one of the trendiest neighbourhoods in London.

Brixton

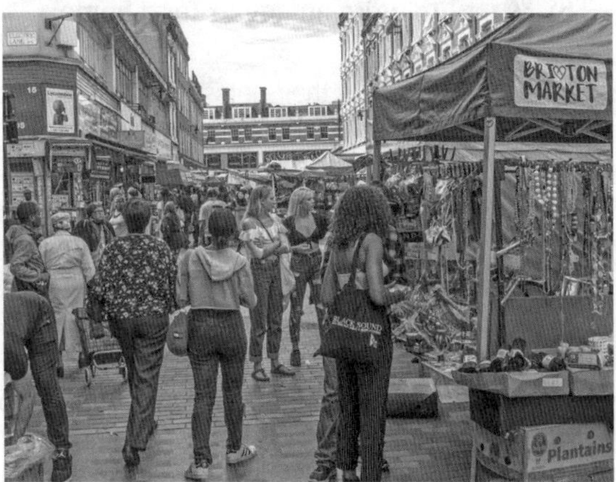

For a less trendy neighbourhood, let's visit Brixton in South London. It was an area popular with the middle classes up to the late 1800s and then it developed into an entertainment centre with a large market, cinemas and pubs. From the 1950s, lots of people from the West Indies settled in Brixton and it developed an African Caribbean culture. Today there is a thriving art scene as well as markets, art galleries, delicatessens, bars, cafés and vintage clothing stores. Brixton Market is now famous and attracts people from all over London.

Review 4

Vocabulary

1 **Aim To consolidate vocabulary from the unit**

- Explain the task.
- Give Ss time to complete it.
- Check Ss' answers.

Answer Key

1 mobile	*4 block*	*7 private*
2 natural	*5 air*	*8 busy*
3 luxury	*6 house*	

2 **Aim To consolidate vocabulary from the unit**

- Explain the task.
- Give Ss time to complete it.
- Check Ss' answers.

Answer Key

1 *king-size*	4 *solar*	7 *dryer*
2 *roof*	5 *basement*	8 *open-plan*
3 *en-suite*	6 *train*	

3 Aim To practise prepositional phrases and phrasal verbs

- Explain the task.
- Give Ss time to complete it.
- Check Ss' answers.

Answer Key

1 *in*	3 *on*	5 *into*
2 *on*	4 *with*	

Grammar

4 Aim To practise comparisons

- Explain the task.
- Give Ss time to complete it.
- Check Ss' answers.

Answer Key

1 *the worst*	4 *more modern*
2 *as cheap*	5 *the most historic*
3 *the least expensive*	

5 Aim To practise types of comparisons

- Explain the task.
- Give Ss time to complete it.
- Check Ss' answers.

Answer Key

1 *enough*	3 *It*	5 *very*
2 *there*	4 *too*	

Everyday English

6 Aim To match exchanges

- Explain the task.
- Give Ss time to complete it.
- Check Ss' answers.

Answer Key

1 *e* 2 *d* 3 *b* 4 *a* 5 *c*

Competences

Ask Ss to assess their own performance in the unit by ticking the items according to how competent they feel for each of the listed activities.

Let's talk

Topic	
In this unit, Ss will explore the topics of ways to communicate, textspeak, body language and feelings.	
5a Reading & Vocabulary	**38-39**
Lesson objectives: To introduce vocabulary for ways to communicate, to read for gist, to read and listen for cohesion and coherence (gapped text), to learn collocations related to communication, to learn prepositional phrases, to practise words easily confused, to learn phrasal verbs with *keep*, to talk about the dangers of brain-to-brain communication, to write about the pros and cons of brain-to-brain communication, to have a class debate **Vocabulary:** Ways to communicate *(verbal, non-verbal, written, visual, drawing, eye contact, facial expressions, gestures, speech, touch, text message, video chat, writing, TV, radio, newspapers, magazines)*; Nouns *(language barrier, element, impact, session, expert)*; Verbs *(interact, govern)*; Phrasal verbs *(get sth across, come up with)*; Adjectives *(paralysed)*; Phrases *(tone of voice, communication breakdown, at risk, commit crimes)*	
5b Grammar in Use	**40-41**
Lesson objectives: To revise future tenses, to revise time clauses, to talk about the future	
5c Skills in Action	**42-43**
Lesson objectives: To learn vocabulary for textspeak, to listen for specific information (multiple choice), to listen and read for specific information, to act out a dialogue and practise everyday English for agreeing/disagreeing & expressing doubt, to learn intonation when expressing feelings, to read for cohesion and coherence (missing sentences), to learn/practise linkers, to write a for-and-against essay, to discuss the value of communication **Vocabulary:** Textspeak *(BB, BRB, CUL, IDK, F2F, ATM, AFK, BBS, tbh, thx, NP, ASAP, WB, PLZ, JK, L8R, HF, GR8, BTW)*	
Culture 5	**44**
Lesson objectives: To listen and read for specific information; To read for gist (match headings to paragraphs), to talk about body language in the UK and in one's country, to prepare a presentation on body language and gestures in one's country **Vocabulary:** Nouns *(globetrotter, bow, balance)*; Verbs *(stare, nod, tend, greet, glance, lean)*; Adjectives *(seasoned, crucial, non-verbal, appropriate, typical, fluent)*; Adverb *(greatly)*; Idioms *(variety is the spice of life)*	
Review 5	**45**
Lesson objectives: To test/consolidate vocabulary and grammar learnt throughout the unit; to practise everyday English	

Go through the objectives box and tell Ss that these are the topics, skills and activities this unit will cover.

5a

Vocabulary

1 Aim To present vocabulary related to ways to communicate

- Ask Ss to look at the mindmap and read the list of ways to communicate.
- Explain/Elicit the meanings of any unknown words or phrases.
- Ss complete the mindmap in their notebooks. Tell Ss some words and phrases fit more than one category.
- Ss do the task in closed pairs.
- Check Ss' answers on the board.

Suggested Answer Key

verbal: *speech, video chat, TV, radio*
non-verbal: *drawing, eye contact, facial expressions, gestures, touch, text message, writing, newspapers/magazines*
written: *drawing, text message, writing, newspapers/magazines*
visual: *drawing, eye contact, facial expressions, gestures, text message, video chat, TV, newspapers/magazines*

Reading & Listening

2 Aim To scan a text; to read for gist

- Ask Ss to scan the text and then elicit whether this idea about the future of communication seems interesting or not to Ss.
- Ask various Ss to share their answers with the class.

Suggested Answer Key

I think it is an interesting idea but I don't think I would like to try it with anyone I didn't already know very well. I wouldn't like strangers to know my thoughts.

3 Aim To listen and read for cohesion and coherence (gapped text)

- Ask Ss to read the text again and then read the sentences (A-H) carefully and match them to the gaps (1-5). Remind Ss there are three extra sentences. As Ss to pay attention to words before and after each gap as this will help them do the task
- Play the recording for Ss to listen and check their answers.
- Then, give Ss time to look up the meanings of the words in bold in the Word List or in their dictionaries and elicit definitions from Ss around the class.

Answer Key

1 E (fully understand ... Misunderstandings)
2 G (control things using thoughts ... computer ... move robotic arm with BCI)
3 A (people unable to talk ... They will be able to communicate)
4 H (mind control ... unwelcome mind-reading ... anyone can access our private thoughts and feelings)
5 D (Possible dangers ... Despite these concerns)

Suggested Answer Key

element (n): *a part of sth*
get sth across (phr v): *to make sb understand sth*
communication breakdowns (phr): *when exchanging information fails*
impact (n): *effect*
sessions (n): *periods of time or meetings for a particular activity*
expert (n): *a person who knows a lot on a particular subject*
at risk (phr): *in danger*
come up with (phr v): *to think of; to suggest an idea*

- Give Ss time to look up the meanings of the words in the ***Check these words*** box in the Word List.
- Play the video for Ss and elicit their comments.

4 Aim To consolidate prepositional phrases from a text

- Give Ss time to read the sentences and fill in the correct prepositions.
- Ask Ss to check their answers in their dictionaries.
- Check Ss' answers.

Answer Key

1 at	3 across	5 from
2 of	4 on	6 about

5 Aim To consolidate new vocabulary & practise collocations

- Ask Ss to look through the text and find the words that pair with the words in the list to make collocations.
- Check Ss' answers.

Answer Key

1 body	3 language	5 national
2 massive	4 mind	6 daily

Suggested Answer Key

Body language *can say a lot about a person.*
BCI would have a ***massive impact*** *on the lives of paralysed people.*
When two people don't speak the same language we call this a ***language barrier****.*
Hypnotism is a type of ***mind control****.*
Brain-to-brain technology could be a threat to ***national security*** *as the safety of a country is extremely important.*
Communicating with others quickly and accurately makes everyone's ***daily life*** *easier.*

6 Aim To understand words easily confused

- Explain the task and give Ss time to use their dictionaries to help them complete it.
- Check Ss' answers and then elicit sentences with the unused words from Ss around the class.

Answer Key

1 communicate	3 talk
2 speak	

Suggested Answer Key

I'd like to ***express*** *my thanks to you for coming to my party.*
Can you ***say*** *that again, please? I didn't hear you.*
Can you ***tell*** *me the time, please?*

7 Aim To learn phrasal verbs with *keep*

- Ask Ss to read the phrasal verbs box and make sure that Ss understand the definitions.
- Then give Ss time to complete the task and check their answers.

Answer Key

1 from	3 down	5 up
2 on	4 out	

Speaking & Writing

8 Aim THINK To expand the topic and develop critical thinking skills

Give Ss time to consider the questions either alone or with a partner and then ask various Ss to share their answers with the class.

Suggested Answer Key

I think one of the dangers of brain-to-brain communication would be that you could get hacked in the same way a computer can get hacked. A stranger could access your thoughts and find out sensitive or private information. I guess a way to prevent this would be to have a sort of a firewall or a security system for your brain that could block them. Maybe this would be a metal hat or something more sophisticated like a microchip.

9 Aim To discuss ways to communicate

- Present the situation and have Ss work in small groups and suggest ways to communicate.

- Then ask various groups to present their ideas to the rest of the class.

Suggested Answer Key

A: *I think I would use gestures as much as I could and use my hands to point to things or try to make simple requests.*

B: *Another suggestion would be to do simple drawings to try and communicate something a bit more complicated.*

C: *What about using a translation app or a phrasebook? I think that would help a lot. etc*

10 Aim ICT To develop research skills; to write and talk about the pros and cons of the topic; to have a class debate

- Ask Ss to work in small groups and then give them time to research the topic of brain-to-brain communication online and make notes about the pros and cons of the topic.
- Tell Ss to use their notes to prepare an argument either in favour of or against the topic.
- Then initiate a class debate where each group contributes to a serious discussion on the topic.

Suggested Answer Key

Pros: *crime may be reduced because criminals may be caught early; the justice system may improve because no innocent people would go to jail*

Cons: *personal relationships would suffer because no thoughts would be private; people may have health problems such as headaches or mental health problems such as anxiety*

A: *I think brain-to-brain communication is a good thing because we could use it to reduce crime. If we could read the minds of criminals, we could catch them early and send them straight to jail.*

B: *Good point. Also, it may put them off committing crimes in the first place if they knew they would get caught.*

C: *Yes, I agree. And this would also have an effect on the justice system because no innocent people would go to jail. If their brain had no specific knowledge about the crime, how could they have committed it?*

D: *Exactly. But if nobody's thoughts are private, that would create a lot of problems. For example, in personal relationships, if no thoughts were private, the relationship would suffer.*

A: *I see your point. I think it may also cause people health problems like headaches if their brain was constantly being read or sent messages by other brains.*

B: *That's a very interesting argument. I think it might also lead to mental health problems like anxiety. If you were worried all the time about someone reading your thoughts or if you were a shy person and didn't want to share your thoughts with anyone, that might cause a lot of stress. etc*

5b Grammar in Use

1 Aim To revise future tenses

- Ask Ss to read the forum entry and identify the tenses in bold. Elicit how each tense is formed. Then Ss match the tenses to the uses in the list.
- Refer Ss to the ***Grammar Reference*** section for more information or to check any points they are unsure of.

Answer Key

start – *present simple – timetables*
'm giving – *present continuous – fixed arrangements in the near future*
'm going to fail – *be going to – predictions based on what we can see or know*
will help – *future simple – predictions based on what we think or imagine*
'll have finished – *future perfect – actions that will have finished before a stated time in the future*
'll be wondering – *future continuous – action in progress at a definite time in the future*
won't fail – *future simple – predictions based on what we think or imagine*

2 Aim To practise future forms

- Give Ss time to complete the task.
- Elicit answers from Ss around the class with reasons.

Answer Key

1 *will ever get (prediction based on what we think or imagine)*
2 *'ll be talking (action in progress at a definite time in the future)*
3 *'m going to buy (action we have already decided to do)*
4 *won't have finished (action that will [not] have finished before a stated time in the future)*
5 *will be updating (action in progress at a definite time in the future)*
6 *launches (timetable)*
7 *is going to be (prediction based on what we can see or know)*
8 *'m meeting (fixed arrangement in the near future)*

3 **Aim** **To practise *will – be going to***

Give Ss time to complete the exercise and then check their answers around the class.

Answer Key

1 *will*	5 *is going to*
2 *will*	6 *will*
3 *am going to*	7 *will*
4 *will*	

4 **Aim** **To practise the present simple and the present continuous (future meaning)**

- Explain the task and give Ss time to complete it.
- Check Ss' answers and elicit reasons from Ss around the class.

Answer Key

1 *takes off (timetable)*
2 *is starting (fixed future arrangement)*
3 *closes (timetable)*
4 *starts (timetable)*
5 *are holding (fixed future arrangement)*
6 *is attending (fixed future arrangement)*

Speaking

5 **Aim** **To practise future forms**

- Explain the task and read out the example.
- Ask Ss to work in closed pairs and complete the task.
- Monitor the activity around the class and then ask some Ss to share their answers with the rest of the class.

Suggested Answer Key

2 *We are going to get wet.*
3 *It usually comes at 4:15.*
4 *I will look after it, I promise.*
5 *I'm working late tonight.*
6 *We are going to miss the bus!*
7 *I am making a cake later and I haven't got enough.*
8 *I will make a sandwich.*

6 **Aim** **To practise the future continuous and the future perfect**

- Explain the task and give Ss time to complete it.
- Check Ss' answers and elicit reasons from Ss around the class.

Answer Key

1 *will be having (action in progress at a definite time in the future – at 5 o'clock tomorrow afternoon)*
2 *will have given (action that will have finished before a stated time in the future – by 6 o'clock next Friday)*
3 *will probably be replying (action in progress at a definite time in the future – all morning)*
4 *will have learnt (action that will have finished before a stated time in the future – by the time she graduates)*
5 *will be recording (action in progress at a definite time in the future – on Thursday at 10 am)*
6 *will have installed (action that will have finished before a stated time in the future – by this time next week)*
7 *will have spoken (action that will have finished before a stated time in the future – by tomorrow afternoon)*
8 *will have been (action that will have finished before a stated time in the future – for three hours by noon)*

Speaking

7 **Aim** **To practise future forms**

- Explain the task and read out the example exchange.
- Then have Ss complete the task in pairs using futures tenses and the sentences in Ex. 6 following the example.
- Monitor the activity around the class and then ask some pairs to ask and answer in front of the rest of the class.

Suggested Answer Key

A: Will you have given a speech by 6 o'clock next Friday?
B: Yes, I will. /No, I won't. I will have finished my assignment by 6 o'clock next Friday.
A: Will you be replying to emails all morning on Monday?
B: Yes, I will. / No, I won't. I will be answering calls all morning on Monday.
A: Will you have learnt sign language by the time you graduate?
B: Yes, I will. /No, I won't. I will have learnt a computing language by the time I graduate.
A: Will you be recording your first podcast on Thursday at 10 am?
B: Yes, I will. /No, I won't. I will be writing an essay on Thursday at 10 am.
A: Will they have installed the optical fibre by this time next week?
B: Yes, they will. /No, they won't. They will have installed a new router by this time next week.
A: Will you have spoken to your manager by tomorrow afternoon?
B: Yes, I will. /No, I won't. I will have spoken to my lecturer by tomorrow afternoon.
A: Will you have been online for three hours by noon?
B: Yes, I will. /No, I won't. I will have been working in the garden for three hours by noon.

8 **Aim** To practise future forms

- Give Ss time to complete the task.
- Check Ss' answers around the class.

Answer Key

1 *will read*	4 *won't have finished*
2 *isn't going to answer/ isn't answering*	5 *are going to drop*
	6 *is flying/will be flying*
3 *will call*	7 *are going to chat*

9 **Aim** To practise future tenses

- Explain the task and give Ss time to complete it.
- Check Ss' answers and elicit reasons from Ss around the class.

Answer Key

1 *D (fixed future arrangement)*
2 *C (action in progress at a definite time in the future)*
3 *A (prediction based on what we think or imagine)*
4 *A (action that will have finished before a stated time in the future)*
5 *C (fixed future arrangement)*

10 **Aim** To revise time clauses

- Direct Ss to the highlighted verbs in the forum on p. 40. Elicit what tenses we use after time words/ phrases and when we use *will* after *when*.
- Refer Ss to the ***Grammar Reference*** section for more information or to check any points they are unsure of.

Suggested Answer Key

Time clauses follow the rule of the sequence of tenses. If the main clause is in the present simple, the present continuous, future tenses or the imperative then the time clause can be in the present simple, the present continuous or the present perfect. When the main clause is in the past simple or the past perfect then the time clause can be in the past simple, the past continuous or the past perfect.
We use will after 'when' when it is used as a question word.

11 **Aim** To practise time clauses

Explain the task and give Ss time to complete it. Then check their answers.

Answer Key

1 *will call, lands*	4 *won't buy, breaks*
2 *will send, leave*	5 *Will, finish*
3 *will have missed, arrive*	

Speaking

12 **Aim** To practise future forms

- Explain the task and ask two Ss to read out the example conversation.
- Then have Ss complete the task in closed pairs.
- Monitor the activity around the class.
- Ask some pairs to act out their dialogues.

Suggested Answer Key

A: I'm going to a concert at the weekend.
B: What are you going to see?
A: I'm going to see "No Time to Die". I've got a spare ticket. Would you like to come?
B: I'd love to. When is it?
A: It's on Saturday at 8 pm at the stadium. Gates open at 6:30 pm.
B: I'll have finished all my chores and homework by then.
A: Great. I'll pick you up at 6 then.
B: OK. Are you going to drive there?
A: Yes, I am. It will be easier than going by train. etc

5c Skills in Action

Vocabulary

1 a) **Aim** To present vocabulary related to textspeak

- Ask Ss to read the abbreviations and the definitions in the lists and match them.
- Elicit answers from Ss around the class.

Answer Key

1 *f*	3 *g*	5 *h*	7 *a*	9 *e*
2 *j*	4 *b*	6 *d*	8 *i*	10 *c*

b) **Aim** To present vocabulary related to textspeak

- Read out the items and elicit Ss' guesses as to what they mean.
- Ask Ss to check their answers online.
- Check Ss' answers.

Answer Key

1 *no problem*	6 *later*
2 *as soon as possible*	7 *have fun*
3 *welcome back*	8 *great*
4 *please*	9 *by the way*
5 *kidding*	

2 **Aim** To talk about textspeak

- Ask Ss to work in closed pairs and discuss the questions.

- Monitor the activity around the class and then ask various pairs to share their answers with the class.

Suggested Answer Key

A: *I use textspeak when I send messages to friends because it is faster and easier than typing everything out in full.*
B: *Yeah, me too. It takes too long to reply if you type properly and slows down the conversation.*

Listening

3 a) **Aim To listen for specific information (multiple choice)**

- Ask Ss to read the questions and the answer choices and then play the recording twice and have Ss choose their answers according to what they hear.
- Check Ss' answers. You can play the recording again with pauses for Ss to check their answers.

Answer Key

1 A   2 B   3 A   4 C

b) **Aim To express an opinion on textspeak**

- Ask Ss to work in closed pairs and discuss the question.
- Monitor the activity around the class and then ask various pairs to share their opinions with the class.

Suggested Answer Key

A: *I believe textspeak does have a negative effect on the way people use language. I think it makes people lazy. For example, they can't be bothered to write a word or phrase out in full and in the end this affects their spelling and their ability to write a sentence well.*
B: *I don't entirely agree. I think it can be used in informal situations to make our language more friendly and personal. Also, it helps us to express our thoughts more quickly so we don't forget them!*

Everyday English

4 **Aim To listen and read for specific information**

Play the recording. Ss listen to and read the dialogue and then elicit an answer to the question.

Answer Key

Jim is confused about the message because he doesn't understand textspeak.

5 **Aim To act out a dialogue and practise everyday English for agreeing/disagreeing and expressing doubt**

- Explain the task and ask Ss to act out a dialogue similar to the one in Ex. 4 in pairs using the prompts.
- Write this diagram on the board for Ss to follow.

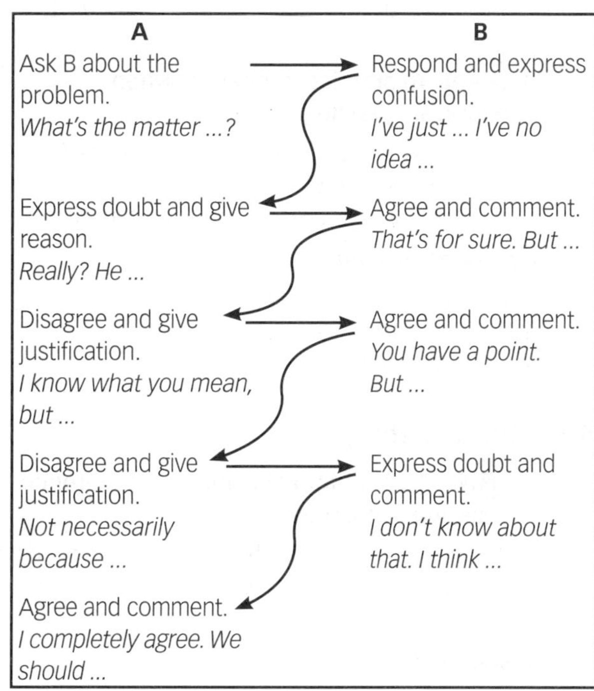

A
B
Ask B about the problem.
What's the matter ...?
Respond and express confusion.
I've just ... I've no idea ...
Express doubt and give reason.
Really? He ...
Agree and comment.
That's for sure. But ...
Disagree and give justification.
I know what you mean, but ...
Agree and comment.
You have a point. But ...
Disagree and give justification.
Not necessarily because ...
Express doubt and comment.
I don't know about that. I think ...
Agree and comment.
I completely agree. We should ...

- Monitor the activity around the class and offer assistance as necessary.
- Then ask some pairs to act out their dialogues in front of the class.

Suggested Answer Key

A: *What's the matter, John?*
B: *I've just looked in on our son and he's preparing a podcast again. I've no idea why he does it.*
A: *Really? He does it because he enjoys it.*
B: *That's for sure. But I think he spends too much time in front of his PC.*
A: *I know what you mean, but podcasting is a great way to develop research skills. You have to know what you're talking about or no one will listen to the podcast.*
B: *You have a point. But I think he doesn't socialise enough.*
A: *Not necessarily. He chats with his listeners all the time and responds to their comments.*
B: *I don't know about that. I think he needs to spend more time in the real world and meet people face-to-face.*
A: *I completely agree. We should talk to him about that.*

Intonation

6 a) **Aim** **To present intonation when expressing feelings**

Play the recording. Elicit how each speaker feels.

Answer Key

a 3 b 1 c 4 d 2

b) **Aim** **To practise intonation when expressing feelings**

- Ask Ss to practise expressing different feelings using the words provided.
- Check Ss' intonation and correct where necessary.

Suggested Answer Key

Yeah! – agreement/enthusiasm
Hey! – irritation/enthusiasm/excitement
Right! – agreement

Reading & Writing

7 a) **Aim** **To read for cohesion and coherence (missing sentences)**

- Give Ss time to read the essay and complete the gaps with a topic sentence from the list (1-4).
- Check Ss' answers.

Answer Key

B 2 C 4

b) **Aim** **To prepare for a writing task**

- Read out the ***Writing Tip*** and tell Ss that this advice will help them to complete the writing task successfully.
- Elicit alternative topic sentences from Ss around the class.

Suggested Answer Key

Face-to-face communication has a number of advantages.
Nevertheless, there are some disadvantages to face-to-face communication.

8 **Aim** **To present/practise linkers**

- Refer Ss to the essay in Ex. 7a and give them time to match the underlined linkers to their uses in the list.
- Check Ss' answers and then elicit synonymous ones from Ss around the class.

Answer Key/Suggested Answer Key

express contrast: *Despite the fact that (In spite of the fact that, Even though)*
add points: *In addition, (Also, Moreover, Furthermore)*
list points: *In the first place, Firstly, Secondly, (To start with, To begin with, First, Second)*
conclude: *In conclusion (To sum up, All in all, Overall)*
give examples: *For instance, For example (In particular, To take one example)*

Writing

9 a) **Aim** **To prepare for a writing task**

- Ask Ss to underline the key words in the rubric and then answer the questions.
- Check Ss' answers.

Suggested Answer Key

Key words: *teacher, essay, pros and cons of using textspeak, 120-180 words*

1 I am going to write an essay for my teacher.
2 I am going to write about the pros and cons of using textspeak.
3 I should write in a formal style.

b) **Aim** **To prepare for a writing task**

Ask Ss to read the arguments and the justifications/examples and match them to each other. The elicit which ones are for/against the topic.

Answer Key

1 c (against) 3 b (against)
2 a (for) 4 d (for)

10 **Aim** **To write a for-and-against essay**

- Tell Ss to use their answers from Ex. 9b and the plan to help them write their essay.
- Give Ss time to complete the task and then ask various Ss to read their essays to the class.
- This task may be assigned as homework.

Suggested Answer Key

These days lots of people use abbreviations when communicating online and in messages. Textspeak is a very popular method of communicating especially with young people. However, what are the pros and cons of using it?
Textspeak has a number of advantages. Firstly, it is a very convenient way to communicate. For instance, it is much faster than writing full sentences and it takes up less space, so it is perfect for sending a quick short message. Secondly, it is fun and creative. People use it to chat with friends and they can invent new abbreviations of their own.
On the other hand, there are some disadvantages to using textspeak. To start with, it promotes misspelling. Therefore, it can have a negative affect on schoolwork. Furthermore, textspeak excludes and confuses some

people. For example, older people might not be familiar with it and so might not understand it.
Overall, I believe that textspeak has its advantages. Despite the fact that it promotes misspelling and excludes some people, it is fast and fun.

VALUES

Ask Ss to read the quotation, then initiate a class discussion about its meanings. Encourage all Ss to participate.

Suggested Answer Key

A: I think the quotation means that we should listen to what someone is saying but we should also try and work out what they are not saying.
B: I agree. I think it refers to paying attention to someone's body language and non-verbal cues when they are speaking to get extra information.
A: Absolutely! We can listen to the tone of someone's voice and look at their facial expressions to find out about their feelings. etc

Culture 5

Listening & Reading

1 Aim To introduce the topic; to listen and read for specific information

- Ask Ss to look at the pictures. Elicit what each one shows and when Ss think the British use them.
- Play the recording. Ss listen to and read the text and find out if their guesses were correct.

Suggested Answer Key

Shaking hands, hugging or kissing on the cheek are greetings. I think the British shake hands when they meet someone for the first time, in formal situations or when some men greet their friends and family. I think the British hug or kiss their friends and family on the cheek. Holding up two fingers means 'two' or 'peace'. I think the British hold up their fingers to show 'two' or 'peace'.

2 Aim To read for gist (matching headings to paragraphs)

- Give Ss time to read the text again and then match the headings to the paragraphs.
- Elicit answers from Ss around the class. Ss justify their answers.

Answer Key

A 3 (varies from country to country)
B 5 (type of greeting people use)
C 1 (listening to a person ... saying)
D 6 (hand signals)
E 2 (don't like ... to them)

- Then give Ss time to explain the words in bold using their dictionaries or the Word List to help them.

Suggested Answer Key

awkward (adj): *uncomfortable*
non-verbal (adj): *unspoken*
appropriate (adj): *suitable*
tends (v): *happens more often than not*
greet (v): *to say 'hello'*
typical (adj): *normal or usual*
glance (v): *to look at sth briefly*
greatly (adv): *a lot*
leaning (v): *moving in a sloping position*
fluent (adj): *being able to speak a language well*

- Give Ss time to look up the meanings of the words in the ***Check these words*** box in the Word List.
- Play the video for Ss and elicit their comments.

Speaking & Writing

3 Aim THINK To develop critical thinking skills; to compare body language in two countries

- Have Ss work in groups and compare body language in their country and in the UK and discuss some gestures that are different.
- Monitor the activity around the class and then ask some groups to share their answers with the class.

Suggested Answer Key

A: In Greece, we greet people we meet for the first time with a handshake and we greet friends and family with a hug and a kiss on each cheek.
B: Yes, that's the same as in the UK except we do two kisses instead of one.
C: In the UK holding up two fingers can be an extremely rude gesture and in Greece holding up five fingers can be an extremely rude gesture.
A: Right. A gesture we have in Greece that is different to the UK is we make a circular motion with the hand to express disbelief or impatience. etc

4 Aim ICT To develop research skills; to give a presentation on gestures and body language in one's country

- Ask Ss to work in small groups and give them time to research online and find out information about gestures and body language in their country and make notes. Then tell Ss to use this information to prepare a presentation for a group of foreign visitors.
- Ask various groups of Ss to make their presentations to the class.
- This task may be assigned as homework.

Suggested Answer Key

Good morning everyone! Welcome to Greece! We are going to tell you about some gestures and body language you should know that will help you during your stay in our country.

The type of greeting people use in Greece depends on whether the situation is formal or informal. A handshake is appropriate for formal situations like business meetings and when you meet someone for the first time. When greeting friends or family members, however, a hug and a kiss on each cheek is the usual greeting.

When Greeks say 'no' they raise their chin in an upwards movement and then down again. This can sometimes be confused with a nod for 'yes' which is common in many other countries. 'Yes' is often indicated with a sideways nod of the head. To avoid confusion, use words!

Hand signals are a type of body language that can differ greatly from place to place. In Greece avoid holding up five fingers when ordering food or drinks because it is an extremely rude gesture. Again, it's best to use your words and not your hands.

In Greece, people aren't really concerned about personal space and may stand quite close to you. They do not do it to make you uncomfortable so don't worry about it.

Body language is a hugely important part of communication and we hope we have been able to help you read a Greek person's non-verbal signals a little better. When you don't understand the language, it is crucial to know a bit about body language. Enjoy your stay!

Review 5

Vocabulary

1 Aim To consolidate vocabulary from the unit

- Explain the task.
- Give Ss time to complete it.
- Check Ss' answers.

Answer Key

1 express | *4 breakdown*
2 body | *5 tone*
3 tell

2 Aim To consolidate vocabulary from the unit

- Explain the task.
- Give Ss time to complete it.
- Check Ss' answers.

Answer Key

1 come *3 get* *5 commit*
2 access *4 interact*

3 Aim To practise prepositional phrases and phrasal verbs

- Explain the task.
- Give Ss time to complete it.
- Check Ss' answers.

Answer Key

1 down *3 on* *5 about*
2 from *4 at*

Grammar

4 Aim To practise future tenses

- Explain the task.
- Give Ss time to complete it.
- Check Ss' answers.

Answer Key

1 is meeting *4 is going to lose*
2 begins *5 will be working*
3 am going to buy

5 Aim To practise future tenses

- Explain the task.
- Give Ss time to complete it.
- Check Ss' answers.

Answer Key

1 will have changed *4 will invent*
2 will be driving *5 is going to learn*
3 will take

Everyday English

6 Aim To match exchanges

- Explain the task.
- Give Ss time to complete it.
- Check Ss' answers.

Answer Key

1 d *2 b* *3 a* *4 c*

Competences

Ask Ss to assess their own performance in the unit by ticking the items according to how competent they feel for each of the listed activities.

Challenges

Topic	
In this unit, Ss will explore the topics of jobs and work values.	
6a Reading & Vocabulary	**46-47**
Lesson objectives: To introduce key vocabulary, to listen and read for gist, to read for key information (multiple matching), to learn collocations related to different careers, to learn prepositional phrases, to practise words easily confused, to learn phrasal verbs with *fill*, to talk about lifestyles, to write about your daily life **Vocabulary:** Jobs *(supermarket cashier, sales assistant, art director, bank clerk, weather reporter, fitness trainer, flight attendant, marketing manager, multimedia developer, rock star, street artist, tour guide)*; Nouns *(listing, spice, code, podcast, crew, contacts, creativity, deadline, locals, client, requirement, goal, citizen)*; Verbs *(delegate, wonder, suit, share, explore, design)*; Phrasal verbs *(hang out, step into)*; Adjectives *(inspirational, independent, passionate, blank)*; Phrase *(squeeze in)*	
6b Grammar in Use	**48-49**
Lesson objectives: To revise/learn modals, to learn modals in the past and modals of deduction, to talk about company rules, to talk about rules at primary school, to make deductions	
6c Skills in Action	**50-51**
Lesson objectives: To learn vocabulary for work values, to listen for general gist, opinion, attitude, etc (multiple matching), to listen and read for specific information, to act out a dialogue and practise everyday English for congratulating, wishing and expressing thanks, to practise reduced pronunciation, to read for lexical cohesion (word formation), to practise congratulating someone, to write an email of congratulations **Vocabulary:** Work values *(punctual, respectful, autonomous, cooperative, creative, responsible)*	
Culture 6	**52**
Lesson objectives: To listen and read for gist, to read for general comprehension (matching headings to paragraphs), to talk about business etiquette in your country and compare it with the USA, to give a presentation on the office etiquette in another country **Vocabulary:** Nouns *(etiquette, gaze, flip-flop, divider, immigrant, punctuality)*, Verb *(crush)*; Phrasal verb *(rock up)*; Adjectives *(bone-crushing, receptive, open plan)*; Adverb *(stateside)*; Phrases *(first name terms, code of conduct, business casual)*	
Review 6	**53**
Lesson objectives: To test/consolidate vocabulary and grammar learnt throughout the unit; to practise everyday English	

Go through the objectives box and tell Ss that these are the topics, skills and activities this unit will cover.

6a

Vocabulary

1 Aim To present vocabulary related to jobs

- Ask Ss to read the words in the lists and then give them time to match them to make job titles.
- Check Ss' answers around the class.

Answer Key

1 h 3 d 5 a 7 i 9 b 11 f
2 k 4 j 6 l 8 g 10 e 12 c

Listening & Reading

2 Aim To read for gist

- Play the recording. Ss listen and read the profiles to match the people to the characteristics.
- Check Ss' answers.

Answer Key

1 sociable 2 artistic 3 enthusiastic

3 Aim To read for key information (multiple matching)

- Ask Ss to read the text, then read the descriptions and match the people to the jobs.
- Check Ss' answers. Ss should justify their choices.
- Then, give Ss time to look up the meanings of the words in bold in the Word List or in their dictionaries and elicit definitions from Ss around the class.

Answer Key

1 C (She's a people person – The main requirement of the job and lifestyle is that you're sociable)
2 E (his true passion is art ... there are lots of rules about where you can and can't create art – Don't worry about breaking the law – your crew has contacts and they always ask for permission first.)
3 A (She'd prefer something more creative and exciting ... She needs something fast-paced and fun! – Every day is different, and you'll need creativity)

Suggested Answer Key

wondered (v): *thought about sth with curiosity*
suits (v): *matches, fits*
independent (adj): *not controlled by a big company*
hanging out (phr v): *spending time with*
creativity (n): *the ability to use skill and imagination to create sth new*
deadlines (n): *points in time by which sth should be done*
share (v): *to divide sth equally with others*

explore (v): *to look around a place to find out more about it*
locals (n): *the people who live in a certain area*
step into (phr v): *to move into*
clients (n): *customers*
requirement (n): *sth that is necessary*
passionate (adj): *having a lot of passion/enthusiasm for sth*
designing (v): *creating plans for sth*
goals (n): *things that you hope to achieve*
blank (adj): *empty*
citizens (n): *people who live in a particular place*

- Give Ss time to look up the meanings of the words in the ***Check these words*** box in the Word List.
- Play the video for Ss and elicit their comments.

4 **Aim** **To consolidate new vocabulary & practise collocations**

- Ask Ss to look through the text and find the words that pair with the words in the list to make collocations.
- Check Ss' answers and then give them time to use the collocations in sentences of their own.

Answer Key

1 social	*4 stylish*	*7 body*
2 time	*5 graphic*	*8 double*
3 free	*6 fitness*	

Suggested Answer Key

*Most people these days use **social media**.*
***Time management** skills are very useful in any job.*
*I like to paint in my **free time**.*
*I don't often eat at **stylish restaurants**.*
***Graphic designers** have an interesting job.*
*Personal trainers often have **fitness blogs**.*
*A healthy **body image** is good for everyone to have.*
*People who have two jobs could be said to have a **double life**.*

5 **Aim** **To consolidate prepositional phrases from a text**

- Give Ss time to read sentences and choose the correct prepositions.
- Then check Ss' answers.

Answer Key

1 to 2 by 3 by 4 on 5 for

6 **Aim** **To understand words easily confused**

- Explain the task and give Ss time to use their dictionaries to help them complete it.
- Check Ss' answers.

Answer Key

1 alive	*3 spectators*	*5 list*
2 live	*4 audience*	*6 listing*

7 **Aim** **To learn phrasal verbs with *fill***

- Ask Ss to read the phrasal verbs box and make sure that Ss understand the definitions.
- Then give Ss time to complete the task and check their answers.

Answer Key

1 in	*3 up*	*5 up*
2 out	*4 in/out*	

Speaking & Writing

8 **Aim** THINK **To consolidate information in a text; to express an opinion**

- Ask Ss to listen to and read the text again.
- Play the recording.
- In pairs, have Ss discuss their opinions.
- Monitor the activity around the class and then ask various pairs to share their opinions and their reasons with the class.

Suggested Answer Key

A: *I would like to be an art director for a week because I think it would be great to eat out at stylish restaurants and meet clients and then get other people to do all the work.*

B: *I see what you mean. But I would rather be a tour guide for a week. I'd like to get to travel to interesting places and learn all about them and then share it all with other people.*

9 **Aim** **To write a short text about your life for a life swap webpage**

- Give Ss time to write a short text about their life including all the points in the list.
- Then have Ss read out their text to the class and find someone who wants to swap with them.

Suggested Answer Key

Job: *shop assistant*
Place: *fashion boutique, Prague, Czech Republic*
qualities/skills needed: *friendly, sociable, knowledge of fashion, organisational skills*
duties: *serving customers, ordering stock, doing window displays*
advantages: *reduced prices, meeting people, learning about fashion trends*

I work as a shop assistant in a fashion boutique in Prague in the Czech Republic. For this kind of work you

need to be friendly and sociable and you need to have knowledge of fashion as well as organisational skills. My daily duties mainly involve serving customers but I also spend some time ordering stock and every week I do the window display. I enjoy my job very much and it has certain advantages such as getting reduced prices on all my clothes but most of all I enjoy it because I like meeting people and learning about fashion trends.

6b Grammar in Use

1 **Aim To learn/revise modals**

- Ask Ss to read the FAQs and match the modal verbs in bold to their uses.
- Check Ss' answers and refer Ss to the ***Grammar Reference*** section for more information or to check any points they are unsure of.

Answer Key

may = *permission*
must = *obligation*
don't have to = *absence of necessity*
should = *advice*
can = *ability*
need to = *necessity*
may = *possibility*

2 **Aim To practise modals**

Give Ss time to complete the exercise and then check their answers around the class.

Answer Key

1 shouldn't	*5 ought to*
2 Can	*6 needn't*
3 don't have to	*7 mustn't*
4 can	*8 may*

3 **Aim To practise modals**

- Give Ss time to complete the sentences with the modals in the list.
- Elicit answers from Ss around the class.

Suggested Answer Key

1 must/have to	*5 must/have to*
2 mustn't/can't	*6 mustn't/can't*
3 must/have to	*7 must/have to*
4 don't have to	*8 don't have to*

4 **Aim To practise modals**

- Explain the task and read out the example and then give Ss time to complete it.
- Elicit answers from Ss around the class.

Suggested Answer Key

1 Would you like some help carrying your bags?
2 May I have Friday off?
3 I may be late tomorrow.
4 Would you like me to make you a cup of coffee?
5 Can/Would you email me the files?
6 I may finish work early today.

5 **Aim To practice modals**

Explain the task and give Ss time to complete it and then check their answers.

Suggested Answer Key

1 She had to deliver the project on Tuesday.
2 You should talk to the manager.
3 Steve may/might get a promotion.
4 You mustn't/can't enter this lab.
5 May/Can I take my break now?
6 They can work under pressure.
7 Shall we meet on Tuesday?
8 Ben has/needs to pick up the group at 8:30.

Speaking

6 **Aim To describe a set of imaginary company rules**

- Give Ss time to discuss what rules a company might have for their staff.
- Monitor the activity around the class and then ask some pairs to share their answers with the class.

Suggested Answer Key

A: Most companies have rules about timekeeping. Staff should all start work on time and not be late.
B: Right. Staff should also dress appropriately and wear the proper uniform as well as use the correct safety equipment.
A: Yes and they must follow the health and safety rules at all times.
B: Absolutely. They must treat their co-workers and customers with respect too.
A: Right. Of course, the rules depend on the company.
B: I agree. Not all companies have the same set of rules. etc

7 **Aim To present/practise modals in the past**

- Go through the theory box with Ss and refer them to the ***Grammar Reference*** section for more information and to clarify any points they are unsure of.
- Alternatively you can write the examples in the theory box on the board and elicit uses.
- Then give Ss time to complete the task.
- Check Ss' answers around the class.

Answer Key

Example in the text: *wasn't able to*

1 *didn't have to*	4 *had to*
2 *couldn't*	5 *wasn't able to*
3 *was able to*	6 *could*

Speaking

8 **Aim To talk about rules**

Explain the task and ask Ss to discuss the rules they had in primary school in pairs. Monitor the activity around the class and then ask some Ss to tell the class.

Suggested Answer Key

A: *I had to be at school for 9 am.*
B: *Really? I had to be there by 8 am.*
A: *I had to sit at the same desk every day.*
B: *Me too. I had to do homework every day.*
A: *I didn't have to. I had to eat my lunch in the school canteen.*
B: *So did I. I had to go outside at break times.*
A: *Me too. I had to change into my gym kit for PE lessons.*
B: *I didn't have to, but we were allowed to wear trainers at primary school.*
A: *We weren't. etc*

9 **Aim To present/practise modals of deduction**

- Go through the theory box with Ss and refer them to the ***Grammar Reference*** section for more information and to clarify any points they are unsure of.
- Then elicit answers to the questions from Ss around the class.

Answer Key

Example in the text: *might not have submitted*

*We use **may/might/could** to express possibility.*
*We use **must** to express positive logical assumption.*
*We use **can't/couldn't** to express negative logical assumption.*

*Modals of deduction in the **present infinitive** are formed with **may/might/could/must + bare infinitive**.*

*Modals of deduction in the **present continuous infinitive** are formed with **may/might/could/must + be + -ing**.*

*Modals of deduction in the **perfect infinitive** are formed with **may/might/could/must + have + past participle**.*

*Modals of deduction in the **perfect continuous infinitive** are formed with **may/might/could/must + have been + -ing**.*

10 **Aim To practise modals of deduction**

Explain the task and give Ss time to complete it. Check Ss' answers.

Answer Key

1 *must*	3 *might*	5 *must*
2 *can't*	4 *could*	6 *can't*

Speaking

11 **Aim To practise making deductions**

- Give Ss time to study the images and then make deductions based on what they show.
- Elicit answers from Ss around the class.

Suggested Answer Key

A *He must be tired. He must have a lot of work to do. He can't be at home. He must be at work. He might work in finance. He might have a presentation to prepare. He could be thinking very hard. He might have missed a deadline. He must have been working for hours. etc*

B *She might be in a meeting. She might be a student. She might be talking about a personal experience. She must know the people. She can't be at home. She might be at work or at college.*

6c Skills in Action

Vocabulary

1 **Aim To present vocabulary related to work values**

- Ask Ss to read the job listing and complete the gaps with the words in the list.
- Explain/Elicit the meanings of any unknown words or phrases or ask Ss to look them up in the Word List.
- Elicit answers from Ss around the class.

Answer Key

1 *cooperative*	4 *respectful*
2 *responsible*	5 *creative*
3 *autonomous*	6 *punctual*

2 **Aim THINK To discuss work values**

- Ask Ss to work in closed pairs. Ss think of three important work values and tell their partner why they are important.
- Ask various students to tell the class.

Suggested Answer Key

A: *My top three work values are cooperation, responsibility and respectfulness. I think it is important to be able to work well with others. I think you have to be responsible in your job so you don't make mistakes and I think you should respect*

the people you work with and they should respect you because then everyone feels valued.
B: *I totally agree with you. For me, though, I think the values of honesty and hard work are also important. I think it would be very difficult to work with people who are dishonest. Also, I think it is important for everyone to be hard-working. It would be awful to be surrounded by lazy people. etc*

Listening

3 Aim To listen for general gist, opinion, attitude, etc (multiple matching)

- Ask Ss to read the sentences (A-H) and find the key words. Play the recording twice. Ss match the speakers to the sentences. Remind Ss there are three extra sentences.
- Check Ss' answers. You can play the recording again with pauses for Ss to check their answers.

Answer Key

1 F 2 D 3 H 4 A 5 C

Everyday English

4 Aim To listen and read for specific information

- Ask Ss to read the first exchange in the dialogue. Elicit Ss' guesses as to what good news Paul has.
- Play the recording for Ss to listen and read and find out if their guesses were correct.

Answer Key

Paul has got a promotion to head manager at his company.

5 Aim To act out a dialogue and practise everyday English for congratulating

- Explain the task and ask Ss to act out a dialogue similar to the one in Ex. 4 in pairs using the prompts.
- Write this diagram on the board for Ss to follow.

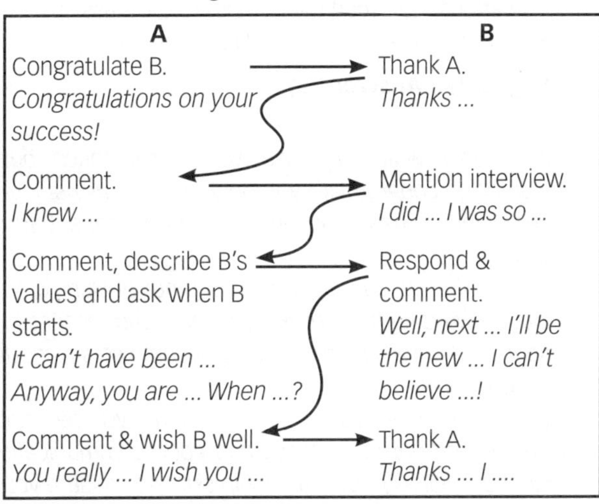

A
B
Congratulate B.
Congratulations on your success!
Thank A.
Thanks ...
Comment.
I knew ...
Mention interview.
I did ... I was so ...
Comment, describe B's values and ask when B starts.
It can't have been ...
Anyway, you are ... When ...?
Respond & comment.
Well, next ... I'll be the new ... I can't believe ...!
Comment & wish B well.
You really ... I wish you ...
Thank A.
Thanks ... I ....

- Monitor the activity around the class and offer assistance as necessary.
- Then ask some pairs to act out their dialogues in front of the class.

Suggested Answer Key

A: *Molly! Congratulations on your success!*
B: *Thanks, Arthur.*
A: *I knew you would get it. You were definitely the best candidate to become head teacher after Doug Redwood retired.*
B: *I did terribly in the interview, though. I was so nervous!*
A: *It can't have been so bad! Anyway, you are the most hard-working teacher in the school. When do you start?*
B: *Well, next term I'll be the official head teacher. I can't believe it!*
A: *You really deserve it. I wish you all the best in your new position, Molly!*
A: *Thanks a lot, Arthur. I really appreciate it.*

Pronunciation

6 a) Aim To learn reduced pronunciation

Play the recording with pauses for Ss to repeat chorally and/or individually. Check Ss' intonation.

b) Aim To practise reduced pronunciation

Ask Ss to use the modal verbs in Ex. 6a to make their own sentences. Ask Ss around the class to say their sentences aloud. Check Ss' pronunciation.

Suggested Answer Key

Could you hold the lift, please?
Would you mind waiting for me?
Should he go to the meeting?
He ought to be more polite.
She has to start work early.

Reading & Writing

7 Aim To read for lexical cohesion (word formation)

- Give Ss time to read the email and complete the gaps with a word formed from the word in brackets.
- Check Ss' answers.

Answer Key

1 delighted
2 reliable
3 surprising
4 demanding
5 ability/abilities
6 achievement

8 a) **Aim** **To identify the style and content of an email**

- Read out the ***Writing Tip*** and tell Ss that this advice will help them to complete the writing task successfully.
- Have Ss read the email in Ex. 7 again and identify the style and any wish it contains.
- Elicit answers from Ss around the class.

Answer Key

The style is semi-formal and the wish is 'best of luck with everything'.

b) **Aim** **To substitute phrases in an email**

- Explain the task and give Ss time to substitute the phrases in the email with suitable alternatives from the list.
- Check Ss' answers.

Answer Key

It's been months since we were last in touch = *I haven't talked to you in ages*
become so successful = *done so well*
I imagine that your new position = *I guess your new job*
be able to rise to the challenge = *manage fine*
required = *you'll need*
congratulations = *well done*
best of luck = *good luck*

Writing

9 **Aim** **To prepare for a writing task; to analyse a rubric**

- Give Ss time to read the rubric and underline the key words.
- Then elicit answers to the questions from Ss around the class.

Suggested Answer Key

Key words: *ex-colleague, new job, manager, electronics shop, email, to congratulate the person, mentioning their skills and work values, and wishing them well for the future (120-180 words)*

1 *I am going to write an email. It is for my ex-colleague.*
2 *I am going to write to congratulate them on their new job, mention their skills and work values and wish them the best for the future.*
3 *I should write in an informal or semi-formal style.*

10 **Aim** THINK **To decide which skills and work values match a role**

- Ask Ss to read the list of skills and work values and give them time to decide in pairs which ones match a manager at an electronics shop.
- Ask various Ss to share their answers with the class.

Suggested Answer Key

A: *I think a manager at an electronics shop should have good communication skills to speak clearly to staff and customers.*
B: *I agree. I think he or she should also have good leadership skills in a position of authority like this.*
A: *Right. They should also be able to work under pressure because they may have a lot of orders for new electronics equipment at the same time.*
B: *Yes. Also, they need to meet customers' needs and make the right decisions. For example, which electronics goods will sell and which won't so they can have enough stock in the shop.*
A: *Good point. As for work values, I think an electronics manager needs to be hard-working, reliable and responsible because they are a role model for the staff.*
B: *Me too. I also think they need to be cooperative because they work with others and flexible to be able to adapt to changing situations.*
A: *I see your point. They should definitely be punctual and polite to set a good example to staff and when dealing with customers.*
B: *True. And they need to be tolerant because they may have to deal with difficult customers.*

11 **Aim** **To develop writing skills; to write an email of congratulations**

- Tell Ss to use their answers from Ex. 10 and the plan to help them write their email for the rubric in Ex. 9.
- Give Ss time to complete the task and then ask various Ss to read their emails to the class.
- This task may be assigned as homework.

Suggested Answer Key

Hi Tom,
It's been a while since we were last in touch, but I wanted to congratulate you on your good news! I was very happy to hear that you are now Manager at Barry's Electronics!
I remember when we worked together at Curry's. You were always so hard-working, reliable and responsible, so it's not surprising that you've become so successful in your career.
I imagine that your new position will be quite demanding but you always had good communication skills as well as good leadership skills so I'm sure you'll

be able to rise to the challenge. After all, you definitely have the ability and the work values required.
Well, that's all from me. Once again, congratulations on your promotion and best of luck with everything.
All the best,
Angie

VALUES

Ask Ss to read the quotation, then initiate a class discussion about its meanings. Encourage all Ss to participate.

Suggested Answer Key

A: I think the quotation means that a person should always challenge themselves in life. This could involve trying new experiences or always trying their best to succeed.
B: I totally agree. I also think it refers to how we should step away from what makes us comfortable and what is familiar and try new and exciting and even scary things and push ourselves to see how far we can go and what we can achieve. etc.

Culture 6

Listening & Reading

1 Aim To introduce the topic; to listen and read for specific information

- Elicit what Ss think office etiquette is like in the USA.
- Play the recording. Ss listen and read the text to find out.

Answer Key

Office etiquette in the USA is pretty informal but punctuality and hard work is expected.

2 Aim To read for gist (matching headings to paragraphs; to present/consolidate new vocabulary

- Give Ss time to read the text again and then match the headings to the paragraphs giving reasons. Remind Ss that there are two extra headings.
- Check Ss' answers and then give them time to explain the words in bold using the Word List or their dictionaries to help them.

Answer Key

1 D (It's important not to do it too softly or too hard.)
2 B (full name, first name terms)
3 F (a receptive and welcoming look on your face)
4 C (trousers, shirt and jacket)
5 H (a room full of cubicles)
6 G (punctuality, late)

Suggested Answer Key

bone-crushing (adj): *very strong and forceful*
receptive (adj): *open to new ideas*
business casual (phr): *a semi-formal style of dress*
open plan (adj): *a large room with few or no dividing walls*
punctuality (n): *being on time*

- Give Ss time to look up the meanings of the words in the ***Check these words*** box in the Word List.
- Play the video for Ss and elicit their comments.

Speaking & Writing

3 Aim THINK To compare office etiquette in two countries

- Have Ss work in closed pairs and discuss the office etiquette in their country and then compare it to the office etiquette in the USA and think of two similarities and differences.
- Monitor the activity around the class and then ask some pairs to share their answers with the class.

Suggested Answer Key

A: In Italy punctuality is not as important as in America.
B: That's right meetings start late and end late here. In America, they start on time and finish quickly.
A: Also, in the USA, people dress fairly casually for work, but in an Italian office everyone is dressed very smartly.
B: That's true. I don't think that happens often in the USA.
A: I think in both countries, the handshake is an important element of business etiquette, though.
B: Yes, I agree. It's important in the USA and in Italy.
A: Also, eye contact and an expression of interest is important in both countries.
B: That's right. I think that is international.

4 Aim ICT To develop research skills; to give a presentation about office etiquette in an English-speaking country

- Give Ss time to research online and find out information about the office etiquette in another English-speaking country and use this information to prepare a presentation.
- Ask various Ss to give their presentation to the class.
- This task may be assigned as homework.

Suggested Answer Key

Have you ever thought about living and working 'down under'? Well if you do, the Australian workplace has some office etiquette rules that you should know about if you are going to work there.

First and foremost, always arrive on time at your workplace and for meetings. Lateness is seen as disrespectful in Australia. When you meet someone for the first time at work, you should always shake hands. That is true for both males and females. In Australia, people at work also always address each other by his or her first name. They rarely or never address people as Mr or Mrs and their last name.

You should show respect to your boss but you should also relate to them as an equal. The management structure of most companies in Australia is not as strictly defined as in many other countries. This is also true for your co-workers. You should speak to everyone in your workplace as an equal and treat everyone with respect.

Eye contact is important and you should look everyone in the eye. Not doing so could make you seem untrustworthy.

Finally, it's a good idea not to rush out of the door at 5 pm in an Australian office. Always try and finish what you are working on before you leave if possible. If you drop everything and go home you may get a reputation as someone who does not really care about the company. This can affect your career.

All in all, most countries have similar rules about how to conduct yourself in an office. If you are polite, respectful and hard-working, you should get along wherever you work but in Australia you should also remember to be punctual but not watch the clock at home time. Thanks for listening. I hope you found this informative. Are there any questions?

Review 6

Vocabulary

1 Aim To consolidate vocabulary from the unit

- Explain the task.
- Give Ss time to complete it.
- Check Ss' answers.

Answer Key

1 attendant *2 polite* *3 multimedia* *4 client* *5 management* *6 alive* *7 reporter* *8 star* *9 requirements* *10 suits*

2 Aim To consolidate vocabulary from the unit

- Explain the task.
- Give Ss time to complete it.
- Check Ss' answers.

Answer Key

1 autonomous *2 punctual* *3 respectful* *4 creative* *5 cooperative* *6 responsible*

3 Aim To practise prepositional phrases and phrasal verbs

- Explain the task.
- Give Ss time to complete it.
- Check Ss' answers.

Answer Key

1 in *2 to* *3 for* *4 up* *5 by* *6 out*

Grammar

4 Aim To practise modals

- Explain the task.
- Give Ss time to complete it.
- Check Ss' answers.

Answer Key

1 wasn't able to *2 don't have to* *3 can* *4 mustn't* *5 Shall* *6 May* *7 must* *8 ought to*

5 Aim To practise modals of deduction

- Explain the task.
- Give Ss time to complete it.
- Check Ss' answers.

Answer Key

1 can't/couldn't have gone
2 may/might/could have been waiting
3 can't be
4 must work

Everyday English

6 Aim To match exchanges

- Explain the task.
- Give Ss time to complete it.
- Check Ss' answers.

Answer Key

1 c *2 e* *3 b* *4 a* *5 d*

Competences

Ask Ss to assess their own performance in the unit by ticking the items according to how competent they feel for each of the listed activities.

Values: Productivity

1 **Aim** **To introduce the topic; to read for gist**

- Read out the question and elicit answers from Ss around the class.
- Ss read the first paragraph to find out if their answers were mentioned.

Answer Key

Productivity can help us get a promotion at work, get better marks in our studies, reach our fitness goals and more.

2 **Aim** **To read for key information (matching headings to paragraphs); to consolidate new vocabulary**

- Ask Ss to read headings A-G and give them time to read the text again and match them to paragraphs 1-7.
- Play the recording for Ss to check their answers.

Answer Key

1 G	*3 E*	*5 D*	*7 C*
2 F	*4 B*	*6 A*	

- Elicit the meanings of the words/phrases in bold in the text from Ss around the class.

Suggested Answer Key

specific (adj): *particular*
motivated (adj): *full of determination*
treat (n): *something pleasant that you allow yourself rarely*
guilty (adj): *feeling like you have done something wrong*
challenging (adj): *difficult*
commute (n): *journey to place of work or study*
capable (adj): *having the ability to do sth*

3 **Aim** **ICT** **To develop critical thinking skills**

Give Ss time to consider their answers and have Ss discuss the question in pairs. Then ask some Ss to share their answers with the class.

Suggested Answer Key

For me, the most important methods are making a good start and having a healthy lifestyle. The first because I get my best work done in the morning and the second because when I don't eat or sleep well, I never do good work.

4 **Aim** **ICT** **To develop research skills; to write about a successful person's productivity secrets**

- Have Ss read the rubric and explain the task. Ask them for examples of successful people.
- Give Ss time to complete the task or assign as homework.
- Ask Ss to read their texts to the class.

Suggested Answer Key

Elon Musk runs Tesla, the electric car company, and SpaceX, the space company, among other things. Musk starts work at 7 am every day and answers emails from other people in the company. This means they have their questions answered by the time they arrive at work. He does two things at the same time quite often, like eating while answering emails. He breaks his day up into five-minute pieces and tries to complete a task every five minutes. Finally, he has people around him who will tell him if he's doing something wrong, and he is always willing to change to become better.

Public Speaking Skills

1 Aim To analyse a rubric

Read the rubric aloud and elicit answers to the questions from Ss around the class.

Answer Key

1 *I am a candidate for mayor of a city.*
2 *I will be speaking to local citizens.*
3 *The purpose of the talk is to persuade them to vote for me.*
4 *I will be talking about the problems of the city and how I plan to solve them.*

2 Aim To analyse a model speech

- Read out the ***Study Skills*** box and tell Ss that this tip will help them to complete the speaking skills task successfully.
- Play the recording. Ss listen to and read the model.
- Elicit answers to the questions from Ss around the class.

Answer Key

Now, what does it take to be a great mayor? hook question
How do I plan to do this? hypophora
Why is this an important issue to me? hypophora
Wouldn't this make a huge difference to our city? rhetorical question
Do you know where this city stands for air quality compared to others in the region? hook question
Do you want a city suitable for the 21st century? rhetorical question

3 Aim ICT To give a speech to win citizens' votes

- Read out the rubric and explain the situation. Give Ss time to consider what they will say and prepare a speech. Remind Ss to include questions.
- Ask various Ss to give their speech to the class.

Suggested Answer Key

Good morning, citizens of Winford. My name is Mandy Marshall. What makes a city great? The place, of course, and the people, but also the government. Winford is a great city, but with better government, it could be greater, and that's why I'm running for mayor.
The first thing I would do is clean the place up! There's too much litter lying on the streets of our city, and who wouldn't want it cleaned up? I would hire a number of new street cleaners, first of all, and I would start fining people who dropped litter on the ground.
Second, there's not enough housing here. How do I know? I was just talking to a young couple with two kids who told me they couldn't find a three-bedroom flat to rent in their price range. My solution would be to make a number of city plots available for building companies to buy – as long as they promise to build family accommodation on them.
Finally, I want to make Winford a city for the future. How would I do that? Two words, citizens – high-speed Internet. I want to make Winford the first city in the region with high-speed Internet in every house.
Clean, high-tech and with plenty of accommodation – doesn't that sound like the city you want to live in? Then vote for me, Mandy Marshall, for mayor of Winford on March 26th. Vote for Mayor Mandy!

High-tech

Topic	
In this unit, Ss will explore the topics of technology and apps.	
7a Reading & Vocabulary	**56-57**
Lesson objectives: To learn vocabulary related to technology, to listen and read for gist, to read for specific information (multiple choice), to learn collocations related to technology, to learn prepositional phrases, to practise words easily confused, to learn phrasal verbs with *drop*, to talk about the IoT, to write a short text about the IoT and have a class debate on it **Vocabulary:** Technology *(artificial intelligence, virtual reality, smart devices, high-speed broadband, the Internet of Things [IOT], digital assistant)*; Nouns *(device, lightbulb, wearable, offender, microchips, sensors, command, the authorities)*; Verbs *(access, manage, maintain, monitor, revolutionised)*; Phrasal verbs *(go off, run out of)*; Adjective *(powerful)*; Adverbs *(remotely, independently, automatically, straightaway)*; Phrase *(industrial equipment, customer behaviour)*	
7b Grammar in Use	**58-59**
Lesson objectives: To revise/learn the passive, to prepare a quiz, to revise/learn personal-impersonal constructions, the causative and reflexive/emphatic pronouns, to talk about a science fair	
7c Skills in Action	**60-61**
Lesson objectives: To learn vocabulary related to apps, to listen for specific information (multiple choice), to listen and read for gist, to act out a dialogue and practise everyday English for expressing opinion – agreement/disagreement, to practise word junctures, to read for lexical cohesion (word formation), to write an opinion essay **Vocabulary:** Apps *(upload a video, browse for sth to buy, chat with friends, monitor exercise, get a taxi, book a stay at a hotel, create and share short videos with music, order food, stream films – TV series – music)*	
Culture 7	**62**
Lesson objectives: To listen and read for gist, to read for general comprehension and key words (text completion), to talk about a science and technology topic, to give a presentation on a science event **Vocabulary:** Nouns *(mission, public, venues, CGI, resource)*; Verbs *(colonise, founded, combining, narrated, depict)*; Adjectives *(intellectual, vital, multimedia, renowned, state-of-the-art)*; Phrases *(play a role, in advance, spreading the word)*	
Review 7	**63**
Lesson objectives: To test/consolidate vocabulary and grammar learnt throughout the unit; to practise everyday English	

Go through the objectives box and tell Ss that these are the topics, skills and activities this unit will cover.

7a

Vocabulary

1 a) Aim To present vocabulary related to technology

- Ask Ss to read the words in the lists and then give them time to match them to make phrases related to technology.
- Check Ss' answers around the class.

Answer Key

1 d 2 a 3 f 4 e 5 b 6 c

b) Aim To practise new vocabulary

- Give Ss time to use the phrases from Ex. 1a to complete the sentences.
- Check Ss' answer around the class.

Answer Key

1 virtual reality
2 Smart devices
3 digital assistant
4 high-speed broadband
5 artificial intelligence

2 Aim To introduce the topic; to generate topic-related vocabulary

- Give Ss time to make a list of all the latest technology they can think of.
- Then ask various Ss to share their list with the class and talk about how often they use technology and what they use it for.

Suggested Answer Key

smartphone, laptop, digital assistant, streaming service, Wi-Fi, wireless headphones/earphones, fitness tracker, VR headset, games console, etc
I use technology every day. I use my smartphone to chat and message my friends as well as make calls. I use my laptop to go online and read articles on the Internet. I use a digital assistant to look things up online for me quickly and to make a shopping list. I use my wireless headphones to listen to music and when I play games online. I use my fitness tracker to count how many steps I walk every day. etc

Reading & Listening

3 Aim To listen and read for gist

- Ask Ss to read the title and elicit their guesses as to what they are going to read about.

- Play the recording. Ss listen and read the text to find out.

Suggested Answer Key

I think I am going to read about smart devices.

4 **Aim To read for specific information (multiple choice)**

- Ask Ss to read the text again, then read the questions and answer choices and choose their answers according to what they read.
- Check Ss' answers. Ss should justify their choices.
- Then, give Ss time to look up the meanings of the words in bold in the Word List or in their dictionaries and elicit definitions from Ss around the class.

Answer Key

1 B *(Ever since the Altair 8800, the first desktop computer, went on sale in 1977, our microchipped friends have become smaller, cheaper and much more powerful.)*
2 A *(These devices all have microchips and sensors which connect to each other, so one smart device can tell another what to do, such as switching itself on or off.)*
3 B *(Sensors have already been installed in some trees in the Amazon Rainforest, so when one is cut down illegally, the authorities track it and catch the offenders.)*
4 D *(In 1956, the first wireless remote control revolutionised TV.)*

Suggested Answer Key

powerful (adj): *having lots of power/force*
microchips (n): *small pieces of electronics that have a circuit*
sensors (n): *devices that can react to light, heat or pressure*
independently (adv): *on its own; without help*
command (n): *an order*
automatically (adv): *without needing sb to operate it*
straightaway (adv): *immediately*
customer behaviour (phr): *the way shoppers/clients act*
maintain (v): *to keep sth in good condition*
monitor (v): *to check sth*
the authorities (n): *the official powers (e.g. government)*
revolutionised (v): *completely changed sth*

- Give Ss time to look up the meanings of the words in the ***Check these words*** box in the Word List.
- Play the video for Ss and elicit their comments.

5 **Aim To consolidate new vocabulary & practise collocations**

- Ask Ss to look through the text and find the words that pair with the words in the list to make collocations.
- Check Ss' answers and then give them time to use the collocations in sentences of their own.

Answer Key

1 *desktop*	3 *coffee*	5 *industrial*
2 *alarm*	4 *bank*	6 *remote*

Suggested Answer Key

*Many people these days have a laptop instead of a **desktop computer**.*
*I use my smartphone as my **alarm clock**.*
*There is a **coffee maker** in the office break room.*
*I often check my **bank account** online.*
*Factories have a lot of **industrial equipment**.*
*We have a **remote control** for the TV, the satellite decoder and the digital streaming service in our house.*

6 **Aim To consolidate prepositional phrases from a text**

- Give Ss time to read the gapped sentences and fill in the gaps with the correct prepositions.
- Then check Ss' answers.

Answer Key

1 *about*	3 *to*	5 *with*
2 *out*	4 *on*	

7 **Aim To understand words easily confused**

- Explain the task and give Ss time to use their dictionaries to help them complete it.
- Check Ss' answers.

Answer Key

1 *reminder*	3 *stationary*
2 *consists*	4 *in the sale*

8 **Aim To learn phrasal verbs with *drop***

- Ask Ss to read the phrasal verbs box and make sure that Ss understand the definitions.
- Then give Ss time to complete the task and check their answers.

Answer Key

1 *out* 2 *off* 3 *by* 4 *off*

Speaking & Writing

9 **Aim THINK To consolidate information in a text; to develop creative thinking skills**

- Ask Ss to read the text again.

- In pairs or small groups, have Ss discuss their ideas.
- Monitor the activity around the class and then ask various pairs to share their ideas with the class.

Suggested Answer Key

A: I would like the IoT to order my groceries when I run out of something in the fridge. How about you?
B: I think I would like it to wake me up in the morning and make my coffee and toast for me.
C: Cool. I'd like it to download all my favourite films and have them ready for me to watch. etc

10 Aim To develop research skills; to write a short text about the IoT and have a class debate

- Give Ss time to research online and write a short text about the IoT.
- Then Ss use their research to have a class debate.
- You can record the debate and provide feedback to each speaker.

Suggested Answer Key

I think the IoT will be useful in the future when lots of people have smart homes and they use it to connect all their devices. For example, they can use it to monitor the heating in their homes and their water usage and make their homes more energy-efficient. They can also use it to keep their homes more secure and have it monitor their security system. They can use it for entertainment purposes and stream movies and music by itself. I think it will save people a lot of time on small tasks because they will not have to go grocery shopping or worry about maintenance because their devices will do these things for them. However, for people who do not have smart homes or use a lot of technology, it will make no difference to their lives and they will carry on as they always have, doing things for themselves and living a life without technology running things for them.

7b Grammar in Use

1 Aim To learn/revise the passive

- Ask Ss to read the announcement and identify all the passive forms.
- Then elicit the tense of each form.

Answer Key

was awarded – past simple
was considered – past simple
is expected – present simple
are being displayed – present continuous
will be held – future simple
is going to be opened – be going to
will be broadcast – future simple
can also be ordered – modal

2 Aim To consolidate the uses of the passive

- Give Ss time to read the sentences and mark them as true or false.
- Check Ss' answers and refer Ss to the ***Grammar Reference*** section for more information or to check any points they are unsure of.

Answer Key

1 F 2 F 3 T 4 T 5 T 6 F

3 Aim To practise the passive

- Give Ss time to choose the correct items.
- Elicit answers with reasons from Ss around the class.

Suggested Answer Key

1 *is written (passive is formed with the verb 'to be' in the appropriate tense + the past participle)*
2 *been invented (present perfect tense with 'yet')*
3 *be cleaned (passive question – bare passive infinitive after 'can')*
4 *are being displayed (present continuous – action happening now)*
5 *be thrown (passive bare infinitive form after 'shouldn't')*
6 *was knocked (past simple passive for an action that was more important than the agent in the past)*
7 *has been shown (present perfect passive for an action that was more important than the agent)*
8 *can be returned (passive bare passive infinitive after 'can')*

4 Aim To practise *with/by* with the passive

- Write on the board: *The app was installed by Tom. The desk is covered with books.*
- Elicit when we use *by/with* to refer to the agent in a passive sentence. Refer Ss to the ***Grammar Reference*** for more details.
- Explain the task and give Ss time to complete it.
- Elicit answers from Ss around the class.

Answer Key

1 *by*	3 *by*	5 *with*
2 *with*	4 *by*	6 *with*

5 Aim To practise the passive

Explain the task and give Ss time to complete it and then check their answers.

Answer Key

1 *IoT devices have been installed at work.*
2 *The computer system is being updated this evening.*
3 *The science fair was called off last Monday.*
4 *The app won't be released until later this year.*
5 *Who were the new computers installed in the office by?*
6 *Can this device be used to stream films and TV series?*
7 *How has your anti-virus software been updated?*
8 *The instructions must be read before the router is installed.*

Speaking

6 Aim ICT To develop research skills; to practise the passive; to prepare a quiz using the passive

- Give Ss time to research online for interesting facts related to technology and then divide the class into teams and have them prepare a quiz.
- Then have Ss do the quiz following the example and keep score.
- The team that gets the most correct answers wins.

Suggested Answer Key

A: Who was the telephone invited by?
B: Alexander Graham Bell.
A: Which company was the first mobile phone sold by?
B: Motorola.
A: Which company was the first smartphone produced by?
B: IBM etc

7 Aim To learn/practise personal – impersonal constructions with the passive

- Go through the theory box with Ss and refer them to the ***Grammar Reference*** section for more information and to clarify any points they are unsure of.
- Then give Ss time to complete the task.
- Check Ss' answers.

Answer Key

1 *... is said that Tyler is an expert at fixing laptops.*
2 *... is believed to be increasing.*
3 *... is said that Claire crashed the computer system.*
4 *... is expected to come out soon.*
5 *... was thought to contain a virus.*
6 *... is claimed that the IoT will change the way we work.*

8 Aim To practise the passive

- Give Ss time to read the text and rewrite it in their notebooks using the passive. Ss can work in closed pairs.
- Ask various Ss to read out their text to the class and check Ss' answers.

Suggested Answer Key

A new app was released at Hereford Tech Fair last week. It is an app that has been created to help blind people in their everyday lives. When a blind person needs help, the app can be opened on their smartphone. This can be done with an audio command. Then a video call is started with a volunteer. Live video footage from the smartphone's camera can be seen by the volunteer. The blind person can be helped to read things or find things by the volunteer. It is said that millions of people will download the app.

9 Aim To present the causative

- Go through the examples with Ss. Elicit the answer. Then explain/elicit how the causative is formed and when we use it.
- Refer Ss to the ***Grammar Reference*** for more information, then, find an example in the text on p. 58.

Answer Key

Max had his laptop fixed suggests that the action was done by another person not Max. We form the causative with ***have + object (thing) + past participle****. We use the causative to say that we have arranged for someone to do something for us.*
Example: *you will have your tickets delivered to your door at no extra charge!*

10 Aim To practise the causative

- Explain the task. Ask Ss to work in closed pairs and do the task.
- Go round the class and monitor the task.
- Check Ss' answers.

Answer Key

1 *... is having her Internet connection checked.*
2 *... have our health monitored.*
3 *... had an app developed.*
4 *... will have its new education software presented by 'Tech Magazine'.*
5 *... have had my computer upgraded by Pete.*

11 Aim To practise the causative

- Explain the task. Ask Ss to work in groups and do the task. Ss can use a variety of tenses as they will

have to decide which activities are/have been/will/ are going to/were done. Ss can use their own ideas if they like.

- Monitor the activity round the class. Then, ask some groups to present their dialogues to the class.

Suggested Answer Key

A: So let's see. Has the venue been booked?
B: Yes, it was booked last Friday.
A: Perfect. What about advertising the fair?
B: We are going to have it advertised in the local press.
C: We will also have posters designed. I expect we will have samples tomorrow to choose from.
D: And we had the flyers printed. I've got them here. Would you like to have a look?
A: They look great. Have the speakers been invited?
B: Jenny had all the speakers invited last week. They all accepted the invitation so we are good with this.
C: Oh, and the equipment we need is going to be set up by Tech Motors. We have already discussed this and they are coming this Monday to see the place and decide what to do.
B: I think that's fine. We will have the stalls delivered next Tuesday as well. etc.

12 Aim To present reflexive/emphatic pronouns

- Read out the examples and elicit which one is reflexive and which one is emphatic and then elicit any examples in the announcements on p. 58.
- Refer Ss to the ***Grammar Reference*** section for more information and to clarify any points they are unsure of.

Answer Key

*The mayor **himself** opened the new technology museum. – emphatic*
*Jane bought **herself** a state-of-the-art smartphone. – reflexive*
Example – a live episode of the show will be broadcast from the fair itself (emphatic)

13 Aim To practise reflexive/emphatic pronouns

- Give Ss time to read the sentences and fill in the correct pronouns.
- Elicit answers from Ss around the class and elicit which are reflexive/emphatic pronouns.

Answer Key

1 himself (reflexive)	*4 himself (emphatic)*
2 yourself (emphatic)	*5 themselves (reflexive)*
3 itself (reflexive)	*6 myself (emphatic)*

Speaking

14 Aim To talk about a science fair; to practise reflexive/emphatic pronouns and the passive

- Explain the task and give Ss time to prepare their answers.
- Then ask Ss around the class to share their answers with the rest of the class.

Suggested Answer Key

Last week I went to a science fair by myself. Lots of new gadgets and devices were being displayed and I really enjoyed myself because it was very interesting. I saw a new app on which your health can be checked through your smartphone and I met the man who invented it. I think I will try to invent an app myself. My app will make tailored fitness programs for people so they can keep themselves fit without having a personal trainer or going to a gym.

7c Skills in Action

Vocabulary

1 Aim To present vocabulary related to apps

- Ask Ss to read the words in the list and then read the quiz and complete the gaps using the words in the list.
- Explain/Elicit the meanings of any unknown words or phrases or ask Ss to look them up in the Word List.
- Elicit answers from Ss around the class.

Answer Key

1 get	*5 book*	*9 chat*
2 monitor	*6 stream*	*10 order*
3 create	*7 browse*	
4 share	*8 upload*	

2 Aim THINK To develop thinking skills; to design an app

- Ask Ss to work in small groups and design an app. They should give it a name and describe what people can use it for.
- Have groups present it to the class and have the class vote for the best idea.

Suggested Answer Key

We have designed an app called Car Share. People can use it to input their starting point and their destination and find people who want to make the same journey and travel together in one car to share petrol costs and reduce the number of cars on the road.

Listening

3 **Aim** **To listen for specific information (multiple choice)**

- Ask Ss to read the questions (1-4) and the answer choices and find the key words. Play the recording twice. Ss choose their answers according to what they hear.
- Check Ss' answers. You can play the recording again with pauses for Ss to check their answers.

Answer Key

1 C 2 B 3 A 4 C

Everyday English

4 **Aim** **To listen and read for gist**

- Ask Ss to read the first exchange in the dialogue. Elicit Ss' guesses as to what Alesha thinks of the app.
- Play the recording for Ss to listen and read and find out if their guesses were correct.

Answer Key

Alesha does not like the app.

5 **Aim** **To act out a dialogue and practise everyday English for expressing opinion – agreement/disagreement**

- Explain the task and ask Ss to act out a dialogue similar to the one in Ex. 4 in pairs using the ideas and the language box.
- Write this diagram on the board for Ss to follow.

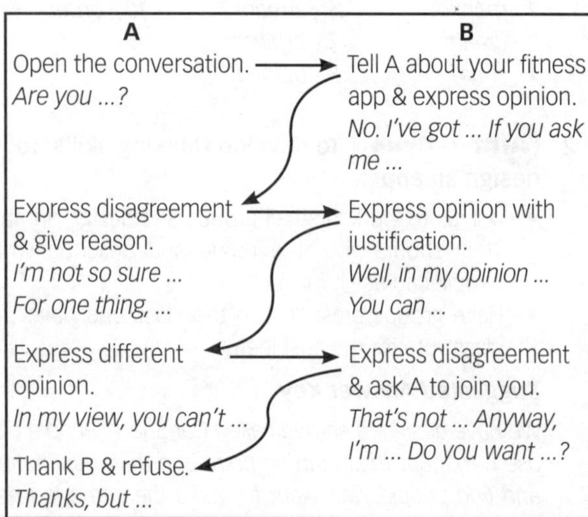

A
B
Open the conversation.
Are you ...?
Tell A about your fitness app & express opinion.
No. I've got ... If you ask me ...
Express disagreement & give reason.
I'm not so sure ...
For one thing, ...
Express opinion with justification.
Well, in my opinion ...
You can ...
Express different opinion.
In my view, you can't ...
Express disagreement & ask A to join you.
That's not ... Anyway, I'm ... Do you want ...?
Thank B & refuse.
Thanks, but ...

- Monitor the activity around the class and offer assistance as necessary.
- Then ask some pairs to act out their dialogues in front of the class.

Suggested Answer Key

A: Are you coming to the gym Alex?
B: No. I've got one of those fitness apps on my phone. I just tell it I want to exercise and it gives me a workout. If you ask me, these sorts of apps are fantastic!
A: I'm not so sure about that. For one thing, they monitor how much exercise you do and can cause you anxiety about your fitness if they say you're not doing enough.
B: Well, in my opinion, they're really useful. You can set your own targets.
A: In my view, you can't be sure how accurate they are because everyone is different.
B: That's not how I see it. Anyway, I'm going for a jog in the park. Do you want to come?
A: Thanks, but I think I'll go to the gym.

Pronunciation

6 **Aim** **To learn word junctures**

- Play the recording multiple times to allow Ss to recognise the sounds between the words that end with a vowel and the words that start with a vowel as underlined.
- Elicit answers.
- Explain that when the first word ends in an *a*, *e*, i vowel sound [/εɪ/, /iː/, /aɪ/], our lips are wide. Then we insert a *Y* sound at the beginning of the next word.
- When the first word ends in an *o*, *u* vowel sound [/əʊ/, /uː/], our lips are round. Then we insert a *W* sound at the beginning of the next word.

Answer Key

1 y 2 y 3 w 4 w

Reading & Writing

7 **a)** **Aim** **To read for lexical cohesion (word formation)**

- Give Ss time to read the essay and complete the gaps with a word formed from the word in brackets.
- Check Ss' answers.

Answer Key

1 excellent
2 effective
3 employees
4 conversations
5 assistance

b) **Aim** **To identify the content of an essay**

- Have Ss read the essay in Ex. 7a again and identify the content of each paragraph.
- Elicit answers from Ss around the class.

Answer Key

Para A – introduces the topic of chatbots & expresses opinion
Para B – gives a justification for opinion
Para C – gives another justification for opinion
Para D – gives opposing opinion
Para E – summarises & restates opinion

8 **Aim To analyse an essay**

- Ask Ss to copy and complete the table in their notebooks with information from the essay.
- Then elicit which opinion is the opposing opinion.

Answer Key

	Viewpoints	***Reasons/Examples***
1	***faster customer service***	• ***has programmed answers*** • *1) online 24 hours a day*
2	*2) save companies money*	• ***fewer members of staff*** • ***needs just one IT technician***
3	***customers do not always like talking to chatbots***	*3) prefer sth more personal*

Point 3 is the opposing viewpoint.

9 a) **Aim To introduce formal style – linking ideas**

- Read out the ***Writing Tip*** and tell Ss that this advice will help them to complete the writing task successfully.
- Elicit what style the essay in Ex. 7a is written in and ask Ss to give reasons. Tell them they can refer to the ***Writing Tip*** for help.

Answer Key

It is written in formal style because it has no contractions, it uses the passive, and it uses formal linking words and phrases.
No contractions: *you have, might not, is not, do not, will not*
Use of passive: *is designed, will be needed, be liked*
Formal linking words/phrases: *Firstly, Furthermore, Moreover, On the other hand, All in all*

b) **Aim To identify formal linking words/phrases**

- Give Ss time to find all the formal linking words/phrases in the essay in Ex. 7a.
- Elicit answers from Ss around the class and elicit what each one expresses.

Answer Key

Firstly – lists a point
Furthermore, Moreover – add points
On the other hand, – expresses contrast
All in all – concludes

Writing

10 a) **Aim To prepare for a writing task; to analyse a rubric**

Ask Ss to read the rubric and elicit answers to the questions.

Answer Key

I am going to write an essay expressing my opinion on gaming apps for my teacher. I should write in formal style.

b) **Aim To listen for specific information/ideas for a writing task**

- Play the recording and ask Ss to listen and make notes on the speakers' viewpoints and reasons/examples.
- Then elicit answers from Ss around the class.

Answer Key

Male

Viewpoints: *too small; use a lot of battery*
Examples/Reasons: *get headaches; phone might stop working halfway through the day*

Female

Viewpoints: *fun; free*
Examples/Reasons: *helps pass time when travelling on the bus; just download and play*

11 **Aim To develop writing skills; to write an opinion essay**

- Tell Ss to use their answers from Ex. 10b and the plan to help them write their essay for the rubric in Ex. 10a.
- Give Ss time to complete the task and then ask various Ss to read their essays to the class.
- This task may be assigned as homework.

Suggested Answer Key

If you own a smartphone, you might have played a game on a mobile app. I believe mobile games are excellent for several reasons.
Firstly, they are a lot of fun. They help pass time when travelling on the bus or the train.
Moreover, they are free. You just download them and play.
On the other hand, some people think the screens are

too small. They think staring at a small screen for a long time might give you headaches. Furthermore, they use a lot of battery. If you play for a long time, your phone might stop working halfway through the day.
All in all, I think mobile games are a great way to pass the time. They may not be liked by some people, but they provide a cheap way to pass the time.

VALUES

Ask Ss to read the quotation, then initiate a class discussion about its meanings. Encourage all Ss to participate.

Suggested Answer Key

A: *I think the quotation means creativity is a way we use our minds to think of fun things to do.*
B: *I totally agree. I also think it refers to how the more intelligent we are, the more creative we can be. etc*

Culture 7

Listening & Reading

1 **Aim To introduce the topic; to listen and read for specific information**

- Ask Ss to read the title and look at the picture.
- Elicit what Ss think the text is about.
- Play the recording. Ss listen and read the text to find out.

Answer Key

The text is about the World Science Festival.

2 **Aim To read for key words (text completion); to present/consolidate new vocabulary**

- Give Ss time to read the text again and then use key words from the text to complete the email.
- Check Ss' answers and then give them time to explain the words in bold using the Word List or their dictionaries to help them.

Answer Key

1 New York	3 events	5 sold out
2 a week	4 show	

Suggested Answer Key

mission (n): *aim/goal*
public (n): *the general population*
founded (v): *started/set up*
venue (n): *places where an event is held*
CGI (n): *computer generated images*
combining (v): *mixing together*
multimedia (adj): *different types of media e.g. film, dance, music*
renowned (adj): *famous/well known*
narrated (v): *described sth orally*
state-of-the-art (adj): *up to date, very modern*
depict (v): *to show*
in advance (phr): *ahead of time*
spreading the word (phr): *telling people about sth*

- Give Ss time to look up the meanings of the words in the ***Check these words*** box in the Word List.
- Play the video for Ss and elicit their comments.

Speaking & Writing

3 **Aim THINK To express a preference; to develop thinking skills**

- Give Ss time to think of a topic from science and technology that they would like to see presented in a stage show and how it could be presented.
- Ask various Ss to share their answers with the class.

Suggested Answer Key

I would like to see a stage show about genetics and gene therapy. I think it could be presented with videos, music and dancers. The presenter could be Michael Mosley from the TV show 'Trust Me I'm a Doctor.' I think he's great!

4 **Aim ICT To develop research skills; to give a presentation on a science event in your country or another country**

- Give Ss time to research online and find out information about a science event in their country or another country and use this information to prepare a presentation.
- Ask various Ss to give their presentation to the class. Tell Ss they may give it in English or in L1.
- This task may be assigned as homework.

Suggested Answer Key

The Big Bang Fair is a science and technology event for aspiring young scientists and engineers in the UK. It takes place every year in March at the NEC in Birmingham. It is the largest even of its kind in the UK and it is free and welcomes young people from all over the country who are interested in STEM (science, technology, engineering and maths) subjects. It is led by Engineering UK and 200 other organisations are involved as well.
The Big Bang Fair gives young people the chance to try out over 100 hands-on activities, see dozens of amazing shows, hear from inspiring engineers and scientists from some of the UK's biggest companies and find out about future career opportunities available in STEM. It also runs competitions to find the Young Scientist and Young Engineer of the Year.
It is a fun and interesting event that brings science and engineering to life for young people.

Review 7

Vocabulary

1 **Aim** **To consolidate vocabulary from the unit**

- Explain the task.
- Give Ss time to complete it.
- Check Ss' answers.

Answer Key

1 monitor
2 booked
3 command
4 streamed
5 consists
6 straightaway
7 tracks

2 **Aim** **To consolidate vocabulary from the unit**

- Explain the task.
- Give Ss time to complete it.
- Check Ss' answers.

Answer Key

1 control
2 reality
3 high-speed
4 behaviour
5 reminder
6 sensors
7 command
8 account
9 artificial
10 share

3 **Aim** **To practise prepositional phrases and phrasal verbs**

- Explain the task.
- Give Ss time to complete it.
- Check Ss' answers.

Answer Key

1 on
2 with
3 off
4 to
5 out

Grammar

4 **Aim** **To practise the passive/causative/impersonal constructions**

- Explain the task.
- Give Ss time to complete it.
- Check Ss' answers.

Answer Key

1 ... computer system is being repaired now.
2 ... had his computer fixed.
3 ... should be returned to the shop.
4 ... was founded by Bill Gates in 1975?
5 ... 'll have the app downloaded.
6 ... is said to be cancelled this year.
7 ... can have your connection checked.
8 ... is expected that the new games console will be popular.

5 **Aim** **To practise reflexive/emphatic pronouns**

- Explain the task.
- Give Ss time to complete it.
- Check Ss' answers.

Answer Key

1 himself (E)
2 yourself (R)
3 herself (E)
4 themselves (R)
5 myself (E)

Everyday English

6 **Aim** **To match exchanges**

- Explain the task.
- Give Ss time to complete it.
- Check Ss' answers.

Answer Key

1 b 2 d 3 a 4 c

Competences

Ask Ss to assess their own performance in the unit by ticking the items according to how competent they feel for each of the listed activities.

8 Better societies

Topic	
In this unit, Ss will explore the topics of world problems and social problems.	
8a Reading & Vocabulary	**64-65**
Lesson objectives: To learn vocabulary related to world problems, to listen and read for gist, to read for key information (multiple choice), to learn collocations related to refugees, to learn prepositional phrases, to practise words easily confused, to learn phrasal verbs with *fall*, to talk about refugees, to write a diary entry in the voice of a refugee **Vocabulary:** World problems *(overpopulation, homelessness, child labour, climate change, poverty, famine, refugees, inequality, wars, illiteracy)*; Nouns *(border, NGO, dean, gear, income, access)*; Verbs *(reason, affected, apply)*; Adjectives *(estimated, neighbouring, miserable, healthy)*; Adverb *(relatively)*	
8b Grammar in Use	**66-67**
Lesson objectives: To revise/learn conditionals types 0-3, to revise/learn wishes, to revise/learn question tags	
8c Skills in Action	**68-69**
Lesson objectives: To learn vocabulary for social problems, to listen for specific information (multiple choice), to listen and read for specific information, to act out a dialogue and practise everyday English for making suggestions and agreeing/disagreeing, to practise diphthongs, to read for lexical cohesion (word formation), to write an article suggesting solutions to a problem **Vocabulary:** Social problems *(depression, animal abuse, unemployment, racism, obesity, stress, addiction, bullying)*	
Culture 8	**70**
Lesson objectives: To read for specific information, to listen and read for gist *(matching headings to paragraphs)*, to think of a motto, to give a presentation on a non-profit organisation in your country **Vocabulary:** Nouns *(mission, power, intern, campaign)*; Verbs *(define, launch, spread, improving, reduce)*; Adjectives *(clean, major)*; Adverb *(regularly)*	
Review 8	**71**
Lesson objectives: To test/consolidate vocabulary and grammar learnt throughout the unit; to practise everyday English	

Go through the objectives box and tell Ss that these are the topics, skills and activities this unit will cover.

8a

Vocabulary

1 Aim To present vocabulary related to world problems

- Ask Ss to read the words in the list and then give them time to discuss them in small groups and decide which ones are the most serious in their country as well as think of other problems.
- Ask various groups to tell the class.

Suggested Answer Key

A: *I think climate change is a very serious problem that is affecting the whole world right now.*
B: *I agree. It's a serious problem in our country, too. There's been a lot of flooding in the winter in recent years and droughts in the summer.*
C: *Poverty is another global problem that we can see in our country.*
A: *That's true. There are food banks in almost every town these days and a lot of homeless people, too.*
B: *That's right. There are a lot of people sleeping rough in towns and cities all over the country.*
A: *So the three most serious problems in our country are climate change, poverty and homelessness. What about any other problems?*
B: *Well, I think pollution is a major problem in our country and around the world and that's why climate change is happening.*
C: *Right. I agree. I think pollution is the biggest problem the world is facing right now because it is what is causing so many other problems. etc*

Reading & Listening

2 Aim To read and listen for gist

- Ask Ss to read the title of the text and look at the picture and elicit their guesses for what the article is going to be about.
- Play the recording. Ss listen and read the text to find out.
- Check Ss' answers.

Answer Key

I think the text is about refugees.

3 **Aim** **To read for specific information (multiple choice)**

- Ask Ss to read the text again, then read the questions and answer choices and choose their answers based on what they read.
- Check Ss' answers. Ss should justify their choices.
- Then give Ss time to look up the meanings of the words in bold in the Word List or in their dictionaries and elicit definitions from Ss around the class.

Answer Key

1 B (relatively peaceful)
2 C (the right to work)
3 A (We were in a refugee camp for years)
4 B (set up a business with another woman from my course)
5 A (they can generate income, create jobs wherever they go)

Suggested Answer Key

estimated (adj): *approximately guessed*
neighbouring (adj): *being/living next to sb/sth*
relatively (adv): *quite*
access (n): *the ability to use*
affected (v): *had an impact on sb/sth*
miserable (adj): *very unhappy*
apply (v): *to officially ask for sth*
healthy (adj): *being good for one's health/well-being*

- Give Ss time to look up the meanings of the words in the ***Check these words*** box in the Word List.
- Play the video for Ss and elicit their comments.

Background Information

Ethiopia is a country in Africa. Its official language is Amharic. Its currency is the Ethiopian birr. Its capital city is Addis Ababa. Other major cities are Dire Dawa and Mekele.

4 **Aim** **To consolidate new vocabulary & practise collocations**

- Ask Ss to look through the text and find the words that pair with the words in the list to make collocations.
- Check Ss' answers and then give them time to use the collocations in sentences of their own.

Answer Key

1 member
2 business
3 refugee
4 international
5 group
6 special

Suggested Answer Key

Everyone wants to be a useful ***member of society****.*
I'd like to be a ***business owner*** *one day.*
There are some ***refugee camps*** *in my country.*
Médecins Sans Frontières is an ***international NGO****.*
I have a friend who goes to ***group therapy****.*
You get ***special treatment*** *at a 5-star hotel.*

5 **Aim** **To consolidate prepositional phrases from a text**

- Give Ss time to read the sentences and fill in the gaps with the correct prepositions.
- Then check Ss' answers.

Answer Key

1 in 2 to 3 with 4 as

6 **Aim** **To understand words easily confused**

- Explain the task and give Ss time to use their dictionaries to help them complete it.
- Check Ss' answers.

Answer Key

1 action
2 ordinary
3 reminds
4 real
5 special

7 **Aim** **To learn phrasal verbs with *fall***

- Ask Ss to read the phrasal verbs box and make sure that Ss understand the definitions.
- Then give Ss time to complete the task and check their answers.

Answer Key

1 through
2 out
3 apart
4 behind
5 apart
6 in with

Speaking & Writing

8 **Aim** **To expand the topic**

- Ask Ss to talk in small groups and discuss other ways the Ethiopian government could improve refugees' conditions.
- Monitor the activity around the class and then ask various groups to share their ideas with the class.

Suggested Answer Key

A: I think the Ethiopian government could improve the facilities at the refugee camps. For example, they could provide better housing with heating and electricity so people didn't have to hunt for wood to make fires to cook over.
B: That's a good idea. Also, people would have more room and conditions would not be so crowded.

C: Obviously, healthcare is important and I think the government could make health services available to refugees so that people in the camps didn't get sick. etc

9 **Aim THINK To write a diary entry in the voice of a refugee; to develop thinking skills**

- Give Ss time to write a diary entry about their daily life as a refugee.
- Then have various Ss read out their diary entries to the class.

Suggested Answer Key

Dear Diary,

Today was another miserable day in the refugee camp. I spent the morning looking for firewood to make a fire to cook over. Then, I queued with the hundreds of others at the gates to get some flour and some rice to cook to eat. I am really unhappy here. I wish I could go to school and study all the subjects I used to back home. I wish I could go to college and get a good job. Then, I could buy a house for me and my family to live in together away from the camp. We would have heating and electricity and all the comforts of a home. One day maybe my dream will come true.

8b Grammar in Use

1 **Aim To learn/revise conditionals 0-3**

- Ask Ss to read the messages in the group chat and match the underlined sentences to what they express.
- Then elicit how we form each type of conditional.
- Check Ss' answers and refer Ss to the ***Grammar Reference*** section for more information or to check any points they are unsure of.

Answer Key

If we carry on polluting the planet like this, there won't be many more New Year's Days left! – a situation that is likely to happen in the present/future (Conditional Type 1)
When children work, they don't go to school and illiteracy rates rise. – a general truth/scientific fact (Conditional Type 0)
If more of us volunteered, we could solve many of the world's problems. – a situation that is unlikely to happen in the present/future (Conditional Type 2)
If the wars had never started, they wouldn't have had to leave their homes. – an unreal situation in the past (Conditional Type 3)
If I were you, I'd do the same. – advice (Conditional Type 2)

We form type 0 conditionals with if/when *+ present simple – present simple.*
We form type 1 conditionals with if *+ present simple – will + bare infinitive.*
We form type 2 conditionals with if *+ past simple – would/could + bare infinitive)*
We form type 3 conditionals with if *+ past perfect –* would *+* have *+ past participle.*

2 **Aim To practise conditionals**

- Give Ss time to complete the task.
- Check Ss' answers and refer Ss to the ***Grammar Reference*** section for more information or to check any points they are unsure of.

Answer Key

1 keeps – type 1
2 melts – type 0
3 would have made – type 3
4 would volunteer – type 2
5 wouldn't have happened – type 3
6 deal – type 1

We use commas to separate the clauses in conditional sentences when the if-clause *is at the beginning of the sentence.*

3 **Aim To practise conditionals**

- Give Ss time to complete the sentences with the correct forms of the verbs in brackets. Have Ss add commas where necessary. Ss can also work in closed pairs if you like.
- Elicit answers from Ss around the class and elicit reasons.

Answer Key

1 would report (advice)
2 get (a situation that is likely to happen in the future) – comma after 'teachers'
3 would have given (an unreal situation in the past) – comma after 'going'
4 doesn't pollute (a scientific fact) – comma after 'car'
5 will disappear (a situation that is likely to happen in the future) – comma after 'continues'
6 had realised (an unreal situation in the past)
7 floods (general truth)
8 wouldn't be (a situation that is unlikely to happen in the future) – comma after 'resources'

4 **Aim To practise conditionals**

- Explain the task. Go through the sentences with Ss and check if they have any unknown words. Give Ss time to complete the task. Ss compare their

answers in closed pairs.
- Elicit answers from Ss around the class.

Answer Key

1 *had finished (type 3)*	5 *would have given (type 3)*
2 *will die (type 1)*	6 *had told (type 3)*
3 *vaccinate (type 0)*	
4 *would donate (type 2)*	

Speaking

5 Aim To practise conditionals

Divide the class into small groups. Explain the task and read out the examples. Then give Ss time to complete it in groups. Monitor the activity around the class.

Suggested Answer Key

A: If I were you,
B: I would volunteer at a homeless shelter.
C: If more people fall into poverty,
D: more people will become homeless.
A: When carbon emissions increase,
B: climate change gets worse.
C: If I had known you didn't have enough money,
D: I would have lent you some. etc.

6 Aim To learn/revise wishes

- Go through the rubric with Ss.
- Direct Ss to the highlighted sentences in the group chat messages on p. 66.
- Have Ss match the highlighted sentences to what they express.
- Then elicit what words we use to introduce wishes.

Answer Key

I wish child labour didn't exist. – a desire for a present situation to be different
I just wish I'd done it sooner! – regret that something didn't happen in the past
I wish people would stop fighting each other. – a desire for something to change

*We use **I wish/If only** to introduce wishes.*

7 Aim To practise wishes

- Give Ss time to complete the task.
- Check Ss' answers around the class.

Answer Key

1 *had baked*	7 *hadn't lost*
2 *knew*	8 *earned*
3 *hadn't driven*	
4 *wasn't/weren't*	
5 *had*	
6 *had taken*	

Speaking

8 Aim To practise wishes

Explain the task and ask Ss to practise making wishes in closed pairs following the example and taking turns. Monitor the activity around the class and then ask some pairs to tell the class.

Suggested Answer Key

A: There is so much poverty in the world.
B: I wish the billionaires would share more of their wealth.
A: Climate change is a big problem.
B: If only everyone would stop using fossil fuels. etc

9 Aim To learn/revise question tags

- Write on the board: *He is late, isn't he? He doesn't walk to work, does he?*
- Elicit answers to the questions in the rubric from Ss around the class.
- Refer Ss to the ***Grammar Reference*** section for more information and to clarify any points they are unsure of.
- Ask Ss to find an example in the group chat messages.

Answer Key

Question tags are short questions at the end of statements.
We use them to ask for confirmation or agreement.
Question tags are formed with the auxiliary or modal verb from the statement and the appropriate subject.
Example from p. 66 – Unless children receive an education, they won't break free from their lives of poverty, will they?

10 Aim To practise question tags

- Give Ss time to complete the sentences with the correct question tags. Check Ss' answers.
- Then play the recording. Ss listen and put a tick in the correct box according to whether the question tag has rising or falling intonation.

Answer Key

1 *shall we*	↘		6 *didn't they*	↘
2 *don't I*	↗		7 *isn't it*	↗
3 *will you*	↗		8 *hasn't she*	↘
4 *isn't he*	↗		9 *did they*	↘
5 *didn't we*	↘		10 *do you*	↗

Speaking

11 Aim To practise question tags

- Explain the task and ask two Ss to read out the examples. Ask Ss to work in pairs and do the task.

- Monitor the activity around the class and then ask some Ss to share their answers with the class.

Suggested Answer Key

A: I'm tired.
B: You didn't stay up late again last night, did you? It's my graduation day on Friday.
A: You are excited, aren't you? etc

8c Skills in Action

Vocabulary

1 **Aim To present vocabulary related to social problems**

- Ask Ss to read the problems in the list and then read the statements (1-8).
- Explain/Elicit the meanings of any unknown words or phrases or ask Ss to look them up in the Word List.
- Then give Ss time to match the problems to the statements.
- Elicit answers from Ss around the class.

Answer Key

1 E 3 A 5 C 7 F
2 D 4 B 6 G 8 H

2 **Aim THINK To categorise problems**

- Elicit the meanings of the words social (related to society) and socio-economic (related to the differences between people because of their financial situation).
- Give Ss time to consider which problems match which category, then ask various Ss to tell the class.

Suggested Answer Key

Social: *depression, animal abuse, racism, obesity, stress, addiction, bullying*
Socio-economic: *unemployment*

Listening

3 **Aim To listen for specific information (multiple choice)**

- Ask Ss to read the sentences (1-4) and the possible answers. Play the recording twice. Ss choose their answers.
- Check Ss' answers. You can play the recording again with pauses for Ss to check their answers.

Answer Key

1 B 2 A 3 C 4 B

Everyday English

4 **Aim To listen and read for specific information**

- Ask Ss to read the first exchange in the dialogue. Elicit Ss' guesses as to what suggestion Dan makes.
- Play the recording for Ss to listen and read and find out if their guesses were correct.

Answer Key

Dan suggests free courses for pet owners to teach them about animal care.

5 **Aim To act out a dialogue and practise everyday English for making suggestions & agreeing/disagreeing**

- Explain the task. Play the recording for Ss to listen to the interview in Ex. 3 again and make notes.
- Give Ss time to use their notes to act out a dialogue similar to the one in Ex. 4 in pairs using the prompts.
- Write this diagram on the board for Ss to follow.

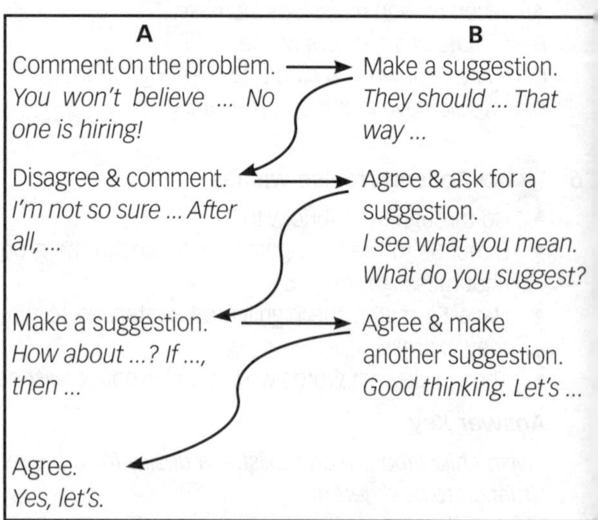

A
B
Comment on the problem.
You won't believe ... No one is hiring!
Make a suggestion.
They should ... That way ...
Disagree & comment.
I'm not so sure ... After all, ...
Agree & ask for a suggestion.
I see what you mean. What do you suggest?
Make a suggestion.
How about ...? If ..., then ...
Agree & make another suggestion.
Good thinking. Let's ...
Agree.
Yes, let's.

- Monitor the activity around the class and offer assistance as necessary.
- Then ask some pairs to act out their dialogues in front of the class.

Suggested Answer Key

A: You won't believe how difficult it is for young people to get a job these days. No one is hiring!
B: They should get more qualifications. That way, they would have a better chance of finding a job!
A: I'm not so sure about that. After all, it's not like I didn't have enough qualifications, is it?
B: I see what you mean. What do you suggest?
A: How about job creation schemes? If the government gave financial help to start-ups, it would mean more people could start their own businesses.

B: *Good thinking. Let's suggest your idea to the local MP.*
A: *Yes, let's.*

Pronunciation

6 a) Aim To learn diphthongs

- Explain that there are eight diphthongs in English (/ɪə/, /eə/, /ʊə/, /eɪ/, /aɪ/, /ɔɪ/, /əʊ/, /aʊ/). Play the recording with pauses for Ss to repeat chorally and/or individually. Check Ss' intonation.
- Then give Ss time to read the sentences and underline the diphthongs in them.
- Check Ss' answers around the class.

Answer Key

1 *Are you sure he didn't know about the animal abuse?*
2 *It's not fair that the puppies have nowhere to play.*
3 *There is a real need in the camp for children's toys.*
4 *Let's try volunteering. How about helping out at the animal shelter?*

b) Aim To practise diphthongs

Ask Ss to work in pairs and take turns to say sentences to each other including diphthongs. Ss identify the diphthongs. Monitor the activity around the class.

Suggested Answer Key

I get upset when I think about animal abuse. I don't know how people can do it.

Reading & Writing

7 a) Aim To read for lexical cohesion (word formation)

- Give Ss time to read the article and complete the gaps with a word formed from the word in brackets.
- Check Ss' answers.

Answer Key

1 *Obesity*	4 *consequently*
2 *overweight*	5 *sensible*
3 *reduction*	6 *ensure*

b) Aim To analyse the content of an article

Elicit what each paragraph is about from Ss around the class.

Answer Key

A *state topic & cause*
B *first suggestion & expected result*
C *second suggestion & expected result*
D *summarise points & state personal opinion*

8 Aim To analyse a model

- Read out the ***Writing Tip*** and tell Ss that this advice will help them to complete the writing task successfully.
- Have Ss read the article in Ex. 7 again and answer the questions.
- Elicit answers from Ss around the class.

Answer Key

The writer suggests decreasing food intake and exercising. The explanations/examples are: regulates the size of portions, take up a sport or walk long distances. The expected results are that by not consuming more food than the body needs and by burning the energy from food, we won't put on weight.
The writer introduces his/her suggestions with: One possible solution is, In this way, Consequently, Another useful suggestion is, This means that

9 Aim To analyse a conclusion

Read out the question. Ask Ss to read the conclusion again and elicit the answer.

Answer Key

a, c

Writing

10 Aim To prepare for a writing task; to analyse a rubric

Give Ss time to read the rubric and elicit answers to the questions from Ss around the class.

Answer Key

1 *I am going to write an article for a local newspaper.*
2 *I should write about animal abuse in our modern society. I should write 120-180 words.*

11 Aim To prepare for a writing task

- Ask Ss to copy the table into their notebooks and complete it using the ideas from Ex. 4 and their own ideas.
- Ask various Ss to share their answers with the class.

Suggested Answer Key

Suggestions	***Explanations/ Examples***	***Expected results***
Report to police	*Abusers would be banned from owning an animal.*	*They would not abuse an animal again.*
Free education	*Pet owners learn about animal care.*	*They won't do anything to harm an animal.*

12 **Aim** **To develop writing skills; to write an article suggesting solutions to a problem**

- Tell Ss to use their answers from Ex. 11 and the plan to help them write their article for the rubric in Ex. 10. Remind Ss to give their article a title.
- Give Ss time to complete the task and then ask various Ss to read their articles to the class.
- This task may be assigned as homework.

Suggested Answer Key

End Animal Abuse

Animal abuse is a serious problem worldwide. Some of it is deliberate and some is because people don't know how to care properly for an animal. So, what can we do about this problem?

One possible solution is to report abusers to the police. Abusers would be banned from owning an animal. This way, they would never abuse an animal again.

Another useful suggestion is to offer free education to pet owners. This means that they would learn about animal care. As a result, they would not do anything to harm an animal.

In conclusion, reporting abusers to the police and educating pet owners are two ways to solve the problem of animal abuse. I believe that this way we can ensure that animals are safe.

VALUES

Ask Ss to read the quotation, then initiate a class discussion about its meaning. Encourage all Ss to participate.

Suggested Answer Key

A: I think the quotation means that we should always be kind to others.
B: I totally agree. I also think it refers to the fact that we should find ways to be kind even in difficult situations where we may not feel like being kind to someone, for example, when that person is mean.
A: Yes, I think you're right. etc

Culture 8

Listening & Reading

1 **Aim** **To introduce the topic; to read for specific information**

- Have Ss look at the picture and elicit what Ss think the Borgen Project is and what problem it addresses.
- Give Ss time to read through the text to find out.

Answer Key

The Borgen Project is a non-governmental project with a mission to demand change from governments. It addresses the problem of extreme poverty.

2 **Aim** **To listen and read for gist (matching headings to paragraphs)**

- Give Ss time to read the text again and then match the headings to the paragraphs giving reasons. Remind Ss that there are two extra headings.
- Check Ss' answers. Ss justify their answers.
- Give Ss time to look up the meanings of the words in bold in the Word List or in their dictionaries and elicit definitions from Ss around the class.

Answer Key

1 D (issue – extreme poverty also lack safe homes, clean drinking water, enough food, access to healthcare or education, work in dangerous conditions)
2 G (solution – mission: to end extreme poverty)
3 A (origins – story behind the Borgen Project)
4 C (actions/activities – volunteers /educate people about how to demand change from their governments/regularly meet with politicians)
5 E (success – the good news is the situation is improving/In 1990, 1.9 billion people living in extreme poverty worldwide. Today, … 702 million)

- Give Ss time to look up the meanings of the words in the ***Check these words*** box in the Word List.
- Play the video for Ss and elicit their comments.

Suggested Answer Key

clean (adj): *not dirty or contaminated*
spread (v): *to expand in order to reach a greater area/ more people etc*
regularly (adv): *happening often*
major (adj): *very important*
improving (v): *getting better*
reduce (v): *to make less*

3 **Aim** **To present/consolidate new vocabulary through antonyms**

Give Ss time to match the words in bold to the antonyms in the list. Check Ss' answers.

Answer Key

clean *≠ polluted*
spread *≠ contain*
regularly *≠ rarely*
major *≠ minor*
improving *≠ worsening*
reduce *≠ increase*

Speaking & Writing

4 Aim THINK To develop thinking skills; to think of a motto

- Have Ss work independently and consider their ideas for a motto for the Borgen Project and how it reflects the aims of the organisation. Ss can work in groups if you like.
- Ask some Ss to share their answers with the class.

Suggested Answer Key

A good motto would be 'We can all end extreme poverty together!' This says that everyone needs to join the project. It also says what the issue is and encourages people to work together.

5 Aim ICT To develop research skills; to give a presentation on a non-profit organisation in your country

- Give Ss time to research online and find out information about a non-profit organisation in their country and use this information to prepare a presentation.
- Ask various Ss to give their presentation to the class.
- This task may be assigned as homework.

Suggested Answer Key

Good morning. Today I am going to talk to you about a non-profit organisation that is helping refugees in Greece.

What's the issue?

During the recent migrant crisis in Europe, hundreds of thousands of refugees have been shipwrecked off the coast of Greece and some people wanted to do what they could to help.

What's the solution?

The Starfish Foundation is a non-governmental organisation with a mission to help refugees and migrants who are shipwreck survivors. These people needed their basic needs meeting. They had no food or clothing and the local people got together to help them.

The origins of the organisation

Restaurant owner Melinda McRostie from Lesbos coordinated with the local people to form the Starfish Foundation in 2015 and help the refugees get access to hot food and dry clothes. They worked together to set up and manage the largest refugee camp on the island.

Actions and activities

In the first two years of operating, the foundation had more than 1,500 volunteers who welcomed, sheltered and took care of over 200,000 people. It also started to work on a national scale, delivering clothes and other items to camps across the country.

Success so far

There are still refugees arriving in Greece but thanks to the Starfish Foundation they receive a warm welcome and all their needs are met. They have access to food, shelter, toiletries, and other items such as mobile phones, as well as education and sports. Starfish will continue to provide assistance wherever needed, both to refugees and to the local community.

Thanks for listening. Are there any questions?

Review 8

Vocabulary

1 Aim To consolidate vocabulary from the unit

- Explain the task.
- Give Ss time to complete it.
- Check Ss' answers.

Answer Key

1 overpopulation, 2 homelessness, 3 famine, 4 poverty, 5 illiteracy, 6 obesity, 7 unemployment, 8 depression

2 Aim To consolidate vocabulary from the unit

- Explain the task.
- Give Ss time to complete it.
- Check Ss' answers.

Answer Key

1 stress, 2 real, 3 Child, 4 Climate, 5 animal, 6 Group, 7 Racism, 8 refugee

3 Aim To practise prepositional phrases and phrasal verbs

- Explain the task.
- Give Ss time to complete it.
- Check Ss' answers.

Answer Key

1 apart, 2 as, 3 out, 4 to, 5 in, 6 through

Grammar

4 Aim To practise conditionals

- Explain the task.
- Give Ss time to complete it.
- Check Ss' answers.

Answer Key

1 would treat 2, 2 will increase 1, 3 don't have 0, 4 would have gone 3

5 **Aim** **To practise wishes**

- Explain the task.
- Give Ss time to complete it.
- Check Ss' answers.

Answer Key

1 had	*3 wasn't/weren't*
2 hadn't ignored	*4 had volunteered*

6 **Aim** **To practise question tags**

- Explain the task.
- Give Ss time to complete it.
- Check Ss' answers.

Answer Key

1 don't you	*3 are they*
2 haven't you	*4 will you*

Everyday English

7 **Aim** **To match exchanges**

- Explain the task.
- Give Ss time to complete it.
- Check Ss' answers.

Answer Key

1 e 2 d 3 b 4 c 5 a

Competences

Ask Ss to assess their own performance in the unit by ticking the items according to how competent they feel for each of the listed activities.

Live & Learn

Topic	
In this unit, Ss will explore the topics of university and education.	
9a Reading & Vocabulary	**72-73**
Lesson objectives: To learn vocabulary related to education & technology, to read for gist, to listen and read for cohesion and coherence (gapped text), to learn collocations related to technology in education, to learn prepositional phrases, to practise words easily confused, to learn phrasal verbs with *check*, to talk about AR apps, to design and present an educational AR app **Vocabulary:** University *(lecture, lecture hall, professor, undergraduate, notes, course, campus)*; Nouns *(effects, nutritionist, constellation, concept, creatures, identification)*; Verbs *(abandoned, experience)*; Adjectives *(overpowering, stimulating, interactive, passive)*; *-ing* form *(beating)*	
9b Grammar in Use	**74-75**
Lesson objectives: learn/revise the infinitive/*-ing* form; to learn revise forms of the infinitive/*-ing* form; to learn/revise relative clauses	
9c Skills in Action	**76-77**
Lesson objectives: To learn vocabulary related to education, to listen for specific information (multiple choice), to listen and read for specific information, to act out a dialogue and practise everyday English for asking for information, to practise intonation in follow-up questions, to read for lexical cohesion (word formation), to write an email asking for information **Vocabulary:** Education *(register, fees, study session, computer labs, official certificate, part-time course, mature students, course description)*	
Culture 9	**78**
Lesson objectives: To listen and read for gist, to read for specific information (comprehension questions), to talk about an education foundation, to write a short article about an educational foundation **Vocabulary:** Nouns *(attitude, mentor, focus, backgrounds)*; Verbs *(promote, reach, runs, achieve)*; Phrasal verbs *(drop out of, points out)*; Adjectives *(financial, impressive, longer)*; Adverb *(nationally)*	
Review 9	**79**
Lesson objectives: To test/consolidate vocabulary and grammar learnt throughout the unit; to practise everyday English	

Go through the objectives box and tell Ss that these are the topics, skills and activities this unit will cover.

9a

Vocabulary

1 a) Aim To introduce the topic; to present vocabulary related to university

- Read out the lists of words/phrases and elicit/explain the meanings of any that are unknown.
- Then give Ss time to complete the task in pairs.
- Check Ss' answers around the class.

Answer Key

1 g 2 b 3 c 4 a 5 d 6 f 7 e

b) Aim To expand the topic

- Give Ss time to discuss the differences between school and university education in pairs.
- Ask various Ss to tell the class.

Suggested Answer Key

A: *University education is very different from school education. First, you don't work from textbooks, but from notes you've taken from lectures and books from the library.*

B: *That's right, and you study one main subject as a course for three or four years before you get your degree. You are the one responsible for studying and handing in work. etc*

Listening & Reading

2 Aim To introduce the topic of a text; to read for gist

- Read out the definition and the question. Give Ss time to skim through the text and find the answer.
- Elicit answers from Ss around the class.

Suggested Answer Key

AR can be used in many ways; first to add to the lecture experience, second to allow them to access information quickly and third to help the student have a broader educational experience.

3 a) Aim To read for cohesion and coherence (gapped text)

- Ask Ss to read the sentences and then give them time to read the text again and use the sentences to complete the gaps in the text.
- Remind Ss that there is one extra sentence.

- Ss should pay attention to the sentences before and after each gap to do the task.
- Once Ss have completed the task, they need to read the completed text to make sure it flows.

b) **Aim To listen for cohesion and coherence; to consolidate new vocabulary**

- Play the recording. Ss listen and read the text to check their answers in Ex. 3a.
- Give Ss time to look up the meanings of the words in bold in the Word List or in their dictionaries and elicit definitions from Ss around the class.

Answer Key

1 E (encourages them to learn – In fact, one study found that technology in the lecture hall makes students 72% more likely to participate.)
2 D (But research has shown that VR can sometimes lead to lower marks. – This is because the world it surrounds the student with is too overpowering, too stimulating)
3 A (however, lays digital images (called auras) on top of the physical world so they see the real world – So, it 'augments' (or adds) images on top of what we can see with the naked eye.)
4 F (On campus, the same technique can be used in nearly every course universities offer. – Medical students can use AR apps to see a 3D human heart beating in their professor's chest)
5 G (Lots of educational AR apps are available that allow students to learn independently, and outside their narrow course of study. – For example, there are apps that act like a hand-held planetarium. – You simply point your phone camera towards the night sky and the app recognises stars and planets, giving you information about them.)
6 C (the best thing about AR, though, is that it gives students a new way to use their smartphones. – AR teaches students that they aren't just for socialising and gaming – they're also really useful learning tools.)

Suggested Answer Key

abandoned (v): *left behind*
experience (v): *to feel or go through sth*
creatures (n): *animals*
beating (v): *making a regular movement*
identification (n): *recognition*
passive (adj): *allowing others to be in control of a situation*

- Give Ss time to look up the meanings of the words in the ***Check these words*** box in the Word List.
- Play the video for Ss and elicit their comments.

4 **Aim To consolidate new vocabulary & practise collocations**

- Ask Ss to look through the text and find the words that pair with the words in the list to make collocations.
- Check Ss' answers and then give them time to use the collocations in sentences of their own.

Answer Key

1 interactive	*3 VR*	*5 video*
2 augmented	*4 digital*	*6 human*

Suggested Answer Key

*Many schools and universities these days use **interactive whiteboards**.*
*The latest technology in education is **augmented reality**.*
***VR headsets** are mostly used in gaming these days.*
*AR lays **digital images** over real images to create a new way of seeing the world.*
***Video chat** is commonly used to keep in touch with people these days.*

5 **Aim To consolidate prepositional phrases from a text**

- Give Ss time to choose the correct prepositions in the sentences.
- Then check Ss' answers.

Answer Key

1 on	*3 at*	*5 to*
2 at	*4 over*	

6 **Aim To understand words easily confused**

- Explain the task and give Ss time to use their dictionaries to help them complete it.
- Check Ss' answers. As an extension, ask Ss to make sentences using the other options.

Answer Key

1 attend	*3 is doing*
2 revise	*4 mark*

7 **Aim To learn phrasal verbs with *check***

- Ask Ss to read the phrasal verbs box and make sure that Ss understand the definitions.
- Then give Ss time to complete the task and check their answers.
- Have Ss make a story with the phrasal verbs and elicit answers from Ss around the class.

Answer Key

1 out	*3 in*	*5 in*
2 off	*4 up on*	

Suggested Answer Key

I checked in at the airport, but I knew I had forgotten something. When I checked in to my hotel in London, the feeling got stronger. Passport, laptop, notes – I checked the items off the list I had in my head. I decided to go and get something to eat and check out the city, but before that I decided to call my daughter to check in on her. That's when I realised what I had forgotten – my phone!

Speaking & Writing

8 Aim THINK To consolidate information in a text; to develop critical thinking skills

- Have Ss discuss the question in pairs and think of three reasons.
- Elicit answers from Ss around the class.

Suggested Answer Key

A: AR apps are a must because, first of all, they make students interested in the lesson. Second, they can provide interesting visual information while a lecture is going on.
B: Yes, and that's really helpful for visual learners who like to see what's actually happening. Finally, they can give students easy access to fields of study outside their own.

9 Aim ICT To develop thinking skills; to design and present an educational AR app

- Give Ss time to research online and find out information about AR apps and think of an educational AR app of their own and prepare a presentation on it.
- Then have Ss give their presentation to the class.

Suggested Answer Key

Our app is called 'Zoom In' and it allows you to zoom in on everyday objects. If you point it at some wood, for example, you can zoom in and see what wood looks like from very close up. It would be especially useful for biology students, we think.

9b Grammar in Use

1 Aim To learn/revise the infinitive/*-ing* form

- Ask Ss to read the text and then give them time to identify all the infinitive/*-ing* forms and list them in a table.
- Elicit answers from Ss around the class.
- Check Ss' answers and refer Ss to the ***Grammar Reference*** section for more information or to check any points they are unsure of.

Answer Key

to-*infinitive*	*infinitive without to*	-ing *form*
to improve *to have* *to challenge*	*can't change* *can improve* *let failure stop*	*(means) believing* *(have difficulty) learning* *(quit) learning* *(continue) working*

2 Aim To practise the infinitive/*-ing* form

- Explain the task and give Ss time to complete it.
- Check Ss' answers and elicit reasons.

Answer Key

1 *finding (have trouble doing sth)*
2 *to discover (only to do sth)*
3 *bring (can't = modal)*
4 *being (after preposition)*
5 *to participate (after 'refuse')*
6 *reading (spend time doing)*
7 *to start (after adjective)*
8 *send (with verb 'make')*
9 *playing (waste time doing sth)*
10 *to hear (after adjective)*

3 Aim To practise the infinitive/*-ing* form

- Give Ss time to complete the sentences.
- Elicit answers from Ss around the class.

Answer Key

1 *to lend, to help*
2 *to study, going*
3 *talking, say*
4 *to watch, doing*
5 *finish, to give*
6 *To be, to stay*

4 Aim To practise forms of the infinitive/*-ing* form

- Read out the theory box and refer Ss to the ***Grammar Reference*** section for more information or to check any points they are unsure of.
- Then explain the task and read out the example.
- Give Ss time to complete the sentences and then check Ss' answers around the class.

Answer Key

2 *to be doing their homework*
3 *to have cheated in her finals*
4 *to get a place at Oxford University*
5 *to have been studying all morning*
6 *to be too strict*

5 **Aim** **To practise the infinitive/-*ing* form**

- Give Ss time to complete the task.
- Check Ss' answers around the class.

Answer Key

1 *working* (mean + -ing *form = involve)*
2 *looking* (try + -ing *form = do sth as an experiment)*
3 *to announce* (regret + to-*infinitive = be sorry)*
4 *to submit* (remember + to-*infinitive = not forget)*
5 *meeting* (forget + -ing *form = not recall)*
6 *to drink* (stop + to-*infinitive = stop temporarily in order to do sth else)*

6 **Aim** **To practise the infinitive/-*ing* form**

- Give Ss time to read the sentences and correct them.
- Check Ss' answers and elicit Ss' reasons.

Answer Key

1 *We heard Lisa give ... (since we heard the whole lecture)*
2 *interrupting (with 'hate' for something you don't like)*
3 *walking (part of his journey was seen by five different people)*
4 *go (to-infinitive after an adjective)*
5 *walking (since you didn't see the completed action)*
6 *to deliver (with 'I'd like')*

Speaking

7 **Aim** **To practise the infinitive/-*ing* form**

- Explain the task, read out the example and give Ss time to complete the task in pairs using the verbs in the list.
- Monitor the activity around the class and then ask some Ss to ask and answer in front of the rest of the class.

Suggested Answer Key

A: *What food do you avoid eating?*
B: *I avoid eating sugar because it's bad for your health. Where have you decided to go for your holidays?*
A: *I've decided to go to the seaside. What country would you love to visit?*
B: *I'd love to visit the USA – New York in particular. Which household chore do you hate doing?*
A: *I hate washing the dishes. What are you looking forward to doing most this year?*
B: *I'm looking forward to going on holiday this summer. What do you regret doing most?*
A: *I regret starting to learn English so late. Which fruit do you like eating the most?*
B: *I like eating strawberries the most. What do you remember doing when you were a child?*
A: *I remember visiting my grandparents every summer.*

8 **Aim** **To learn/revise relatives & relative clauses**

- Read out the rubric and refer Ss to the text on p. 74 again.
- Read out the examples and refer Ss to the ***Grammar Reference*** section for more information and to check any points they are unsure of.
- Then elicit answers to the questions in the rubric from Ss around the class.

Answer Key

The second contains a defining relative clause. The first sentence contains a non-defining relative clause.
The non-defining relative clause can be omitted.
The 'which' in the second sentence can be replaced with 'that'.
Example from text: *students with a fixed mindset who have difficulty learning ... (defining)*

9 **Aim** **To practise relative clauses**

- Explain the task and give Ss time to complete it.
- Elicit answers from Ss around the class.

Answer Key

1 *Do you know the reason why Peter left the lecture early today? D (can be omitted)*
2 *Jane, whose son goes to an expensive college in the USA, earns a high wage. ND*
3 *Advanced Logic is the module that I find the most challenging. D (can be omitted)*
4 *Mr Richards, who inspired me to become a teacher, has recently retired. ND*
5 *The gym where we work out is not far from the college. D*
6 *Do you remember the day when Professor Rodgers came into the lecture in costume? D (can be omitted)*
7 *Lisa, who's agreed to help me with my essay, has a degree in Philosophy. ND*
8 *Is that book which you're reading any good? D (can be omitted)*

10 **Aim** **To practise relative clauses**

- Explain the task and read out the example.
- Then give Ss time to complete the task in their notebooks.
- Check Ss' answers around the class.

Answer Key

2 *I'll never forget the day when my daughter graduated from university.*
3 *This is the reason why James should go to a private college.*
4 *Alice reads a lot of novels which she borrows from the library.*

5 *The university has 200 foreign students, many of whom are from Asia.*
6 *Steve, whose father is a celebrity chef, studies Marketing.*
7 *This is the town where I went to college.*
8 *Paul did a study on volcanoes that was impressive.*

Speaking

11 Aim To practise relative clauses

- Have Ss work in groups of four and complete the task following the example.
- Monitor the activity around the class.

Suggested Answer Key

S1: It's a male film actor.
S2: It's an American actor.
S3: It's the actor who starred in the John Wick films.
S4: It's Keanu Reeves. etc

9c Skills in Action

Vocabulary

1 Aim To present vocabulary related to education

- Ask Ss to read the words in the list and then read the advert and complete the gaps using the words in the list.
- Explain/Elicit the meanings of any unknown words or phrases or ask Ss to look them up in the Word List.
- Elicit answers from Ss around the class.

Answer Key

1 Register	*4 Study*	*7 certificate*
2 part-time	*5 labs*	*8 description*
3 mature	*6 Fees*	

2 Aim THINK To expand the topic; to express an opinion

- Give Ss time to consider their opinions and discuss the pros and cons of taking evening classes in groups.
- Monitor the activity around the class and then ask various Ss to share their opinions with the class.

Suggested Answer Key

A: One advantage of taking evening classes is that you can work during the day and study at night.
B: Yes – or look after your children during the day, then study at night.
C: A disadvantage is that you have to study at night, and can't go out.
A: That's true. You don't have much free time. etc

Listening

3 Aim To listen for specific information (multiple choice)

- Ask Ss to read the questions and answer choices and find the keywords. Play the recording twice. Ss choose their answers according to what they hear.
- Check Ss' answers. You can play the recording again with pauses for Ss to check their answers.

Answer Key

1 C   2 B   3 C   4 C

Everyday English

4 Aim To listen and read for specific information

- Ask Ss to read the first exchange in the dialogue. Read out the question. Elicit Ss' guesses as to what questions Peter will ask about the course.
- Play the recording for Ss to listen and read and find out if their guesses were correct.

Answer Key

He asks about fees and accommodation.

5 Aim To act out a dialogue and practise everyday English for asking for information

- Explain the task and ask Ss to act out a dialogue similar to the one in Ex. 4 in pairs using the advert in Ex. 1 and the phrases in the language box.
- Write this diagram on the board for Ss to follow.

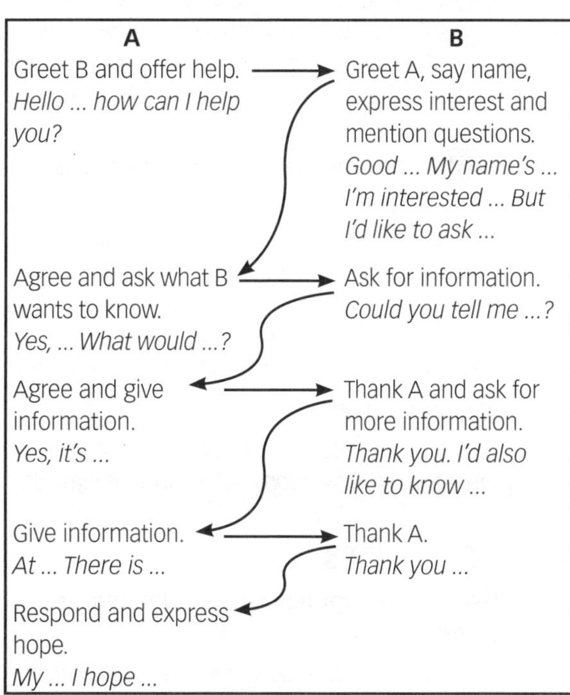

A
B
Greet B and offer help.
Hello ... how can I help you?
Greet A, say name, express interest and mention questions.
Good ... My name's ... I'm interested ... But I'd like to ask ...
Agree and ask what B wants to know.
Yes, ... What would ...?
Ask for information.
Could you tell me ...?
Agree and give information.
Yes, it's ...
Thank A and ask for more information.
Thank you. I'd also like to know ...
Give information.
At ... There is ...
Thank A.
Thank you ...
Respond and express hope.
My ... I hope ...

- Monitor the activity around the class and offer assistance as necessary.
- Then ask some pairs to act out their dialogues in front of the class.

Suggested Answer Key

A: Hello, Sart College. How can I help you?
B: Good morning. My name's Fran Smith. I'm interested in attending the Introduction to Computer Science course, but I'd like to ask you some questions first.
A: Yes, of course. What would you like to know?
B: Could you tell me how long each study session is
A: Yes, they are two hours each.
B: Thank you. I'd also like to know what time the classes start every evening.
A: At 7 pm. There is more information on our website.
B: Thank you for your help.
A: My pleasure. I hope to see you in September!

Intonation

6 a) Aim To learn intonation in follow-up questions

- Play the recording twice and have Ss listen and read the examples.
- Elicit how we form follow-up questions and what intonation the speaker uses to express each emotion.

Answer Key

Follow-up question are short questions we use to quickly respond to information we have been given. They are formed with auxiliary verb/modals + pronoun + a question mark. A speaker uses falling intonation to show interest and rising intonation to show surprise.

b) Aim To practise follow-up questions

- Ask Ss to work in pairs and take turns making statements and asking follow-up questions following the example.
- Have Ss indicate whether each question expresses surprise or interest.
- Walk around the class and check Ss' intonation.

Suggested Answer Key

A: My brother finishes university next month!
B: Does he? (falling intonation – showing interest)

Reading & Writing

7 Aim To read for lexical cohesion (word formation)

- Give Ss time to read the email and complete the gaps with a word formed from the word in brackets.
- Check Ss' answers.

Answer Key

1 *connection*	4 *additional*
2 *registration/ registering*	5 *equipment*
3 *completely*	6 *deeply*

8 Aim To analyse a model

- Ask Ss to read the email again and answer the questions.
- Elicit answers from Ss around the class.

Answer Key

1 *The first paragraph expresses interest in the course the second asks about the deadline for registration, the third about extra cost and the last thanks the course coordinator.*
2 *Yes, it does.*
3 *The email starts with 'Dear' and the name of the course coordinator. Since he has put a name at the start, he ends with 'Yours sincerely'.*

9 a) Aim To identify examples of formal style

- Read out the ***Writing Tip*** and tell Ss that this advice will help them to complete the writing task successfully.
- Then have Ss read the email again and find examples of formal style.
- Elicit answers from Ss around the class.

Answer Key

full verb forms: *I am writing; I have been learning, etc*
the passive: *will the ticket price be covered*
complex sentences: *Although it is likely that I will be free on the dates of the course, I am still not completely certain, so I would be interested to know the latest day possible when I could register.*
formal linkers: *Although, However*

b) Aim To compare formal and informal style

- Read out the informal phrases (1-5) and give Ss time to match them to the highlighted formal phrases in the email.
- Check Ss' answers.

Answer Key

1 *could you tell me if there will be any additional costs during the course*
2 *I am interested in attending your course*
3 *I imagine that the course will include some concerts*
4 *I am still not completely certain*
5 *I would now consider myself an advanced player*

Writing

10 a) Aim To prepare for a writing task; to analyse a rubric

- Ask Ss to read the rubric and answers the questions.
- Elicit answers from Ss around the class.

Answer Key

1 *I am going to write an email asking for information. It is to Jane Kemp, the course coordinator.*
2 *It should be formal.*
3 *I need to ask about student accommodation and meals.*
4 *I should write between 120 and 180 words.*

b) Aim To develop writing skills; to write an email asking for information

- Give Ss time to use their answers in Ex. 10a to write their email in answer to the task. Tell Ss to follow the plan and use formal style.
- Ask various Ss to read out their email to the class.
- This task may be assigned as homework.

Suggested Answer Key

Dear Ms Kemp,
I am writing in connection with your advertisement for a summer English course. I am a 19-year-old student who will start university in the UK in October, so I would like to bring my English up to the best level possible. For that reason, I am interested in attending your course, but I have some questions.
First of all, I want to ask if there is accommodation available. If there is, is it included in the price of the course?
Second, I need to know about meals. Are breakfast, lunch and dinner provided, or just one or two of these meals? Do we have to pay extra for meals, or are they included in the £800 fee?
I would be deeply grateful for your help. I look forward to hearing from you.
Yours sincerely,
Sofia Lorenzo

VALUES

Ask Ss to read the quotation, then initiate a class discussion about its meanings. Encourage all Ss to participate.

Suggested Answer Key

A: I think the quotation means that it is always difficult at first to learn something new but once we are familiar, it is easy.
B: I totally agree. I also think it refers to the fact that the benefits of education are many and have value. etc

Culture 9

Listening & Reading

1 Aim To introduce the topic; to listen and read for specific information

- Read the questions aloud. Elicit Ss' guesses in answer to them.
- Play the recording. Ss listen and read the text to find out the answers and whether their guesses were correct.

Answer Key

LeBron James is a basketball player and the founder of a number of programs to help children with their education. I Promise is a programme which helps children from Akron, where LeBron James grew up, with their education.

2 Aim To read for specific information (answer questions)

- Give Ss time to read the text again and answer the questions.
- Check Ss' answers.

Answer Key

1 *16*
2 *to change young people's attitude towards education*
3 *He grew up there.*
4 *Mentors support and motivate them.*
5 *It opens for longer hours.*

- Then give Ss time to look up the meanings of the words in bold in the Word List or in their dictionaries.
- Elicit explanations from Ss around the class.

Suggested Answer Key

impressive (adj): *amazing*
reach (v): *to get to a point*
nationally (adv): *across a country*
runs (v): *is in charge of and controls sth*
focus (n): *the main emphasis*
backgrounds (n): *upbringings and family circumstances*
achieve (v): *to succeed*
longer (adj): *more*
points out (phr v): *draws attention to*

- Give Ss time to look up the meanings of the words in the ***Check these words*** box in the Word List.
- Play the video for Ss and elicit their comments.

Speaking & Writing

3 Aim THINK To develop critical thinking skills

Give Ss time to consider their answers to the questions and ask various Ss to share their answers with the class.

Suggested Answer Key

My foundation is called Second Chance. It's for students who had to quit university for money, health or family reasons and now want to go back as mature students. I would give students help with their living costs as well as a sum of money to buy a laptop or tablet for their notes.

4 Aim ICT To develop research skills; to write about an educational foundation

- Give Ss time to research online and find out information about an educational foundation and make notes about it under the headings provided. Then have Ss use their notes to write a short article.
- Ask various Ss to read their articles to the class.
- This task may be assigned as homework.

Suggested Answer Key

name of foundation *– Sir John Cass's Foundation*
main aim of foundation *– to support education for young people in London*
who foundation helps *– young people in central London*
success of the foundation *– it has helped countless Londoners get a good start in life with an education*

London's Old Friend

Sir John Cass's Foundation is one of the oldest and biggest educational charities in London. It began in 1748 in order to support education for young people in London. The aim of the Foundation is to help in the education of young people in central London through giving money to individuals, and supporting educational institutions and organisations. Since its beginnings, it has helped countless Londoners get a good start in life with an education. Keep up the good work!

Review 9

Vocabulary

1 Aim To consolidate vocabulary from the unit

- Explain the task.
- Give Ss time to complete it.
- Check Ss' answers.

Answer Key

1 whiteboard　3 register　5 quit
2 encourage　4 mature　6 attitude

2 Aim To consolidate vocabulary from the unit

- Explain the task.
- Give Ss time to complete it.
- Check Ss' answers.

Answer Key

1 experience　3 campus　5 run
2 beating　4 identify　6 promote

3 Aim To practise prepositional phrases and phrasal verbs

- Explain the task.
- Give Ss time to complete it.
- Check Ss' answers.

Answer Key

1 over　3 in　5 at
2 out　4 up　6 at

Grammar

4 Aim To practise the infinitive/*-ing* form

- Explain the task.
- Give Ss time to complete it.
- Check Ss' answers.

Answer Key

1 finish　5 to help　9 playing
2 working　6 buying　10 to graduate
3 leave　7 to exercise
4 go　8 studying

5 Aim To practise relative clauses

- Explain the task.
- Give Ss time to complete it.
- Check Ss' answers.

Answer Key

1. *Do you know the name of the person who invented the light bulb?*
2. *I'll never forget the day when Professor Logan entered our lecture hall.*
3. *Do you know the reason why Ken left?*
4. *Our Maths test, which I haven't prepared for, is going to be really difficult.*
5. *Phil, who used to be an actor, agreed to teach drama at the college.*
6. *That's the library where I used to study when I was in secondary school.*

Everyday English

6 **Aim** **To match exchanges**

- Explain the task.
- Give Ss time to complete it.
- Check Ss' answers.

Answer Key

1 d *2 a* *3 c* *4 b*

Competences

Ask Ss to assess their own performance in the unit by ticking the items according to how competent they feel for each of the listed activities.

Values: Compassion

1 **Aim To introduce the topic; to listen and read for gist**

- Read out the questions and elicit answers from Ss around the class.
- Play the recording. Ss listen to and read the text to find out if their answers were mentioned.

Suggested Answer Key

We show compassion when we see someone is suffering – for example, if they've failed an exam. We show compassion by hugging someone, listening to them, giving them comforting words or doing something for them. With strangers, compassion might just be about being nice.

2 **Aim To read for gist (multiple matching)**

- Ask Ss to read situations A-E and check understanding. Then give them time to read the text again and match them to the ways of showing compassion 1-5 in the text.
- Check Ss' answers.

Answer Key

A 3　B 2　C 4　D 5　E 1

3 **Aim To consolidate new vocabulary**

- Ask Ss to guess the meaning of the words/phrases in bold in the text from the context.
- Then give Ss time to check them in the Word List or in their dictionaries.

Suggested Answer Key

desire (n): *want, wish*
supportive (adj): *showing you want to help sb*
mindset (n): *way of thinking*
comforting (adj): *making sb feel better*
gestures (n): *movements of the hands*
deserve (v): *to earn sth because of good behaviour*
appropriate (adj): *suitable under the circumstances*

4 **Aim THINK To personalise the topic**

Give Ss time to consider their answers and have Ss discuss the question in pairs. Then ask some Ss to share their answers with the class.

Suggested Answer Key

For me, the most important way of showing compassion is a hug. When a friend puts their arms around me, nothing seems very bad.

5 **Aim To encourage compassion; to apply knowledge to specific situations; to discuss ways of showing compassion**

- Have Ss read the situations.
- Give Ss time to discuss the situations.
- Ask various Ss to tell the class how they would show compassion in these situations.

Suggested Answer Key

A: If my younger sister was having trouble with a subject at school, I would help her with it.
B: Yes. Or if I wasn't very good either, I'd find a friend that was. Now, if my best friend's pet passed away, I'd just give her a big hug.
A: Yes. There's not much you can say. Now, if my friend can't find a job, I'd help them with their CV.
B: Yes, and I'd look through the wanted ads with them.
A: Finally, what if a stranger lost their phone?
B: Well, I might try to help them find it ...
A: Yes, or use my phone to call theirs. Someone else might have found it.

Public Speaking Skills

1 **Aim** **To analyse a rubric**

Read the rubric aloud and elicit the answer to the question.

Answer Key

It asks for a ceremonial speech.

2 **Aim** **To analyse a model speech**

- Read out the ***Study Skills*** box and tell Ss that this tip will help them to complete the speaking skills task successfully.
- Read the rubric and explain the task.
- Play the recording. Ss listen to and read the model.
- Elicit answers to the question from Ss around the class.

Answer Key

Now, we've come to the highlight of the evening. That's right, it's my great honour to present the Volunteer of the Year Award. (using key phrases)
but the important thing to remember is:
everything helps. (changing your volume)
The winner of this year's Sheltered Volunteer of the Year Award is, of course, ... Ayesha Abad. (taking a pause)

3 **Aim** **ICT** **To give a speech presenting an award**

- Read out the rubric and explain the situation. Give Ss time to brainstorm, consider what they will say and prepare a speech. Remind Ss to include emphasis techniques.
- Ask various Ss to give their speech to the class.

Suggested Answer Key

Good evening, everyone. My name is James Nailer and I'm the President of the National Teachers Organisation. Let me just start by saying how proud I am of the amazing work our teachers have done this year. I think we should all give ourselves a round of applause! Now, what we've all been waiting for. That's right, it's my great honour to present the National Teacher of the Year Award.
The National Teacher of the Year Award, now in its 15th year, honours a teacher in our organisation who has done something special with their year.
It's important to remember, though, that this award isn't for the teacher who has worked the most hours or got the best marks. As I always say, teaching is making children's lives different so it is the children that we ask to vote.
The winner of this year's award is a woman who teaches full-time and has three children, but found time to set up an after-school programme to look after and give extra tuition to children whose parents were at work till late. This meant children who often fall behind at school were actually coming top of their class!
So, without further ado, let's welcome this person on stage to collect her award. The winner of this year's Teacher of the Year Award is, of course, ... Gabby McCloud. Congratulations Gabby!

Green minds

Topic	
In this unit, Ss will explore the topics environmental problems and carbon footprints.	
10a Reading & Vocabulary	**82-83**
Lesson objectives: To learn vocabulary related to environmental problems & waste, to listen and read for gist, to read for specific information (T/F/DS statements), to learn collocations related to the environment, to learn prepositional phrases, to practise words easily confused, to learn phrasal verbs with *head*, to talk about organisms, to write a short text about a species that helps the environment **Vocabulary:** Environmental problems *(air/light/noise/ water pollution, acid rain, climate change, global warming, population growth, waste production, endangered species)*; Waste *(newspapers, vegetable peelings, plastic bags, leaflets and delivery menus, drinking straws, cardboard boxes, eggshells, batteries, food tins, mobile phones, tea leaves and coffee grounds, drink cans, cartons, cut grass, glass bottles, pizza boxes, jars, disposable water bottles)*; Nouns *(push, bacteria, infection, hyena, jackal, vulture, turkey vulture, plain, sea cucumber, threat, mess, scavenger)*; Verb *(wander)*; Phrasal verbs *(break down, suck up)*; Adjectives *(rotting, purifying)*; Phrase *(stomach acid)*	
10b Grammar in Use	**84-85**
Lesson objectives: To revise/learn reported speech, to act out a dialogue about a tree-planting event	
10c Skills in Action	**86-87**
Lesson objectives: To learn vocabulary related to carbon footprints, to listen for key information (multiple matching), to listen and read for specific information, to act out a dialogue and practise everyday English for making proposals – agreeing/ disagreeing, to practise intonation in prepositions, to read for lexical cohesion (word formation), to write a proposal **Vocabulary:** Carbon footprints *(carpool, local, energy-efficient, economy, paperless, electric, detergent, reusable, organic, compost)*	
Culture 10	**88**
Lesson objectives: To listen and read for specific information, to read for key information (multiple choice), to talk about an environmental event, to give a presentation on an environmental event **Vocabulary:** Nouns *(supervision, driftwood)*; Verbs *(wonder, promote, run)*	
Review 10	**89**
Lesson objectives: To test/consolidate vocabulary and grammar learnt throughout the unit; to practise everyday English	

Go through the objectives box and tell Ss that these are the topics, skills and activities this unit will cover.

10a

Vocabulary

1 a) Aim To present vocabulary related to environmental problems

- Ask Ss to read the words in the lists and then give them time to match them to make phrases related to the environment.
- Check Ss' answers around the class.

Answer Key

1 *pollution*	5 *growth*
2 *rain*	6 *production*
3 *change*	7 *species*
4 *warming*	

b) Aim To consolidate the topic; to practise new vocabulary

- Give Ss time to consider which of the problems in Ex. 1a are the most serious in their country.
- Ask various Ss to tell the class.

Suggested Answer Key

Waste production is the most serious problem in my country, since we don't have a very good recycling system.

2 Aim To present vocabulary related to waste

- Give Ss time to read the list of waste and explain/elicit the meanings of any unknown words/phrases. Then, give them time to decide which items go in which bins.
- Have Ss compare their answers with their partner and then have some Ss share their answers with the class.

Suggested Answer Key

Glass: *glass bottles, jars*
Paper: *newspapers, leaflets and delivery menus, paper egg cartons*
Plastic: *plastic packaging, disposable water bottles*
Organic: *vegetable peelings, tree leaves, cardboard boxes, eggshells, tea leaves and coffee grounds, cut grass*
Metal: *food tins, drink cans, tin foil*
In none of the bins: *batteries, mobile phones*

Reading & Listening

3 **Aim To listen and read for gist**

- Ask Ss to name any of the animals/organisms in the pictures that they can. They elicit how they think the writer feels about them.
- Play the recording. Ss listen and read the text to find out.

Suggested Answer Key

In the pictures, we can see bacteria, a vulture and a sea cucumber. The author feels very positive about them as they help the environment.

4 **Aim To read for specific information (T/F/DS statements)**

- Ask Ss to read the text again, then read the statements and mark them as T/F/DS according to what they read.
- Check Ss' answers. Ss should justify their choices.
- Then, give Ss time to look up the meanings of the words in bold in the Word List or in their dictionaries and elicit definitions from Ss around the class.

Answer Key

1 F (150 to 200 species becoming extinct every day)
2 F (Even in the EU ... only 48% of household waste is presently recycled.)
3 DS
4 T (And bacteria might even save the planet from our waste. Scientists recently discovered a type of bacteria that 'eats' plastic)
5 T (Scavengers are the animals that feed on the bodies of dead animals.)
6 DS
7 F (strange-looking sea creature)
8 DS
9 T (These are just a few of the eco-friends we have.)
10 F (But they can't head off environmental disaster alone.)

Suggested Answer Key

under threat (phr): *facing the possibility of danger*
mess (n): *a problematic situation*
scavenger (n): *an animal that feeds on dead bodies*
purifying (adj): *cleansing*

- Give Ss time to look up the meanings of the words in the ***Check these words*** box in the Word List.
- Play the video for Ss and elicit their comments.

5 **Aim To consolidate new vocabulary & practise collocations**

- Ask Ss to look through the text and find the words that pair with the words in the list to make collocations.
- Check Ss' answers and then give them time to use the collocations in sentences of their own.
- As an extension, ask Ss to find more collocations in the text and make sentences using them.

Answer Key

1 power	*4 stomach*	*7 coral*
2 vital	*5 rotting*	*8 marine*
3 deep	*6 natural*	

Suggested Answer Key

Power stations *generate electric power.*
Scavengers play a ***vital role*** *in keeping the planet clean.*
Some bacteria help break down waste; without them the ground would soon be covered in ***deep layers*** *of biological waste.*
Stomach acid *helps our bodies break down food.*
Rotting meat *can make you sick if you eat it.*
The ***natural world*** *is all of the animals, plants, and other things existing in nature.*
Marine biologists *study the oceans.*
A ***coral reef*** *is an underwater ecosystem.*

6 **Aim To consolidate prepositional phrases from a text**

- Give Ss time to read the gapped sentences and fill in the gaps with the correct prepositions.
- Then check Ss' answers.

Answer Key

1 under	*3 in*	*5 in*
2 at	*4 on*	

7 **Aim To understand words easily confused**

- Explain the task and give Ss time to use their dictionaries to help them complete it. Ss can work in closed pairs.
- Check Ss' answers and then elicit sentences using the other words from Ss around the class.

Answer Key

1 clean 2 signs 3 dead 4 alone

I only go swimming if the water is ***clear****.*
Animals can send ***signals*** *to each other through non-verbal communication.*
There are lot of plants and animals on Earth that are ***deadly*** *to humans.*
It must be very ***lonely*** *to live on a deserted island.*

8 **Aim** **To learn phrasal verbs with *head***

- Ask Ss to read the phrasal verbs box and make sure that Ss understand the definitions.
- Then give Ss time to complete the task.
- Check their answers.
- As an extension, ask Ss to work in pairs or groups. One S makes a sentence using one of the definitions of the phrasal verbs in the box. The other(s) say the same sentence using the appropriate phrasal verb.

Answer Key

1 off 2 up 3 out 4 off 5 for

Speaking & Writing

9 **Aim** THINK **To consolidate information in a text; to develop critical thinking skills**

- Ask Ss to read the text again.
- In pairs or small groups, have Ss discuss the importance of the organisms and decide on the most important.
- Monitor the activity around the class and then ask various pairs to share their answers with the class.

Suggested Answer Key

A: In my opinion, sea cucumbers are the most important. If the sea didn't get cleaned, all the fish would die, and then what would we eat?
B: I don't agree. Apart from the sea cucumber, there are other organisms that clean the water. Bacteria, for example, do that job in the sea and on land, and that's why I think they are the most important.
C: I agree with you. Also, they have a very important role to play inside our bodies, helping with digestion. etc

10 **Aim** **To develop research skills; to develop presentation skills; to give a presentation on an organism that helps the environment**

- Give Ss time to research online and find out information about another species that helps the environment and prepare a digital presentation on it. Ss can use images and key points on their slides.
- Then have Ss give their presentation to the class.

Suggested Answer Key

Good morning, everyone. I'd like to tell you about the vital role bees play in nature.
Bees pollinate so many plant and tree species that their work provides 80% of the crops we eat (apples, pears, tomatoes, onions and lots more). The trees they pollinate also create natural habitats, replacing the ones we've destroyed through deforestation. On top of all that, bees are a sign of a thriving ecosystem – the more bees, the more plants and trees, the healthier the environment. Bees play such a vital role in the food chain that naturalist and broadcaster Sir David Attenborough warned that humans would only have four years left to live if bees became extinct. He wasn't the first to say this. The playwright Maurice Maeterlinck said it over a century ago and Albert Einstein also used it.
So remember, without bees, we would have no food. Are there any questions? ...Thank you.

10b Grammar in Use

1 **Aim** **To learn/revise reported speech**

- Ask Ss to read the article and sentences A-C and find the reported speech in the text for sentences A-C.
- Then elicit how the pronouns and tenses change in each one.
- Check Ss' answers and refer Ss to the ***Grammar Reference*** section for more information or to check any points they are unsure of.

Answer Key

A The environmentalist Annie Leonard warned that there was no such thing as 'away', and that when we threw something away, it had to go somewhere.
B He said that what was going to get us through the future was radical change.
C Reynolds said that he was embarrassed to be a human and certainly was embarrassed to be an architect.

Suggested Answer Key

Tenses move from present to past, for example the present simple becomes the past simple.
Pronouns change to reflect that someone else is reporting the speakers' words now, for example from 'I' to 'he'.

2 **Aim** **To practise reported speech**

- Explain the task and give Ss time to complete it.
- Check Ss' answers and refer Ss to the ***Grammar Reference*** section for more information or to check any points they are unsure of.

Answer Key

1 said (with 'that'), had planted (past simple → past perfect), previous (yesterday → the previous day)
2 said (with 'that'), she (I → she), needed (present simple → past simple)
3 told (with 'us'), become (tense remains the same for a general truth), every (general truth – no change)
4 me (to agree with 'me' in the first sentence), he (to agree with 'David' in the first sentence), my (to agree with 'your' in the first sentence)
5 she (to agree with 'Jo'), been picking (past continuous → past perfect continuous), before (the day before)

6 *told (with 'Amy'), was working (present continuous → past continuous), that ('this' → 'that')*

3 **Aim** **To practise reported speech**

- Give Ss time to rewrite the sentences.
- Elicit answers from Ss around the class.

Answer Key

1 *Dr Jones said (that) the company was going to reduce its waste by 50%.*
2 *Harry told Ann (that) he might need some help with the recycling that day.*
3 *Brooke said (that) they had installed a rainwater collector in their house.*
4 *Jack said (that) he had been growing his own food for the past two years.*
5 *The scientist said (that) they had seen some signs of new growth in the forest the week before/previous week.*
6 *Lily told Max (that) Dan had been volunteering at the bird sanctuary the previous summer/the summer before.*

4 **Aim** **To learn/revise reported questions**

- Ask Ss to study the examples and then elicit answers to the questions from Ss around the class.
- Refer Ss to the ***Grammar Reference*** section for more information or to check any points they are unsure of.

Suggested Answer Key

We report ***wh-****questions with the question word followed by the question in the form of a statement and a full stop.*
We report ***Yes/No*** *questions with 'if' or 'whether' followed by the question in the form of a statement and a full stop.*

5 **Aim** **To practise reported questions**

Explain the task and give Ss time to complete it and then check their answers.

Answer Key

1 *Jamila asked if/whether she was doing enough to help the environment.*
2 *Jamila asked where she could get rid of used batteries.*
3 *Jamila asked if/whether electric cars cost a lot of money.*
4 *Jamila asked when the organic food shop had opened.*
5 *Jamila asked which colour bin milk cartons went in.*
6 *Jamila asked how much water her bath used.*

6 **Aim** **To learn/revise reported orders**

- Ask Ss to read the examples and then elicit how we form reported orders.
- Refer Ss to the ***Grammar Reference*** section for more information or to check any points they are unsure of.

Suggested Answer Key

We report orders with the verb tell *and the infinitive.*

7 **Aim** **To practise reported orders**

- Give Ss time to read the email and then write the reported orders.
- Check Ss' answers around the class.

Answer Key

2 *He told us to wear gloves.*
3 *He told us to put all the rubbish in black plastic bags.*
4 *He told us to leave the bags near the coffee shop.*
5 *He told us not to waste any time.*
6 *He told us to enjoy ourselves.*

8 **Aim** **To practise reported speech**

- Give Ss time to rewrite the dialogue in reported speech in their notebooks.
- Check Ss' answers by asking various Ss around the class to read out a sentence at a time.

Answer Key

Amy asked Ben if he was doing anything that weekend, and Ben said he had wanted to go to a football match, but it had been cancelled. Amy said Ben could help her in her garden. She said she was building a birdhouse. Ben said that that sounded like a good idea, and asked what time he should be there. Amy said he could come any time he wanted, but he should call first. Ben asked her to give him her number. He said he didn't think he had it.

9 **Aim** **To practise reported speech with reporting verbs**

- Give Ss time to read the sentence and rewrite them in reported speech and the reporting verb in the list.
- Ask various Ss to read out their answers.

Answer Key

1 *Rory apologised to Amy for throwing the rubbish in the wrong bin.*
2 *Sam reminded me to take the recycling out.*
3 *Dan allowed me to plant a tree in the garden.*
4 *Fiona warned us to not to leave litter on the beach.*
5 *Polly promised Tony that she would be at the animal shelter on time.*

10

6 *Oliver boasted that no one did more to help the environment than him.*
7 *Cal invited me to the Save the Whales meeting the following day/the day after.*
8 *Max suggested creating a garden on our their rooftop.*
9 *Steve admitted putting the wrong rubbish in the recycling bin.*
10 *Beth complained about my missing the tree planting on Sunday.*

Speaking

10 Aim To act out a dialogue about an environmental event; to practise reported speech

- Divide the class into groups of three and have two of the Ss act out a dialogue about organising an event to plant trees in the local part. The third member of the groups takes notes. Monitor the activity around the class.
- Then ask the third member from each group to report what the other two speakers said during their dialogue using his/her notes.

Suggested Answer Key

A: *So first of all, where are we going to get the trees?*
B: *Maybe we could buy some from local nurseries. etc*
C: *Ann asked where they were going to get the trees. Bob suggested buying some from local nurseries. etc*

10c Skills in Action

Vocabulary

1 Aim To present vocabulary related to carbon footprints

- Ask Ss to read the words in the list and then read the quiz and complete the gaps using the words in the list.
- Explain/Elicit the meanings of any unknown words or phrases or ask Ss to look them up in the Word List.
- Elicit answers from Ss around the class.

Answer Key

1 *detergent*	6 *local*
2 *organic*	7 *energy-efficient*
3 *paperless*	8 *electric*
4 *reusable*	9 *economy*
5 *carpool*	10 *compost*

2 Aim To do a quiz

- Give Ss time to do the quiz and then check their score.
- Ask Ss to discuss in pairs what they can do to improve their carbon footprints.

Ss' own answers

Listening

3 Aim To listen for key information (multiple matching)

- Ask Ss to read the statements and find the keywords Play the recording twice. Ss match the statements to the speakers according to what they hear.
- Check Ss' answers. You can play the recording again with pauses for Ss to check their answers.

Answer Key

1 E 2 C 3 A 4 D

Everyday English

4 Aim To listen and read for specific information

- Read out the question. Elicit Ss' guesses as to what suggestions Sam makes.
- Play the recording for Ss to listen and read and find out if their guesses were correct.

Answer Key

He proposes going paperless, issuing green challenges and putting recycling bins on every floor.

5 Aim To act out a dialogue and practise everyday English for making proposals – agreeing/disagreeing

- Explain the task and ask Ss to act out a dialogue similar to the one in Ex. 4 in pairs using the ideas and the language box.
- Write this diagram on the board for Ss to follow.

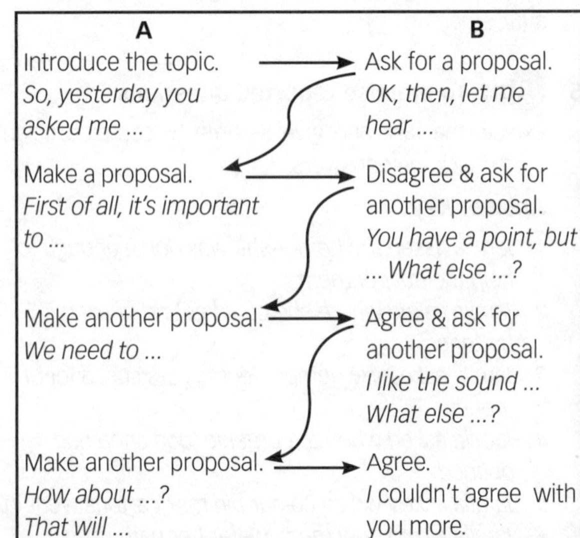
A
B
Introduce the topic.
So, yesterday you asked me ...
Ask for a proposal.
OK, then, let me hear ...
Make a proposal.
First of all, it's important to ...
Disagree & ask for another proposal.
You have a point, but ... What else ...?
Make another proposal.
We need to ...
Agree & ask for another proposal.
I like the sound ... What else ...?
Make another proposal.
How about ...? That will ...
Agree.
I couldn't agree with you more.

- Monitor the activity around the class and offer assistance as necessary.
- Then ask some pairs to act out their dialogues in front of the class.

Suggested Answer Key

A: So, yesterday you asked me for ideas on how to make the house greener.
A: OK, then, let me hear your first one.
A: First of all, it's important to have energy-efficient appliances. That way we wouldn't use so much electricity – which would save money, too!
B: You have a point, but changing them all immediately would cost a lot of money. What else do you have?
A: We need to start growing our own organic food. It's good for the planet and healthier for us.
B: I like the sound of that. What else do you propose?
A: How about composting our food waste? That will reduce our rubbish and we can put the compost on our organic garden.
B: I couldn't agree with you more.

Intonation

6 a) Aim To learn intonation in prepositions

- Play the recording twice and have Ss underline the stressed prepositions.
- Then elicit when prepositions are stressed.

Answer Key

1 *Come on!*
2 *There's no one to go with.*
3 *I can't rely on her.*
4 *Who's he talking to?*
5 *Pick it up.*

Prepositions are usually weak in English. We can stress them when we want to give emphasis or when they appear at the end of questions.

b) Aim To practise intonation in prepositions

Ask various Ss around the class to read the sentences. Check Ss' intonation.

Answer key

- *Don't throw that out!*
- *Animals depend on us.*
- *Let's head off.*
- *Who are you waiting for?*

Reading & Writing

7 Aim To read for lexical cohesion (word formation)

- Give Ss time to read the email and complete the gaps with a word formed from the word in brackets.
- Check Ss' answers.

Answer Key

1 *requested*
2 *reducing*
3 *drastically*
4 *clearly*
5 *recommendations*
6 *greenest*

8 Aim To identify the content of a proposal

- Read out the ***Writing Tip*** and tell Ss that this advice will help them to complete the writing task successfully.
- Then have Ss read the proposal again and complete the lettered gaps with the headings in the list. Remind Ss there are two extra headings.
- Check Ss' answers.

Answer Key

A *Stay local*
B *Waste nothing*
C *Clean and green*

Writing

9 Aim To prepare for a writing task; to analyse a rubric

Ask Ss to read the rubric and elicit answers to the questions.

Answer Key

1 *I am going to write a proposal for my manager about making the office more eco-friendly.*
2 *I should write about office supplies, saving energy and going paperless. I should write between 120 and 180 words.*

10 a) Aim To prepare for a writing task

- Ask Ss to read the suggestions and then match them with the reasons/examples.
- Check Ss' answers around the class and elicit which headings from Ex. 9 they match.
- Elicit any other suggestions.

Answer Key

1 b *Going paperless*
2 c *Saving energy*
3 a *Office supplies*

Suggested Answer Key

I propose that someone in the office is made responsible for checking that all lights and appliances are switched off at the end of the working day. That way, a lot of energy can be saved overnight, for example, by not leaving computers on when not in use.
A second suggestion could be to bring in desk plants. Not only do they create a pleasant working atmosphere, but they also supply the office with extra oxygen.

b) **Aim** **To develop writing skills; to write a proposal**

- Tell Ss to use their answers from Ex. 10a and the plan to help them write their proposal for the rubric in Ex. 9. Remind Ss to use headings.
- Give Ss time to complete the task and then ask various Ss to read their proposals to the class.
- This task may be assigned as homework.

Suggested Answer Key

To: *Martin Oberman, Manager*
From: *Becky O'Rourke*
Subject: *Going green*
Introduction
As you requested, I am writing this proposal to suggest how the office can become more eco-friendly.
Going paperless
First of all, we should store all our files digitally, and put bills and statements online. This way, we will save paper and reduce the need for printouts.
Saving energy
A second step would be switching to energy-efficient appliances to reduce our energy consumption. For example, we can buy LED light bulbs and use fans instead of air-conditioning in summer.
Office supplies
Finally, we can buy recycled paper and other eco-friendly products. If we do this, it will lead to fewer trees being cut down and less water pollution.
Conclusion
I strongly believe that if we carry out the above recommendations, we will become one of the greenest offices in the city.

VALUES

Ask Ss to read the quotation, then initiate a class discussion about its meanings. Encourage all Ss to participate.

Suggested Answer Key

A: I think the quotation means that we share the Earth as our home. We all live here.
B: I totally agree. I also think it refers to the fact that it's where we come from and where we will all end up. etc

Culture 10

Listening & Reading

1 **Aim** **To introduce the topic; to listen and read for specific information**

- Ask Ss to read the title and look at the picture.
- Have Ss read the statements and guess which ones are true.
- Play the recording. Ss listen and read the text to find out.

Answer Key

2 T (held annually)
3 T (volunteers who run their own events all over the country)
4 T (attracts over 120,000 participants)
6 T (e-newsletter ... social media sites for updates.)

2 **Aim** **To read for specific information (multiple choice)**

- Give Ss time to read the text again and read the questions and answer choices and choose their answers.
- Check Ss' answers.

Answer Key

1 B (it's a fun eight days of events for all the family to educate them about the sea, its ecosystems and the challenges it faces)
2 A (The most popular activities are water sport days, when people of all ages go snorkelling, kayaking and exploring areas of the sea under the supervision of experienced guides.)
3 C (Subscribe to our e-newsletter for more details and don't forget to check out social media sites for updates.)

- Give Ss time to look up the meanings of the words in the ***Check these words*** box in the Word List.
- Play the video for Ss and elicit their comments.

Speaking & Writing

3 **Aim** THINK **To practise creative thinking**

- Give Ss time to work in pairs and think of an event that would be fun and interesting as part of Seaweek.
- Ask various Ss to share their answers with the class.

Suggested Answer Key

We would organise a beach clean-up at our local beach. We would bring all our friends and take photos of the beach before and after to post online.

4 **Aim** ICT **To develop research skills; to give a presentation on an environmental event in your country or another country**

- Give Ss time to research online and find out information about an environmental event similar to Seaweek in their country or another country and use this information to make notes under the headings provided and then prepare a presentation

- Ask various Ss to give their presentations to the class.
- This task may be assigned as homework.

Suggested Answer Key

what it is *– The Festival of Nature*
who organises it *– the Natural History Consortium*
what happens *– lectures, films, events and special appearances from celebrity environmentalists*

The Festival of Nature is an annual science festival in the UK. It is organised by the Natural History Consortium and takes place in different locations around the towns of Bristol and Bath every June. There are lectures, films, events and special appearances from celebrity environmentalists like David Attenborough.

Review 10

Vocabulary

1 Aim To consolidate vocabulary from the unit

- Explain the task.
- Give Ss time to complete it.
- Check Ss' answers.

Answer Key

1 food	*4 products*	*7 play*
2 acid	*5 growth*	*8 noise*
3 peelings	*6 plastic*	

2 Aim To consolidate vocabulary from the unit

- Explain the task.
- Give Ss time to complete it.
- Check Ss' answers.

Answer Key

1 electric	*5 carbon*	*9 rotting*
2 warming	*6 reusable*	*10 compost*
3 organic	*7 carpool*	
4 rain	*8 economy*	

3 Aim To practise prepositional phrases and phrasal verbs

- Explain the task.
- Give Ss time to complete it.
- Check Ss' answers.

Answer Key

1 up	*3 out*	*5 5 in*
2 at	*4 under*	

Grammar

4 Aim To practise reported speech

- Explain the task.
- Give Ss time to complete it.
- Check Ss' answers.

Answer Key

1 He told us to switch off the lights before we left.
2 Amy asked what a sea cucumber was like.
3 Mia said she had had trouble getting to work that day.
4 Nina asked Sam if he had taken out the recycling.
5 Kevin said that Luke had to go before 5:00.
6 Rachel said to Steve that the beach clean-up would be cancelled if it rained the following day.

5 Aim To practise reported speech and reporting verbs

- Explain the task.
- Give Ss time to complete it.
- Check Ss' answers.

Answer Key

1 Fran advised Sue to cycle every day.
2 Zoe reminded Henry to buy rechargeable batteries.
3 Kim apologised for being late for the meeting.
4 Harry boasted about cleaning up the beach all by himself.
5 Debbie warned me not to put used batteries in the recycling bin.

Everyday English

6 Aim To match exchanges

- Explain the task.
- Give Ss time to complete it.
- Check Ss' answers.

Answer Key

1 c 2 b 3 d 4 e 5 a

Competences

Ask Ss to assess their own performance in the unit by ticking the items according to how competent they feel for each of the listed activities.

Buying, buying, bought!

Topic	
In this unit, Ss will explore the topics of marketing, advertising, online shopping and customer complaints.	
11a Reading & Vocabulary	**90-91**
Lesson objectives: To learn vocabulary related to marketing & advertising, to listen and read for specific information, to read for key information (matching headings to paragraphs), to learn collocations related to advertising, to learn prepositional phrases, to practise words easily confused, to learn phrasal verbs with *call*, to talk about advertising, to write an outline for an advertisement **Vocabulary:** Marketing & Advertising *(spot, slogan, jingle, commercial, target audience, digital marketing, window display, market research, roadside hoarding, prime time)*; Nouns *(limit, worry, decisions)*; Verbs *(grab, support, experience, create, rush, encourage, spot)*; Adjectives *(sneaky, retail, scarce, positive, annoying, effective, aware)*; Adverb *(deeply)*	
11b Grammar in Use	**92-93**
Lesson objectives: To revise/learn determiners; to revise/learn countable/uncountable nouns; to revise/learn quantifiers & partitives; to revise/learn *some/any/no/every* & compounds	
11c Skills in Action	**94-95**
Lesson objectives: To learn vocabulary for online shopping – customer complaints, to listen for specific information (sentence completion), to listen and read for specific information, to act out a dialogue and practise everyday English for complaining about a product, to practise intonation in exclamations, to read for lexical cohesion (text completion), to complete a complaint form **Vocabulary:** Online shopping – customer complaints *(damaged, cracked, missing, scratched, torn, weak, broken, dead)*	
Culture 11	**96**
Lesson objectives: To listen and read for specific information, to read for key information (completing a summary), to talk about Black Friday, to give a presentation on a popular sales period in your country **Vocabulary:** Nouns *(stocks, crash, investor, retailer, accounts, profits, traffic jams, shoplifting, bargains)*; Verbs *(originate, record, spread)*; Adjectives *(bankrupt, estimated, Cyber)*; Adverb *(worldwide)*; Preposition *(including)*; Phrase *(financial crisis)*	
Review 11	**97**
Lesson objectives: To test/consolidate vocabulary and grammar learnt throughout the unit; to practise everyday English	

Go through the objectives box and tell Ss that these are the topics, skills and activities this unit will cover.

11a

Vocabulary

1 Aim To present vocabulary related to marketing & advertising

- Ask Ss to read the words in the list and then give them time to use them to complete the sentences.
- Have Ss check their answers in their dictionaries.

Answer Key

1	*research*	6	*jingle*
2	*slogan*	7	*display*
3	*hoarding*	8	*time*
4	*spot*	9	*marketing*
5	*commercial*	10	*audience*

Listening & Reading

2 Aim To apply prior experience to the topic; to listen and read for specific information

- Ask Ss to think of their favourite advertisement and think about the reasons they like it.
- Play the recording. Ss listen and read the text to find out if any of the techniques mentioned are used in their favourite advertisement.
- Ask various Ss to tell the class.

Ss' own answers

3 Aim To read for key information (matching headings to paragraphs)

- Ask Ss to read the text again, then read the headings and match them to the paragraphs based on what they read. Ask Ss to look for key words to help them do the task.
- Check Ss' answers.
- Then give Ss time to look up the meanings of the words in bold in the Word List or in their dictionaries and elicit definitions from Ss around the class.

Answer Key

1 B (Leave it to the experts – it's best to ask the professionals.)
2 F (No time to lose – put a time limit on an offer)
3 E (Everyone else is doing it – encourage us to buy products because most other people do, or at least that's how it seems.)
4 A (We like what we recognise – tend to feel more comfortable with things that we know something about.)

5 C *(An amusing distraction – When we see a funny ad, we often stop thinking about whether it would be a good idea to buy the product – we just learn to associate it with a positive feeling.)*
6 D *(Free from its control – The next time you find yourself putting items you hadn't planned to buy in your shopping trolley, ask yourself why. Do you really need the product, or is it actually the power of advertising?)*

Suggested Answer Key

positive (adj): *good*
create (v): *to think of*
limit (n): *the extent of sth*
rushing (v): *hurrying*
encourage (v): *to persuade sb to do sth*
worry (n): *a feeling of concern*
spot (v): *to see*
annoying (adj): *causing mild anger*
effective (adj): *successful*
deeply (adv): *to a great extent*
aware (adj): *having knowledge of sth*
decisions (n): *choices made after thinking about sth*

- Give Ss time to look up the meanings of the words in the ***Check these words*** box in the Word List.
- Play the video for Ss and elicit their comments.

4 Aim THINK To consolidate information in a text

Give Ss time to consider their answers and then ask various Ss around the class to tell the class about an advertising technique from the text using their own words.

Suggested Answer Key

When an advert is funny it sticks in your mind. Then when you go shopping you will often buy the product whose ad made you laugh because it made you feel good.
When advertisers want to encourage customers to buy something they often say it is on sale at a special low price for a short time so that customers think they should buy it now before the price goes up.

5 Aim To consolidate new vocabulary & practise collocations

- Ask Ss to look through the text and find the words that pair with the words in the list to make collocations.
- Check Ss' answers and then give them time to use the collocations in sentences of their own.

Answer Key

1 retail	*5 time*
2 positive	*6 positive*
3 advertising	*7 common*
4 human	*8 shopping*

Suggested Answer Key

*The **retail world** is one of the largest advertisers in business.*
*When we have a **positive experience** with a product, we usually tell people.*
***Advertising agencies** create the ads we see.*
*Advertisers know a lot about the **human mind** and prepare adverts to attract customers.*
*Many times advertisements say an offer has a **time limit**, that is, the special offer will last for a few days.*
*When we see a funny ad, we associate the **positive feeling** from laughing with the product.*
*When it comes to advertisements, we have to use our **common sense** and buy things we need.*
*Don't fill up your **shopping trolley** at the supermarket without thinking about if you really need everything.*

6 Aim To consolidate prepositional phrases from a text

- Give Ss time to read the gapped text and fill in the gaps with the correct prepositions.
- Then check Ss' answers.

Answer Key

1 on	*3 of*	*5 with*
2 out	*4 from*	

7 Aim To understand words easily confused

- Explain the task and give Ss time to use their dictionaries to help them complete it.
- Check Ss' answers.
- As an extension, ask Ss to make sentences using the other options.

Answer Key

1 produce	*3 samples*
2 receipt	*4 clients*

8 Aim To learn phrasal verbs with *call*

- Ask Ss to read the phrasal verbs box and make sure that Ss understand the definitions.
- Then give Ss time to complete the task and check their answers.
- As an extension, ask Ss to make up a story using the phrasal verbs in the box.

Answer Key

1 back	*3 after*	*5 for*
2 off	*4 for*	*6 in*

Speaking & Writing

9 Aim THINK To develop critical thinking skills; to express an opinion

- Ask Ss to talk in small groups and discuss which advertising method they think is the most effective, giving reasons for their opinions.
- Monitor the activity around the class and then ask various groups to share their ideas with the class.
- Optional extension: Ask Ss to discuss whether advertising to children is ethical or unethical and why.

Suggested Answer Key

A: I think FOMO is the most effective because I have fallen for it myself.

B: I see your point, but once you realise the product will be on offer again in the future, you can avoid that trick. I think repetition is the most successful technique because you don't realise that the reason you choose a certain brand is because you have become familiar with it.

C: I know what you mean. I agree with you. It's the techniques that we don't notice that are the most effective. etc

10 Aim ICT To develop research skills; to write an outline for an advertisement

- Give Ss time to work in pairs and research online for information about a new piece of technology and get some ideas for an advertisement for it and create an outline.
- Have Ss create their adverts and present them to the class. The class can vote for the best one.

Suggested Answer Key

Our advert is for a virtual assistant. We call it Trudy. In our video advert we would show people of all ages using it to make their lives easier. We would show older people using it to make shopping lists, read out recipes, and get the latest news. We would show children using it to play music and give them help with their homework. We would show men getting the sports results and the TV programme. We would use FOMO and tell the customers that they have to buy one at the amazing low price because it is for a limited time. We would also use the bandwagon technique and tell customers that it is the must-have gadget in every modern home and lots of people have bought it already.

11b Grammar in Use

1 Aim To learn/revise determiners

- Ask Ss to read the blog and match the determiners in bold to the descriptions in the list.
- Check Ss' answers and refer Ss to the ***Grammar Reference*** section for more information or to check any points they are unsure of.

Answer Key

another: *has a positive meaning, refers to an additional part of something already mentioned*
all: *has a positive meaning, takes a plural verb*
each: *has a positive meaning, is used with singular countable nouns,*
every: *has a positive meaning, is used with singular countable nouns,*
either: *has a positive meaning, takes either a verb in the singular or plural depending on the subject which follows it.*
neither: *has a negative meaning*
both: *has a positive meaning, takes a plural verb*

2 Aim To practise determiners

- Give Ss time to complete the task.
- Check Ss' answers and refer Ss to the ***Grammar Reference*** section for more information or to check any points they are unsure of.

Answer Key

1. *Neither (refers to two things/people, has a negative meaning)*
2. *All (refers to more than two things/people, has a positive meaning)*
3. *either (refers to two things/people, has a positive meaning)*
4. *None (refers to more than two things/people, has a negative meaning)*
5. *All (refers to more than two things/people, has a positive meaning)*
6. *each (used for separate things)*
7. *all her (used for every part of sth)*
8. *Both (used for two things/people)*

3 Aim To practise determiners

- Give Ss time to read the sentences and correct the mistakes.
- Elicit answers from Ss around the class and elicit reasons.

Answer Key

1 *Both Liam and his brother **go** to the mall on Saturdays.*
2 *Either Tracy's **or** Lacy's will have the bag you're looking for.*
3 *The two girls were comparing their new clothes with each **other**.*
4 *Mary came out of the shop with lots of shopping bags in **each** hand.*
5 *Neither advert **is** very funny, if you ask me.*
6 *Sally never shops online, and Matt doesn't **either**.*
7 *All the items in the display **are** reduced in price.*
8 *Neither the restaurant nor the café **is** open on Sundays.*

4 Aim To practise determiners

- Explain the task and give Ss time to complete it by rewriting the sentences sing the words in brackets.
- Elicit answers from Ss around the class.

Answer Key

1 *Neither James nor Susan likes TV commercials.*
2 *None of the customers were satisfied with the product.*
3 *Either Channel X or Channel Y will broadcast the ad.*
4 *Both using social media and sending emails are good ways of advertising.*
5 *Marge spent the whole morning shopping.*
6 *We're giving every one of our customers a five-pound voucher today.*

Speaking

5 Aim To practise determiners

- Divide the class into pairs. Explain the task and read out the examples. Then give Ss time to complete it in pairs.
- Monitor the activity around the class. Then have some Ss share their answers with the class.

Suggested Answer Key

When I go grocery shopping, I either go to the supermarket or the corner shop.
Both the greengrocer's and the newsagent's are near my house.
All the shops near me are family-owned.
Neither of the two local supermarkets is expensive. etc

6 a) Aim To learn/revise countable/uncountable nouns

- Ask Ss to go through the blog entry in Ex. 1 and identify all the countable/uncountable nouns.
- Check Ss' answers around the class.

Answer Key

Countable: *sale, event, store, year, retailer, price, customer, bargain, tip, shopper, morning, day, offer, queue, item, TV, ad, email, detail, product, app, difference, deal*
Uncountable: *world, jewellery, information, homework, social media*

b) Aim To present quantifiers used with countable/uncountable nous

- Ask Ss to look at the highlighted words in the blog and elicit which ones we use with countable/uncountable nouns from Ss around the class.
- Refer Ss to the ***Grammar Reference*** section for more information or to check any points they are unsure of.

Answer Key

We use ***a few*** with plural countable nouns.
We use ***plenty of*** with plural countable and uncountable nouns.
We use ***how much*** with uncountable nouns in interrogative sentences.
We use ***several*** with countable nouns.
We use ***a/an*** with singular countable nouns.

7 Aim To practise quantifiers

- Explain the task and give Ss time to complete it.
- Refer Ss to the ***Grammar Reference*** section for more information or to check any points they are unsure of.
- Check Ss' answers.

Answer Key

1 *some (we don't use 'a/an' with uncountable nouns), a few (plural noun, not many but enough)*
2 *enough (used with uncountable noun in the negative to show that there is less of sth than required), plenty (used with an uncountable noun)*
3 *too many (used with a plural countable noun to show that sth is more than required), few (used with a plural countable noun to mean 'hardly any')*
4 *any (used in a negative sentence with a plural countable noun), a couple of (used with a countable plural noun)*
5 *all (used with a plural countable noun to show the whole quantity) plenty of (used with an uncountable noun to mean 'a lot of')*
6 *any (used in an interrogative sentence with an uncountable noun), lots ('of' is omitted at the end of a sentence)*

8 **Aim To practise quantifiers**

- Explain the task and give Ss time to complete it.
- Check Ss' answers.

Answer Key

1 *a lot of*	6 *plenty*
2 *much*	7 *a few*
3 *many*	8 *little*
4 *Both*	9 *enough*
5 *all*	10 *a little*

9 **Aim To practise partitives**

- Explain the task, read out the example and give Ss time to complete it.
- Check Ss' answers.

Answer Key

2 *tube*	5 *bag*	8 *bowl*
3 *bottle*	6 *pot*	9 *packet*
4 *jar*	7 *carton*	10 *box*

Speaking

10 **Aim To practise countable/uncountable nouns, partitives and determiners**

- Ask Ss to work in pairs and act out a dialogue deciding what to buy for a dinner party using countable/uncountable nouns, partitives and determiners appropriately.
- Monitor the activity around the class and then ask some pairs to act out their dialogue in front of the class.

Suggested Answer Key

A: *There are a lot of people coming to dinner so we need to buy plenty of food.*
B: *OK. What are you going to cook? How many courses will there be?*
A: *I will cook a roast dinner with chicken and potatoes, a starter and a dessert.*
B: *That's a lot of work.*
A: *I guess it is. Well, we will need to buy 2 whole chickens and 5 kilos of potatoes.*
B: *OK. What about other vegetables?*
A: *Yes. Get 2 kilos of carrots and a packet of frozen peas.*
B: *We can buy a cake for dessert.*
A: *Yes and we can have melon as a starter. So buy two melons, please.*
B: *OK. See you later.*

11 **Aim To practise *some/any/no/every* & compounds**

- Explain the task and give Ss time to complete it.
- Refer Ss to the ***Grammar Reference*** section for more information and to clarify any points they are unsure of.

Answer Key

1 *everywhere*	4 *anybody*
2 *anyone*	5 *some*
3 *nothing, somewhere*	6 *Everyone*

12 **Aim To practise *some/any/no/every* & compounds**

- Explain the task and give Ss time to complete it.
- Then check Ss' answers around the class.

Answer Key

1 *some, anywhere*
2 *anyone, some*
3 *everyone, something*
4 *No one, everywhere*
5 *somewhere, every, nothing*
6 *anyone, Someone*

Speaking

13 **Aim To practise *some/any/no/every* & compounds**

- Explain the task and read out the example exchange and then ask Ss to look at the picture and work in pairs and talk about it using some/any/no/every & compounds.
- Monitor the activity around the class and then ask some Ss to share their answers with the class.

Suggested Answer Key

A: *This shop looks like it has got everything. There are some nice things in the window.*
B: *Good. I need to buy something to wear to the party on Saturday. I've got nothing to wear.*
A: *I'm sure you can find some nice clothes here. I need to buy something for my sister. It's her birthday after all. etc*

11c Skills in Action

Vocabulary

1 **Aim To present vocabulary related to online shopping – customer complaints**

- Ask Ss to read the words in the list and then read the statements (A-H) and fill in the gaps (1-8).
- Explain/Elicit the meanings of any unknown words or phrases or ask Ss to look them up in the Word List.
- Elicit answers from Ss around the class.

Answer Key

1 *scratched*	5 *weak*
2 *missing*	6 *torn*
3 *dead*	7 *broken*
4 *cracked*	8 *damaged*

2 Aim THINK To consolidate new vocabulary and expand the topic

- Give Ss time to match the complaints to the products in the list.
- Then give Ss time to think of other problems for each product.
- Elicit answers from Ss around the class.

Suggested Answer Key

A e-reader (cracked screen)
B shirt (wrong size)
C wireless video game controller (wrong colour)
D microwave (plate missing)
E Wi-Fi booster (light display not working)
F book (wrong language)
G suitcase (wheel missing)
H digital camera (cracked screen)

Listening

3 Aim To listen for specific information (gap fill)

- Ask Ss to read the sentences (1-6). Play the recording twice. Ss listen and complete the gaps.
- Check Ss' answers.
- You can play the recording again with pauses for Ss to check their answers.

Answer Key

1 difficulty	*4 70/seventy*
2 15/fifteen days	*5 home*
3 8/eight	*6 payment card*

Everyday English

4 Aim To listen and read for specific information

- Ask Ss to read the first exchange in the dialogue. Elicit Ss' guesses as to how the customer's problem was solved.
- Play the recording for Ss to listen and read and find out if their guesses were correct.

Answer Key

The customer will return the item and get a refund.

5 Aim To act out a dialogue and practise everyday English for complaining about a product

- Explain the task and ask Ss to act out a dialogue similar to the one in Ex. 4 using the ideas in the language box.
- Write this diagram on the board for Ss to follow.

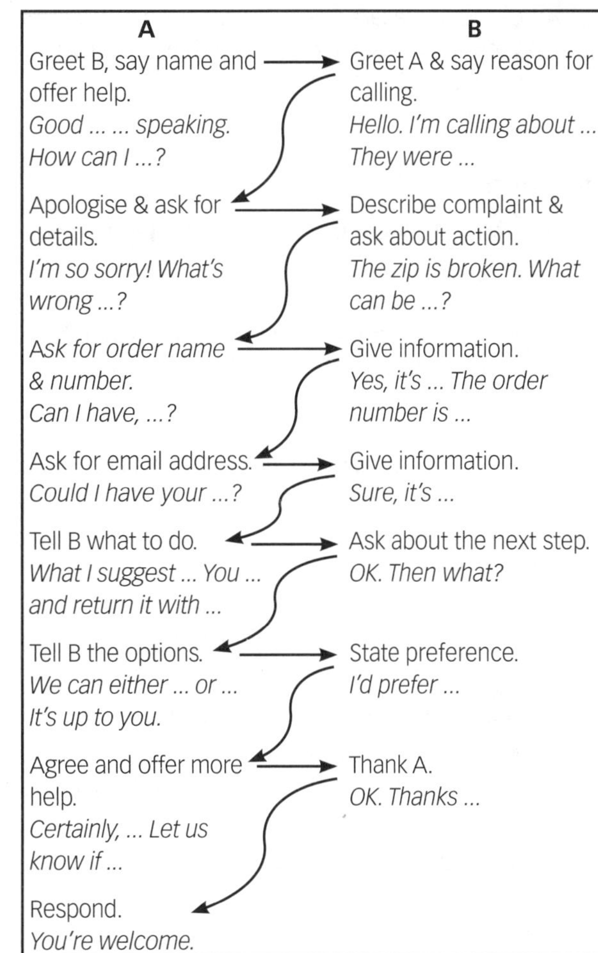

A
B
Greet B, say name and offer help.
Good … … speaking. How can I …?
Greet A & say reason for calling.
Hello. I'm calling about … They were …
Apologise & ask for details.
I'm so sorry! What's wrong …?
Describe complaint & ask about action.
The zip is broken. What can be …?
Ask for order name & number.
Can I have, …?
Give information.
Yes, it's … The order number is …
Ask for email address.
Could I have your …?
Give information.
Sure, it's …
Tell B what to do.
What I suggest … You … and return it with …
Ask about the next step.
OK. Then what?
Tell B the options.
We can either … or … It's up to you.
State preference.
I'd prefer …
Agree and offer more help.
Certainly, … Let us know if …
Thank A.
OK. Thanks …
Respond.
You're welcome.

- Monitor the activity around the class and offer assistance as necessary.
- Then ask some pairs to act out their dialogues in front of the class.

Suggested Answer Key

A: Good afternoon. Tony speaking. How can I help?
B: Hello. I'm calling about a pair of jeans I ordered from you last week. They were damaged when they arrived. What can be done about it?
A: I'm so sorry! What's wrong with them exactly?
B: The zip is broken.
A: Can I have your name and order number?
B: Yes, it's Linda Raby. The order number is 891569.
A: Could I have your email address as well?
B: Sure, it's lindar@amail.com.
A: What I suggest is for me to email you a return slip. You print it out, fill in the details and return it to us with the jeans.
B: OK. Then what?
A: We can either exchange it for a new pair or give you a full refund. It's up to you.
B: I'd prefer a new pair, please.

A: Certainly, madam. The email has been sent. Let us know if there is anything else we can do for you.
B: OK. Thanks for your help.
A: You're welcome.

Intonation

6 a) **Aim To learn intonation in exclamations**

- Elicit when we use *what, how, such, so* in exclamations.
- Give Ss time to fill in the missing words in the exclamations.
- Then play the recording for Ss to check their answers.
- Then play the recording again with pauses for Ss to repeat chorally and/or individually. Check Ss' intonation.

Answer Key

1 How	*3 such an*
2 so	*4 What a*

b) **Aim To practise exclamations**

- Give Ss time to think of similar sentences. Ask Ss around the class to share them with the class.
- Check Ss' intonation.

Suggested Answer Key

What a bargain!
How cheap!
You've been such a great help.
It's so expensive!

Reading & Writing

7 a) **Aim To read for lexical cohesion (text completion)**

- Give Ss time to read the text and complete the gaps with a word from the list.
- Check Ss' answers.

Answer Key

1 some	*3 someone*	*5 nothing*
2 no	*4 every*	*6 any*

b) **Aim To analyse the content of a complaint form**

Elicit what information is contained in the complaint form and in what order it appears. Have Ss choose three of the options in the list. Elicit Ss' answers.

Answer Key

- *when and where the product was purchased/ordered*
- *what was wrong with the product*
- *action requested*

8 **Aim To present language in complaints**

- Read out the ***Writing Tip*** and tell Ss that this advice will help them to complete the writing task successfully.
- Have Ss read the sentences and identify the strength of the tone in each one.
- Elicit answers from Ss around the class and elicit the language tone used in the form in Ex. 7.

Answer Key

Mild, polite language = 1, 2, 5
Strong, insulting language = 3, 4, 6
Mild, polite language is used in the form in Ex. 7.

Writing

9 **Aim To prepare for a writing task; to analyse a rubric**

Give Ss time to read the rubric and elicit answers to the questions from Ss around the class.

Answer Key

1 *I am going to complete a complaint form.*
2 *A person at the store is going to read it.*
3 *I should write about a faulty electronic device I bought.*
4 *I should write 120-180 words.*

10 a) **Aim To prepare for a writing task**

- Ask Ss to copy the headings into their notebooks and make notes using their own ideas.
- Ask various Ss to share their answers with the class.

Suggested Answer Key

product – a games console
when/where purchased – ten days ago from the online store
problem – one of the controllers doesn't work and the cable to connect it to the TV is loose
action requested – a new games console

b) **Aim To develop writing skills; to complete a complaint form**

- Tell Ss to use their answers from Ex. 10a and the plan to help them complete a complaint form for the rubric in Ex. 9.
- Give Ss time to complete the task and then ask various Ss to read their forms to the class.
- This task may be assigned as homework.

Suggested Answer Key

Customer Complaint Form
Name: *John Taylor*
Contact details (phone/email): *020 776 8569 253*
Product description: *Quasar 2100 games console*
Order number: *692514*
Location of purchase: *company website*
Date of purchase: *1/8/....*
Date of complaint: *11/8/....*
I am writing to complain about a games console model Quasar 2100 that I ordered from your company website ten days ago.
First of all, it did not arrive within three working days, as promised. Then, when I tried to use it for the first time, I noticed that one of the game controllers does not work. Furthermore, the cable that connects the games console to the TV is loose. I plugged it in, but it does not seem to connect properly and from time to time the screen goes black.
I would therefore like to return the games console in exchange for a new one. If this is not possible, I would like a full refund. Thank you in advance.
Signature:
J. Taylor

VALUES

Ask Ss to read the quotation, then initiate a class discussion about its meaning. Encourage all Ss to participate.

Suggested Answer Key

A: *I think the quotation means that when we are polite we can make people softer like a melting candle.*
B: *I totally agree. I also think it refers to the fact that politeness improves human nature. For example, when you are polite to someone they are polite back.*
A: *Yes, I think you're right. etc*

Culture 11

Listening & Reading

1 **Aim To introduce the topic; to listen and read for specific information**

- Have Ss look at the picture and read the title and elicit whether any Ss know the answer to the question.
- Play the recording. Ss listen and read the text to find out.

Suggested Answer Key

I think it got its name because of something to do with the stock market in the past.

2 **Aim To read for key information (text completion)**

- Give Ss time to read the text again and then complete the summary using one word in each gap.
- Check Ss' answers.

Answer Key

1 *Thanksgiving*
2 *crash*
3 *profit*
4 *police*
5 *four*

- Then give Ss time to look up the meanings of the words in bold using the Word List or their dictionaries.
- Elicit explanations from Ss around the class.

Suggested Answer Key

worldwide (adv): *all around the world*
accounts (n): *financial records*
recorded (v): *made a record of (wrote down)*
profits (n): *money made after costs*
traffic jams (n): *situations where there so many cars on the road that it is blocked*
shoplifting (n): *the crime of taking something from a shop without paying*
spread (v): *moved across an area*
including (prep): *being part of sth else*
Cyber (adj): *relating to computers and the Internet*
bargains (n): *things sold at a lower price than usual*

- Give Ss time to look up the meanings of the words in the ***Check these words*** box in the Word List.
- Play the video for Ss and elicit their comments.

Speaking & Writing

3 **Aim THINK To develop critical thinking skills**

- Read out the question and have Ss consider their answers and then compare their answers with their partner.
- Ask various Ss to share their answers with the class.

Suggested Answer Key

Businesses participate in Black Friday for a number of reasons. First, it increases sales. Second, it is a good way to sell stock that they may have had for a while. Also, it can attract new customers and increase brand awareness.

4 **Aim ICT To develop research skills; to write a short article about a popular sales period**

- Give Ss time to research online and find out information about a popular sales period in their

country or another country and use this information to write a short article.
- Ask various Ss to read their article to the class.
- This task may be assigned as homework.

Suggested Answer Key

In the UK, the Boxing Day sales are a very popular sales period. Boxing Day is the name for the day after Christmas Day. It gets its name because of the Christmas gift box employers would give to their staff on this day. The box was usually filled with special food as well as money to celebrate Christmas with. People who worked as servants usually got this day off instead of Christmas Day.
Boxing Day sales are very popular because the reductions are huge and there are lots of bargains to find, especially Christmas-related items. A lot of people go shopping on this day to buy late Christmas presents or early ones for the following Christmas. There are usually long queues outside the shops and some people even sleep outside the shops overnight to be the first ones to get the bargains.

Review 11

Vocabulary

1 Aim To consolidate vocabulary from the unit

- Explain the task.
- Give Ss time to complete it.
- Check Ss' answers.

Answer Key

1 hoardings	*4 spot*	*7 grab*
2 window	*5 limit*	*8 spot*
3 marketing	*6 slogans*	

2 Aim To consolidate vocabulary from the unit

- Explain the task.
- Give Ss time to complete it.
- Check Ss' answers.

Answer Key

1 broken	*3 torn*	*5 weak*
2 scratched	*4 cracked*	

3 Aim To practise prepositional phrases and phrasal verbs

- Explain the task.
- Give Ss time to complete it.
- Check Ss' answers.

Answer Key

1 in	*3 about*	*5 at*
2 on	*4 after*	

Grammar

4 Aim To practise determiners

- Explain the task.
- Give Ss time to complete it.
- Check Ss' answers.

Answer Key

1 Both January and June are busy sales months.
2 Either John or May is giving the presentation.
3 We've spent the whole budget on advertising.
4 Sheila liked none of the jeans in the shop.
5 Neither Lynn nor her sisters shop online.
6 There are no ads on this TV channel.

5 Aim To practise quantifiers

- Explain the task.
- Give Ss time to complete it.
- Check Ss' answers.

Answer Key

1 too	*3 some*	*5 plenty of*
2 a few	*4 much*	

6 Aim To practise *some/any/every/no* & compounds

- Explain the task.
- Give Ss time to complete it.
- Check Ss' answers.

Answer Key

1 nowhere	*3 anything*	*5 someone*
2 some	*4 everything*	

Everyday English

7 Aim To match exchanges

- Explain the task.
- Give Ss time to complete it.
- Check Ss' answers.

Answer Key

1 c 2 d 3 e 4 b 5 a

Competences

Ask Ss to assess their own performance in the unit by ticking the items according to how competent they feel for each of the listed activities.

Health is wealth

Topic	
In this unit, Ss will explore the topics of food and healthy living.	
12a Reading & Vocabulary	**98-99**
Lesson objectives: To introduce vocabulary related to food, to listen and read for gist, to read for specific information (multiple choice), to learn collocations related to food, to learn prepositional phrases, to practise words easily confused, to learn phrasal verbs with *cut*, to talk about cultured meat, to give a presentation on future food **Vocabulary:** Food *(carbohydrates, protein, fibre, fat, wholegrain bread and cereals, beans, peas, nuts, seeds, lentils, fruit, vegetables, dairy products, dark chocolate, olives, eggs, avocados, coconuts, oily fish, seafood, lean meat and poultry, eggs, beans, peas, soy products, pasta, rice, sugar, honey, soft drinks, bread, potatoes)*;Nouns *(culture, breakthrough, pesticide, fertiliser, audience, point, creature, vegan)*; Phrasal Verb *(set up)*; Adjectives *(moral, concerned, mushy, affordable)*	
12b Grammar in Use	**100-101**
Lesson objectives: To learn clauses of concession; clauses of result/purpose/reason; intensifiers	
12c Skills in Action	**102-103**
Lesson objectives: To learn vocabulary related to healthy living, to listen for key information (multiple matching), to listen and read for specific information, to act out a dialogue and practise everyday English for asking for/giving advice, to practise intonation in direct/indirect questions, to read for lexical cohesion (word formation), to write a forum post **Vocabulary:** Healthy living *(floss, limit, eliminate, consume, maintain, exercise, remove, apply)*	
Culture 12	**104**
Lesson objectives: To listen and read for specific information, to read for key information (matching headings to paragraphs), to talk about and compare healthcare systems, to write a short article about a healthcare system **Vocabulary:** Nouns *(structure, healthcare, National Insurance contributions, life expectancy, in vitro fertilisation {IVF}, budget, residents)*; Verbs *(mentioned, launched)*; Phrasal verbs *(wipe out, set up)*; Adjectives *(quality, limited, unique)*	
Review 12	**105**
Lesson objectives: To test/consolidate vocabulary and grammar learnt throughout the unit; to practise everyday English	

Go through the objectives box and tell Ss that these are the topics, skills and activities this unit will cover.

12a

Vocabulary

1 **Aim To introduce the topic; to present vocabulary related to food**

- Read out the question and elicit/explain the meanings of any unknown words.
- Then give Ss time to complete the task in pairs.
- Check Ss' answers around the class.

Suggested Answer Key

A: *I think protein helps build and repair muscle tissue.*
B: *I think you're right. I think carbohydrates give the body energy.*
A: *Do you think fat protects the organs?*
B: *I'm not sure about that. I think it helps keep the digestive system healthy though.*
A: *Right. Fibre must help the body absorb vitamins.*
B: *I guess so.*

2 a) **Aim To expand on the topic; to present more vocabulary related to food**

- Give Ss time to consider which of the foods in the list are rich in carbohydrates, fibre, protein or fat.
- Ask various Ss to tell the class.

Answer Key

1 Fibre	*3 Protein*
2 Fat	*4 Carbohydrates*

b) **Aim To generate topic-related vocabulary**

- Give Ss time to think of another item to add to each list in Ex. 2a.
- Elicit answers from Ss around the class.

Suggested Answer Key

Carbohydrates = *starchy vegetables e.g. beetroot*
Protein = *quinoa*
Fibre = *wholewheet pasta*
Fat = *olive oil*

Reading & Listening

3 **Aim To listen and read for gist**

- Ask Ss to read the questions and elicit their guesses in answer to them.
- Play the recording. Ss listen and read the text to find out.

Suggested Answer Key
Cultured meat is made in a lab from animal cells. The positive impact it has on the environment is that it saves resources such as land and water and it cuts down on pollution.

4 a) Aim To read for specific information (multiple choice)

- Ask Ss to read the text again, then read the questions and answer choices and choose their answers according to what they read.
- Check Ss' answers. Ss should justify their choices.

Answer Key
1 D (Taking all this into account, cultured meat could play a huge role in saving our planet.)
2 B (This meat doesn't look like a chicken breast or beef steak,though. Instead, cultured meat is more 'mushy')
3 A (One American company says it costs them $50 to make a single chicken nugget! So, it will be some time before cultured meat is affordable for customers.)
4 C (Right now, animal farming is the cause of 18% of greenhouse gas emissions – more than all cars, trucks, planes and trains put together!)

b) Aim To consolidate new vocabulary

Give Ss time to look up the meanings of the words in bold in the Word List or in their dictionaries and elicit definitions from Ss around the class.

Suggested Answer Key
concerned (adj): *worried*
mushy (adj): *having a soft consistency*
audience (n): *the people watching sth live*
affordable (adj): *able to be bought for a reasonable price*
point (n): *reason for sth*
creature (n): *living organism (animal)*
vegan (n): *a person who does not eat any animal products*

- Give Ss time to look up the meanings of the words in the ***Check these words*** box in the Word List.
- Play the video for Ss and elicit their comments.

5 Aim To consolidate prepositional phrases from a text

- Give Ss time to read the gapped sentences and fill in the gaps with the correct prepositions.
- Then check Ss' answers.

Answer Key
1 about 3 in 5 on
2 of 4 of

6 Aim To consolidate new vocabulary & practise collocations

- Ask Ss to look through the text and find the words that pair with the words in the list to make collocations.
- Check Ss' answers and then give them time to use the collocations in sentences of their own.

Answer Key
1 healthy 5 chicken
2 processed 6 moral
3 global 7 animal
4 animal 8 water and soil

Suggested Answer Key
*It is important to have a **healthy diet** with lots of vegetables and fruit.*
*We shouldn't eat a lot of **processed foods** as they have been changed from their natural state.*
***Global warming** occurs when carbon dioxide (CO_2) and greenhouse gases collect in the atmosphere and absorb sunlight that has bounced off the Earth's surface.*
*Cultured meat is made from **animal cells** without harming the animal.*
*Cultured meat doesn't look like a **chicken breast**.*
*There is a strong **moral reason** to eat cultured meat.*
***Animal farming** creates a lot of **water and soil pollution**.*

7 Aim To understand words easily confused

- Explain the task and give Ss time to use their dictionaries to help them complete it.
- Check Ss' answers and then elicit sentences using the other words from Ss around the class.

Answer Key
1 raises 3 affect
2 choice 4 produces

8 Aim To learn phrasal verbs with *cut*

- Ask Ss to read the phrasal verbs box and make sure that Ss understand the definitions.
- Then give Ss time to complete the task and check their answers.

Answer Key
1 off 3 down on 5 out
2 off 4 off 6 in

Speaking & Writing

9 **Aim** THINK **To consolidate information in a text; to develop critical thinking skills**

- Play the recording. Have Ss listen and take notes.
- Then ask Ss to read the fourth paragraph in the text again and make notes.
- Have Ss use their notes to have a class debate on cultured meat using the statements provided as a basis. Record the debate and monitor the activity.

Suggested Answer Key

A: *I don't think cultured meat is the food of the future because I think we should be encouraging people to cut down on their meat consumption and giving them another source of meat does not do this.*
B: *I totally agree. I think it would be better for people to eat less meat and become vegetarian or vegan. That would help cut down on pollution caused by animal farming.*
C: *I see what you mean. But what about the farmers? They have to make a living.*
D: *Yes, but they can still be farmers without raising animals. They can grow crops.*
E: *I think we should all think about the animals more and the people less. I mean, people will always have food to eat. We don't have to eat meat at all. I think keeping animals to kill for meat is cruel.*
F: *Yes, but we are meat-eaters by nature. If we eat cultured meat instead of animals, it might be the food of the future. etc*

10 **Aim** ICT **To develop research skills; to give a presentation on food of the future**

- Give Ss time to research online and find out information about future foods and prepare a presentation on it.
- Then have Ss give their presentation to the class.

Suggested Answer Key

Good morning everyone. Sadly, there is still hunger around the world and as the population grows we need to look at new food sources to help feed everyone, as well as tackle some of the other problems we face, such as global warming and climate change, brought about by too much pollution. Today I am going to talk to you about two possible foods of the future which may help to solve these problems.
First of all, insects are a possible food of the future because they are high in protein and cost less to raise than larger animals. Producing insects for food needs less land, less energy and less water than raising beef cattle. However, some insects contain heavy metals which could be a health concern. Also, a lot of people, especially in the West, are scared of insects and may not choose to eat them.
Another possible food of the future is seaweed. It can be a food source for people and animals. Growing food in the sea would help to save resources such as land and fresh water as neither of these are needed to grow seaweed. Growing seaweed cuts down on carbon emissions too because it absorbs carbon from the sea. Certain types of seaweed have lots of vitamins and protein.
Overall, there are other options which use what nature provides rather than producing processed foods in factories. We should consider them, don't you agree? Thanks for listening. Are there any questions?

12b Grammar in Use

1 **Aim** **To learn/revise clauses of concession**

- Ask Ss to read the theory box and then read the article and find two examples.
- Check Ss' answers and refer Ss to the ***Grammar Reference*** section for more information or to check any points they are unsure of. Direct Ss' attention to how clauses of concession are formed.

Answer Key

While most fruits don't contain much protein, these small red berries are packed with it.
Originally, goji berries were only grown in the Himalaya region in Asia, but now many countries around the world grow them ...

2 **Aim** **To practise clauses of concession**

- Explain the task and give Ss time to complete it.
- Check Ss' answers.

Answer Key

1 *whereas*	3 *but*	5 *though*
2 *yet*	4 *Despite*	6 *Although*

3 **Aim** **To practise clauses of concession**

- Give Ss time to complete the sentences.
- Elicit answers from Ss around the class.

Answer Key

1 *Jason went to bed early, he feels tired today*
2 *Sue is really fit, her husband doesn't do any exercise at all*
3 *of taking up yoga, Jessica still feels stressed*
4 *not liking vegetables, George tries to eat at least one portion a day*
5 *Greta is a talented cook, she rarely makes dinner for her family*

Speaking

4 **Aim** **To practise clauses of concession**

Ask Ss to work in pairs and talk about a person they know using clauses of concession and following the examples.

Suggested Answer Key

A: Although Lisa is very slim, she rarely exercises.
B: Despite always getting high marks, Julie doesn't like Maths.

5 **Aim** **To learn/revise clauses of result/purpose/ reason**

- Ask Ss to read the theory and then match the types of clauses to the highlighted sections of the text in Ex. 1.
- Check Ss' answers and refer Ss to the ***Grammar Reference*** section for more information or to check any points they are unsure of.

Answer Key

Clause of result *– goji berries have so much protein that you can get 14% of your daily recommended intake from a 100-gram serving.*
Clause of reason *– Due to the fact that they are so nutritious, goji berries are fast becoming the most popular superfood on the market.*
Clause of purpose *– many countries around the world grow them so that they can be sold fresher and for a cheaper price to local consumers.*

6 **Aim** **To practise clauses of result/purpose/ reason**

- Give Ss time to read the sentences and choose the correct items.
- Check Ss' answers.

Answer Key

1 A 2 C 3 B 4 C 5 C 6 A

7 **Aim** **To practise clauses of result/purpose/ reason**

- Give Ss time to read and complete the sentences.
- Check Ss' answers around the class.

Answer Key

1 in order not to	*5 in case*
2 Therefore	*6 Now that*
3 such	*7 The reason for*
4 as	*8 so that*

8 **Aim** **To practise clauses of result/purpose/ reason**

- Give Ss time to rewrite the sentences.
- Check Ss' answers by asking various Ss around the class to read out a sentence at a time.

Suggested Answer Key

1 *He went to bed early so as not to feel tired at work.*
2 *The reason why Lisa's not joining us at the cinema is that she's got an upset stomach.*
3 *Take some aspirin with you on the trip in case you get a headache.*
4 *Brian had such terrible backache that he had to take the day off work.*
5 *The runners drank lots of water so that they didn't get dehydrated.*

Speaking

9 **Aim** **To practise clauses of result/purpose/ reason**

- Explain the task and read out the examples.
- Then have Ss complete the task in pairs.
- Monitor the activity round the class and then ask some pairs to share their answers with the class.

Suggested Answer Key

A: The reason I am tired is that I went to bed late.
B: You should get an early night tonight so that you aren't tired tomorrow.
A: I will set a reminder so that I don't forget. etc

10 **Aim** **To learn/revise intensifiers**

- Ask Ss to read the theory and refer them to the ***Grammar Reference*** section for more information or to check any points they are unsure of.
- Then ask Ss to find an example in the text in Ex. 1.

Answer Key

absolutely huge

11 **Aim** **To practise intensifiers**

- Give Ss time to complete the task.
- Check Ss' answers.

Answer Key

1 extremely	*4 extremely*
2 very	*5 lot*
3 really	*6 completely*

12 **Aim** **To practise intensifiers**

- Explain the task and read out the example.
- Give Ss time to complete the task and then check their answers.

Answer Key

2 *George felt absolutely awful when he had the flu.*
3 *The care John received at the hospital was really excellent.*
4 *The rooms here are far more spacious than in most hospitals.*
5 *Getting enough sleep each night is extremely important for your health.*
6 *We've got some totally brilliant news – Kate is pregnant!*

Speaking

13 Aim To practise intensifiers

Have Ss work in pairs and practise making each other's sentences stronger following the example.

Suggested Answer Key

A: Are you hungry?
B: Yes, I'm absolutely starving.

A: Tom is a good student.
B: Yes, he's a great deal better than me.

12c Skills in Action

Vocabulary

1 a) Aim To present vocabulary related to healthy living

- Ask Ss to read the words in the list and then read the tip list and complete the gaps.
- Explain/Elicit the meanings of any unknown words or phrases or ask Ss to look them up in the Word List.
- Elicit answers from Ss around the class.

Answer Key

1 *Maintain*	4 *Consume*	7 *Eliminate*
2 *Apply*	5 *Floss*	8 *Remove*
3 *Exercise*	6 *Limit*	

b) Aim THINK To expand on the topic

Give Ss time to think of two more healthy living tips for teens and elicit answers from Ss around the class.

Suggested Answer Key

Get some fresh air by spending time outside every day.
Shower regularly, especially in hot weather.

Listening

2 Aim To listen for key information (multiple matching)

- Ask Ss to read the statements and find the key words. Play the recording twice. Ss match the statements to the speakers according to what they hear.
- Check Ss' answers. You can play the recording again with pauses for Ss to check their answers.

Answer Key

1 C 2 D 3 E 4 A

Everyday English

3 Aim To listen and read for specific information

- Ask Ss to read the first exchange in the dialogue. Read out the question. Elicit Ss' guesses as to what advice Jane will get.
- Play the recording for Ss to listen and read and find out if their guesses were correct.

Suggested Answer Key

I think she will be advised to get some vaccines and travel insurance.

4 Aim To act out a dialogue and practise everyday English for asking for/giving advice

- Explain the task and ask Ss to act out a dialogue similar to the one in Ex. 3 in pairs using the ideas provided or ideas of their own and the phrases in the language box.
- Write this diagram on the board for Ss to follow.

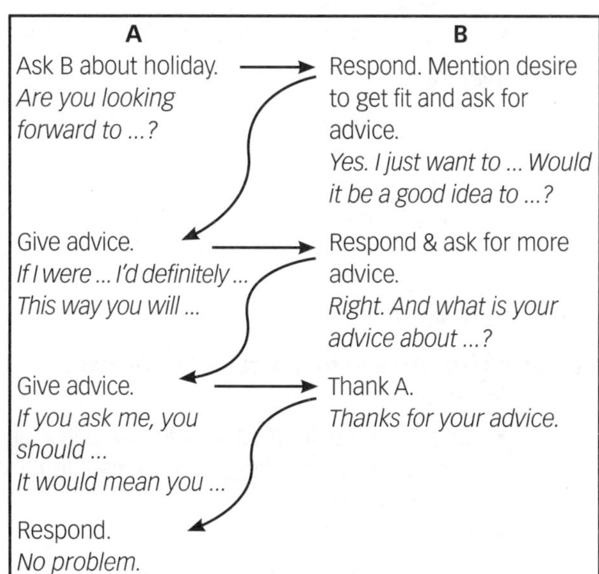

A
B
Ask B about holiday.
Are you looking forward to ...?
Respond. Mention desire to get fit and ask for advice.
Yes. I just want to ... Would it be a good idea to ...?
Give advice.
If I were ... I'd definitely ...
This way you will ...
Respond & ask for more advice.
Right. And what is your advice about ...?
Give advice.
If you ask me, you should ...
It would mean you ...
Thank A.
Thanks for your advice.
Respond.
No problem.

- Monitor the activity around the class and offer assistance as necessary.

- Then ask some pairs to act out their dialogues in front of the class.

Suggested Answer Key

A: Are you looking forward to going on your hiking holiday this summer, John?
B: Yes, I guess so. I just want to get fitter before I go. Would it be a good idea to join a gym?
A: If I were in your shoes, I'd definitely start an exercise routine either at a gym or by yourself. This way you will build up your fitness.
B: Right. And what is your advice about healthy eating? To be honest, I'm not sure if it's worth the effort.
A: If you ask me, I think you should definitely limit sugary food and drinks. Eating more nutritious meals will make you feel healthier and stronger.
B: Thanks for your advice, Lucy.
A: No problem.

Intonation

5 a) Aim To learn intonation in direct/indirect questions

Play the recording twice and have Ss listen and note the difference in intonation between the direct question and the indirect question.

b) Aim To practise direct/indirect questions and their intonation

- Give Ss time to rewrite the questions as indirect questions using the phrases in brackets.
- Then have Ss take turns saying the indirect questions to their partner.
- Walk around the class and check Ss' intonation.

Answer Key

1 *Would you mind telling me where the nearest hospital is?*
2 *Do you know when Frank is having his operation?*
3 *Could you tell me who that man over there is?*
4 *Do you have any idea how I can reach Bob?*

Reading & Writing

6 a) Aim To read for lexical cohesion (word formation)

- Give Ss time to read the forum entry and complete the gaps with a word formed from the word in brackets.
- Check Ss' answers on the board.

Answer Key

1 *impressive*	5 *accidentally*
2 *safety*	6 *importantly*
3 *handle*	7 *tasty*
4 *immediately*	

b) Aim To analyse a text

Elicit what each paragraph is about from Ss around the class.

Answer Key

Para 1 *– introduces the topic of health & safety in the kitchen*
Para 2 *– first piece of advice (washing hands)*
Para 3 *– second piece of advice (avoiding accidents)*
Para 4 *– third piece of advice (being prepared)*
Para 5 *– conclusion*

7 Aim To identify elements in a forum post

- Read out the ***Writing Tip*** and tell Ss that this advice will help them to complete the writing task successfully.
- Then have Ss read the forum post again and answer the questions.
- Elicit answers from Ss around the class.

Answer Key

The writer has used bold for words introducing the three main points. They have used italics in the last paragraph (will).
They want to emphasise safety.
Yes, I think the title is appropriate.

Writing

8 Aim To prepare for a writing task; to analyse a rubric

Ask Ss to read the rubric and elicit answers to the questions.

Answer Key

1 *I am going to write a forum post for people who plan to travel abroad.*
2 *I am going to write about health advice. I should include an introduction and a conclusion and a separate paragraph for each piece of advice.*
3 *My forum post should be 120-180 words.*

9 a) Aim To prepare for a writing task; brainstorming

- Ask Ss to read the pieces of advice and then match them with the reasons/expected results.
- Check Ss' answers around the class.

Answer Key

1 c *2 b* *3 a*

b) Aim To develop writing skills; to write a forum post

- Tell Ss to use their answers from Ex. 9a and the plan to help them write their forum post for the rubric in Ex. 8. Remind Ss to use an appropriate title.
- Give Ss time to complete the task and then ask various Ss to read their forum post to the class.
- This task may be assigned as homework.

Suggested Answer Key

Staying safe when travelling

Hi everyone!
In this forum, I've read a lot of posts about impressive trips, but I've never come across a post about health advice. So, here are some tips about how you can stay safe while travelling.
***First**, take out travel insurance before you travel. This way, your health expenses will be covered in case of an emergency.*
***Secondly**, you should get vaccines before your trip especially if you are going somewhere tropical. By doing this, you can protect yourself from catching certain diseases.*
***Lastly**, you need to be careful when you are eating out. For example, don't eat in dirty restaurants no matter **how** traditional they look. This will help avoid getting food poisoning and certain illnesses.*
So, that's it. Keep these tips in mind when planning your next trip so you can keep safe while travelling.
Leave a comment if you can think of anything else!

VALUES

Ask Ss to read the quotation, then initiate a class discussion about its meanings. Encourage all Ss to participate.

Suggested Answer Key

A: I think the quotation means that a life without health is empty.
B: I totally agree. I also think it refers to the fact that life would be meaningless without health as a river without water would be. etc

Culture 12

Listening & Reading

1 Aim To introduce the topic; to listen and read for specific information

- Go through the questions with Ss.
- Play the recording. Ss listen and read the text to find out the answers.
- Then give Ss time to look up the meanings of the words in bold in the Word List or in their dictionaries.
- Elicit explanations from Ss around the class.

Answer Key

The NHS is the National Health Service in the UK.
Aneurin Bevan was the Health Secretary who launched the NHS in 1948.
In vitro fertilisation (IVF) is a fertility treatment developed by the NHS in 1978.
The Organ Donor Register was set up in 1994 by the NHS.

Suggested Answer Key

mentioned (v): *said*
launched (v): *set up; started*
quality (adj): *how good or bad sth is*
residents (n): *people who live in a place*
set up (phr v): *established*
limited (adj): *small in amount or number*
unique (adj): *one of a kind*

2 Aim To read for key information (matching headings to paragraphs)

- Give Ss time to read the text again and match the headings to the paragraphs. Remind Ss that two headings are extra.
- Check Ss' answers.

Answer Key

1 G (Admired by the Nation – Ask a British person what they are most proud of about their country)
2 F (One Man's Vision – It was launched on 5th July, 1948 by the Health Secretary Aneurin Bevan, who believed that quality healthcare should be available to everyone, both rich and poor, in the country.
3 E (How It's Paid For – On average, this means each British person pays around £2,000 per year to the NHS.)
4 D (A List of Achievements – the NHS has done a lot to improve the health of the British public.)
5 H (Problems with the System – Despite its many successes, the NHS has still received some criticism.)
6 B (Giving Peace of Mind – British people know that they will always receive healthcare from the best doctors and nurses.)

- Give Ss time to look up the meanings of the words in the ***Check these words*** box in the Word List.
- Play the video for Ss and elicit their comments.

Speaking & Writing

3 Aim THINK To practise critical thinking skills

- Give Ss time to consider their answers to the question and then initiate a class debate sharing their opinions and reasons.
- Monitor the debate.

Suggested Answer Key

A: *I think it is much better to have a national health service because not everyone can afford private healthcare.*
B: *I agree. With private healthcare only rich people get the best treatment and poorer people suffer and die needlessly.*
C: *Yes. Without free healthcare, many sick people go into debt to pay their medical bills if they have an accident or if they get sick. etc*

4 Aim ICT To develop research skills; to write about the healthcare system in your country

- Give Ss time to research online and find out information about the healthcare system in their country. Then have Ss use this information to make notes under the headings provided and then write a short article.
- Ask various Ss to read their articles to the class.
- This task may be assigned as homework.

Suggested Answer Key

how it started – *after WW2, Italy established social health insurance controlled by sickness funds, in 1978 it set up its national health service – the SSN (Servizio Sanitario Nazionale)*
services it provides – *free family doctors, free prescriptions, free specialist doctors and tests, free emergency medicine*
achievements – *1994 – first national health plan – outlines national health targets and guarantees the same standards for all citizens; 1997 innovations in organ transplantation*
problems – *planned surgeries have a long waiting list, standard of care varies by region*
what citizens think of it – *citizens are very proud of it*

The National Health Service in Italy
How it started
After WW2, Italy established social health insurance which was controlled by sickness funds. Then in 1978 it set up its national health service – the SSN (Servizio Sanitario Nazionale).
Services it provides
The SSN provides free family doctors, free prescriptions, free specialist doctors and tests, and free emergency medicine to everyone.
Achievements
In 1994, the SSN came up with the first national health plan. This outlines national health targets and guarantees the same standards for all citizens. In 1997, the SSN made innovations in organ transplantation and set up the Mediterranean Institute for Transplantation and Advanced Specialized Therapies.
Problems
There are some problems with the system, though. For example, planned surgeries have a long waiting list and the standard of care varies by region.
Nevertheless, the Italian people know they will receive healthcare from the best doctors and nurses when they need it. That is why the Italian people are very proud of the SSN.

Review 12

Vocabulary

1 Aim To consolidate vocabulary from the unit

- Explain the task.
- Give Ss time to complete it.
- Check Ss' answers.

Answer Key

1 apply	*5 major*
2 eliminate	*6 produces*
3 moral	*7 organs*
4 certain	

2 Aim To consolidate vocabulary from the unit

- Explain the task.
- Give Ss time to complete it.
- Check Ss' answers.

Answer Key

1 d	*3 f*	*5 b*	*7 e*
2 g	*4 a*	*6 h*	*8 c*

3 Aim To practise prepositional phrases and phrasal verbs

- Explain the task.
- Give Ss time to complete it.
- Check Ss' answers.

Answer Key

1 of	*4 out*
2 in	*5 down*
3 about	

Grammar

4 Aim To practise clauses of concession/result/purpose/reason

- Explain the task.
- Give Ss time to complete it.
- Check Ss' answers.

Answer Key

1 *Although she went on a diet, she didn't lose any weight.*
2 *The reason she eats so much protein is that she's a bodybuilder.*
3 *Lisa's a vegetarian, whereas her brother eats a lot of meat.*
4 *Tim eats a lot of fast food in spite of being a fitness trainer.*
5 *Take a bottle of water with you in case you feel thirsty.*

5 Aim To practise intensifiers

- Explain the task.
- Give Ss time to complete it.
- Check Ss' answers.

Answer Key

1 *totally*	3 *absolutely*	5 *absolutely*
2 *really*	4 *far*	

Everyday English

6 Aim To match exchanges

- Explain the task.
- Give Ss time to complete it.
- Check Ss' answers.

Answer Key

1 *b* 2 *d* 3 *a* 4 *c*

Competences

Ask Ss to assess their own performance in the unit by ticking the items according to how competent they feel for each of the listed activities.

Values: Commitment

1 **Aim** **To introduce the topic; to listen and read for gist**

- Read out the question and elicit ideas from Ss around the class.
- Play the recording. Ss listen and read the text to find out if their ideas were mentioned.

Suggested Answer Key

The advice given is to set realistic goals, keep a record of any progress and allow yourself to make mistakes.

2 **Aim** **To read for key information (T/F/DS statements); to consolidate new vocabulary**

- Ask Ss to read statements 1-5 and explain any unknown vocabulary.
- Give Ss time to read the text again and decide if the statements are true, false or if the information is not stated in the text.
- Check Ss' answers.

Answer Key

1 T 2 F 3 F 4 T 5 DS

- Elicit explanations of the words/phrases in bold in the text from Ss around the class.
- Give Ss time to look up the meanings in the Word List or in their dictionaries.

Suggested Answer Key

habits (n): *things you do regularly, without thinking about it*
keep on track (phr): *continue following a plan*
realistic (adj): *possible to achieve*
uncomplicated (adj): *simple*
intensive (adj): *very difficult and using a lot of energy*
dread (v): *not want to do something very strongly*
progress (n): *development*
motivated (adj): *wanting to do something*
abandoning (v): *giving up*
turn it around (phr): *change sth from failing into working*

3 **Aim** THINK **To encourage critical thinking skills**

Explain the task and give Ss time to consider their answers. Then ask Ss to share their ideas with the class.

Suggested Answer Key

The most important situation where you need to show commitment is parenthood, because you need to be there for your children. Another situation where it's important is with a relationship, since your partner needs to know they can rely on you.

4 **Aim** **To encourage commitment; to use prior knowledge; to write a lifestyle plan**

- Explain the task to Ss.
- Give Ss time to complete the task or assign it as homework.
- Ask various Ss to read their plan to the class.

Suggested Answer Key

My lifestyle plan

Diet
I am going to eat yoghurt for breakfast, a salad for lunch and chicken or beef with vegetables for dinner every day.
Exercise
I'm going to cycle to work every day instead of taking the bus. I'm going to go for a long walk every evening after dinner.
Sleep
I'm going to go to bed early enough to get eight hours of sleep every night.
How I will stick to the plan
I won't worry if I miss any on these routines once a week. I'll keep a record of my weight every week. Once a month, I'll treat myself to a dessert.

Public Speaking Skills

1 **Aim To analyse a rubric**

Read the rubric aloud and elicit the answers to the question from the class.

Answer Key

It is asking for an informative speech.

2 **Aim To analyse a model talk; to practise non-verbal communication**

- Read out the ***Study Skills*** box and tell Ss that this tip will help them to complete the speaking skills task successfully.
- Play the recording. Ss listen to and read the model.
- Give pairs time to decide on their non-verbal communication. Then ask some pairs to do the talk again, with one reading it out and the other doing the non-verbal communication.

Ss' own answers

3 **Aim To give a talk about exam preparation**

- Read out the rubric and explain the situation. Give Ss time to research and prepare their talks. Remind Ss to plan what non-verbal communication they will use.
- Ask various Ss to give their speech to the class.

Suggested Answer Key

Good morning, everyone. Today I'm going to talk to you about exam preparation, and how to be in the best possible shape on the day of your exam.
The first and most important step is, of course, revision. If you don't know the material, you won't do well in the exam, will you? But pay attention to how you revise. Very little information that you read when tired, for example, is remembered. Study in short bursts of around 20 minutes each – studies have shown that this is the maximum time we can really concentrate for.
On the day before the exam, get a good night's sleep. There is nothing more important for exam success than a rested mind and body. If you find it hard to get to sleep, a long walk before bed or a session of exercise can help.
Finally, be careful what you eat before the exam. If your exam is in the morning, something like porridge or a cereal with fairly low sugar and high fibre and complex carbohydrates is good. Sugar is burned very quickly by the body, and will probably be gone before you enter the exam hall. Complex carbohydrates, however, take a lot longer to burn, giving you energy all morning.
Follow these three simple steps and I guarantee you success on the day of your exam. Thank you for listening.

CLIL: PSHE

Reading & Listening

1 a) Aim To introduce the topic; to do a quiz (multiple choice)

- Ask Ss to read the quiz and answer the questions.
- Check Ss' answers.

Answer Key

1 C	*3 A*	*5 B*	*7 B*
2 C	*4 A*	*6 A*	*8 A*

b) Aim To listen for confirmation; to consolidate new vocabulary

- Play the recording for Ss to listen and check their answers and then give them time to look up the meanings of the words in bold in the Word List or in their dictionaries.
- Elicit explanations from Ss around the class.

Suggested Answer Key

handheld (adj): *used by holding in your hand*
requires (v): *makes it necessary for sb to do sth*
approved (adj): *officially allowed*
priority (n): *the right to go first*
campaign (n): *an organised group of actions*
term (n): *the word or phrase used to describe sth*

- Then give Ss time to look up the meanings of the words in the ***Check these words*** box in the Word List or in their dictionaries.

2 Aim To read for comprehension

- Give Ss time to read the fact file and then read the quiz again and match the facts to the questions.
- Check Ss' answers around the class.

Answer Key

a 7	*c 2*	*e 4*	*g 5*
b 6	*d 1*	*f 3*	*h 8*

Speaking & Writing

3 Aim THINK To express an opinion

- Ask Ss to discuss the question in pairs and decide which of the rules/laws they think is/are the most important and why.
- Monitor the activity around the class and then ask some pairs to share their answers with the rest of the class.

Suggested Answer Key

A: The rule about driving through a zebra crossing is the most important to me. That's because I mostly travel on foot, and I realise that it's very important to be careful when you cross the road.

B: I see. The most important rule for me is about what cyclists should do at a junction. I often see cyclists break this rule and cycle through red lights, so I think it's important for them to learn to obey it for everyone's safety.

4 Aim ICT To develop research skills; to write a quiz

- Ask Ss to work in small groups and research online for more information about road safety and use it to compile a quiz of their own.
- Tell them to consider, motorists, motorcyclists, cyclists and pedestrians.
- Ask various groups to present their quiz to the class.
- This task may be assigned as homework.

Suggested Answer Key

1 What percentage of road traffic deaths involves motorcyclists?
A 5% B 23% C 69%

2 How do most cycling accidents happen?
A being hit by a car from behind
B being hit by a car from the side
C being hit by a car head-on

3 Which countries have the most car accidents?
A lower-income countries
B middle-income countries
C higher-income countries

4 In which country are pedestrians at least risk of being in an accident?
A Netherlands B Russia C South Africa

Answers: *1 B 2 C 3 B 4 A*

Reading & Listening

1 **Aim** **To introduce the topic; to listen and read for specific information**

- Play the recording. Ss listen and read the text to find out the answer to the question.
- Elicit answers from Ss around the class.

Answer Key

Our voice works using a power source (the air we breathe), a vibrator (our larynx) and a resonator (the resonance tract).

2 **Aim** **To consolidate information in a text**

- Draw Ss' attention to the diagram and the highlighted words/phrases in the text.
- Give Ss time to read the text again and complete the labels in the diagram.
- Check Ss' answers around the class.

Answer Key

1 nasal cavity	*3 larynx*	*5 trachea*
2 oral cavity	*4 lungs*	*6 diaphragm*

3 **Aim** **To read for specific information (answer questions)**

- Give Ss time to read the questions and then read the text again and answer them.
- Check Ss' answers around the class.
- Then give Ss time to look up the meanings of the words/phrases in bold in the Word List or in their dictionaries.
- Elicit explanations from Ss around the class.

Answer Key

1 *The vocal folds get the energy to work from the air that we breathe.*
2 *Air travels up from our lungs through the windpipe with the help of the diaphragm.*
3 *The voice box is at the top of the windpipe.*
4 *The vocal folds are inside the voice box.*
5 *When the vocal folds are closed, we can swallow food or speak.*
6 *The vocal folds make a simple buzzing sound.*
7 *The resonance tract helps us to form words by using muscles in our throat and tongue.*

Suggested Answer Key

communication tool (phr): *sth that helps us exchange information*
rushes (v): *moves fast*
stream (n): *a continuous flow*
powerful (adj): *strong*
situated (adj): *located; placed*
swallow (v): *to cause or allow sth to move down the throat*
transformed (v): *changed*
released (v): *let out*

- Then give Ss time to look up the meanings of the words in the ***Check these words*** box in the Word List or in their dictionaries.

Speaking & Writing

4 **Aim** **To consolidate information in a text**

Ask various Ss around the class to explain how our voice works using the diagram.

Suggested Answer Key

How our voice works

We use the air we breathe as the power source for our voice. When we breathe in, this air goes to the ***lungs****, and when we want to speak it is pushed up the* ***trachea****, with the help of the* ***diaphragm****, towards our mouth. When this air reaches the* ***larynx*** *at the top of the trachea, the two vocal folds there close and vibrate. This produces a buzzing sound, and it is transformed into words through muscles in the* ***nasal cavity****, the* ***oral cavity****, the throat and sinuses. Finally, recognisable sounds are released through our mouth as speech.*

5 **Aim** **ICT** **To develop research skills; to write an explanatory text**

- Ask Ss to work in small groups and research online for information about how our ears work and use it to write an explanatory text.
- Tell them to include a diagram.
- Ask various groups to explain how our ears work to the class.
- This task may be assigned as homework.

Suggested Answer Key

How our ears work

Our ears are the parts of our body that allow us to hear sound. The ear has three main parts, and each part works together to help us hear. Firstly, the outer ear is made up of the pinna and the ear canal. The pinna is the part of the ear you can see at the side of someone's head. It's shaped a bit like a shell and it collect sounds, so they can travel down the ear canal.
A sound then passes into the middle ear. Between the outer ear and the middle ear there is the eardrum, a thin piece of tissue stretching across the ear canal. It moves when sounds hit it, causing three tiny bones in

CLIL: Biology

the ear to vibrate. These bones are called the ossicles. Then, these vibrations pass into the inner ear. There, the cochlea, which looks a bit like a snail, turns the vibrations into nerve signals. These nerve signals then travel along the cochlear nerve, or auditory nerve, to the brain. Finally, we hear the sound.

MIDDLE EAR

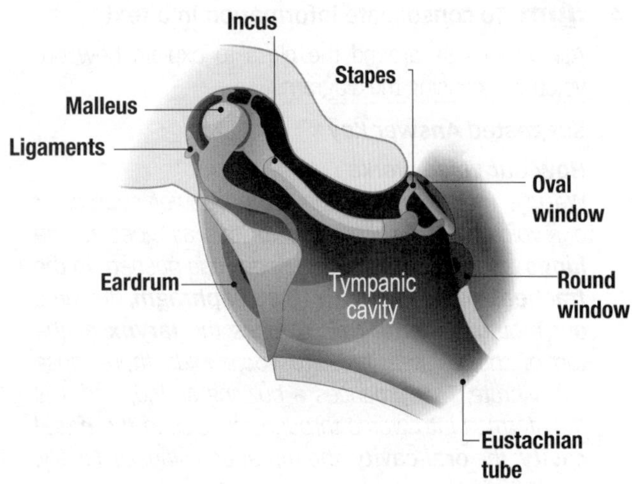

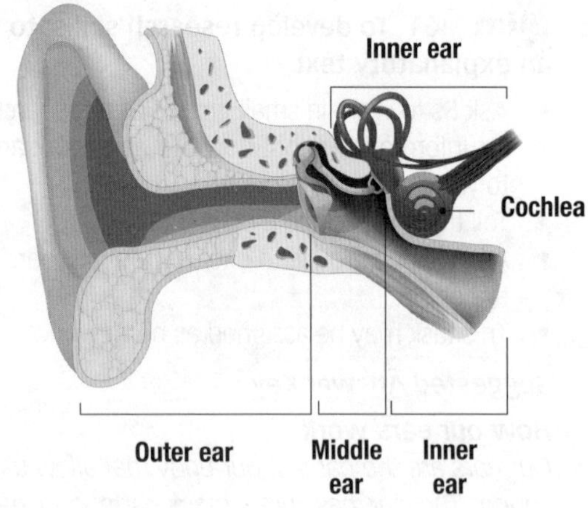

Reading & Listening

1 Aim To listen and read for gist

- Ask Ss to read the title and look at the pictures. Elicit what they think the education system was like in Victorian England.
- Play the recording. Ss listen and read and find out.

Suggested Answer Key

In Victorian England, the education system included basic schooling for the poor for the first time. Only the rich, though, could pay to attend private schools and universities.

2 Aim To read for gist (matching headings to paragraphs); to consolidate new vocabulary

- Ask Ss to read the headings and then read the text again and match the headings to the paragraphs. Remind Ss that three of the headings are extra.
- Check Ss' answers.
- Then give Ss time to look up the meanings of the words in bold in the Word List or in their dictionaries and find the explanations.
- Elicit explanations from Ss around the class.

Answer Key

1 E 2 I 3 A 4 B 5 H 6 C

Suggested Answer Key

support (v): *help*
luxury (n): *sth expensive but not considered essential*
time off (phr): *time away from work*
academic qualifications (phr): *proof that sb has passed an exam, completed a course, etc. in a school, university, etc*
logic (n): *the science of explaining the reason for something using formal methods*

- Then give Ss time to look up the meanings of the words in the ***Check these words*** box in the Word List or in their dictionaries.

Speaking & Writing

3 Aim THINK To compare two education systems

Have Ss consider how the Victorian education system differs from education systems today and make a list and compare it with a partner. Then have various Ss tell the class.

Suggested Answer Key

A: Firstly, you had to pay for school and university in Victorian England, but in most countries today you can go to school for free although university is only free in a few countries.

B: That's true. And today, I think there are a lot of male teachers in primary schools, but in Victorian England, the teachers were usually female.

A: Also, it took a long time for women to be able to get a higher education – right up until about 100 years ago.

B: I know, but sadly in some countries still today women are not able to go to university.

4 Aim ICT To develop research skills

- Have Ss work in small groups and give them time to research online and find out information about the education system in the 19th century in their country or in another country and make notes under the headings provided.
- Then have various groups present their information to the class.

Suggested Answer Key

Education in 19th-century France

Up until the 19th century, most schools in France, both primary and secondary, were run by the Catholic Church as were the universities which had been established in the 12th century.

They were mostly attended by boys from rich families. They offered basic instruction in maths, reading and writing as well as religious studies.

It wasn't until 1850 that elementary education was broadened and made available to both sexes, but still girls were only allowed to be tutored by teachers from the church.

In 1879, colleges and secondary education opened to women. In 1880, universities opened to women as well as teacher training schools, and free public secondary education was given to women. In 1882, elementary education for all children became compulsory. Around the 1870s scholarship funding was provided at universities, as well as laboratory facilities for scientists and medical faculties. During the 19th century, a number of higher education grandes écoles were established to support industry and commerce and offered subjects related to manufacturing and business.

CLIL: Environmental Studies

Listening & Speaking

1 **Aim To introduce the topic; to listen and read for specific information**

Have Ss look at the symbols in the text. Play the recording. Ss listen and read and find out what they mean.

Answer Key

Symbol 1 means that an object can be recycled.
Symbol 2 means that an object is made of plastic.
Symbol 3 means that a glass object should be recycled in a correct recycling bin.
Symbol 4 means that an object is made of recyclable aluminium.
Symbol 5 means that an object is made of recyclable steel.
Symbol 6 means that an object has been made using wood in an environmentally friendly way.
Symbol 7 means that an electrical item shouldn't be thrown into the normal rubbish.
Symbol 8 means that an object can be turned into fertiliser.
Symbol 9 means that people shouldn't litter.
Symbol 10 means that the makers of a product pay towards the cost of recycling, but the item may not be recyclable.

2 **Aim To read for key information (multiple matching); to consolidate new vocabulary**

- Ask Ss to read the statements and then read the text again and match the statements to the paragraphs.
- Check Ss' answers around the class.
- Then give Ss time to look up the meanings of the words/phrases in bold in the Word List or in their dictionaries. Elicit explanations from Ss around the class.

Answer Key

1 D	*3 F*	*5 J*	*7 H*	*9 B*
2 E	*4 G*	*6 I*	*8 A*	*10 C*

Suggested Answer Key

reminds (v): *helps you remember*
bottle bank (n): *a large container where you can put bottles for recycling*
wrappers (n): *coverings protecting something for sale, usually food*
managed (v): *organised; taken care of*
council (n): *the group of people who work for the state in a town, city, etc.*
citizens (n): *people who live in a town, city, etc.*

- Then give Ss time to look up the meanings of the words in the ***Check these words*** box in the Word List or in their dictionaries.

Speaking & Writing

3 **Aim**  **To develop creative thinking skills**

Have Ss consider their answers to the question and then ask various Ss to share their ideas with the class.

Suggested Answer Key

Symbol 1 could be seen on the cardboard boxes used for cereal.
Symbol 2 could be seen on the containers used by take-away food restaurants.
Symbol 3 could be seen on any glass bottle or jar such as sauce bottles and jam jars.
Symbol 4 could be seen on kitchen pots.
Symbol 5 could be seen on kitchen utensils.
Symbol 6 could be seen on furniture, such as chairs and desks.
Symbol 7 could be seen toasters.
Symbol 8 could be seen on coffee filters.
Symbol 9 could be seen on public signs, for example in a park.
Symbol 10 could be seen on kitchen appliances, such as fridges and cookers.

4 **Aim ICT To develop research skills; to make a poster**

- Ask Ss to work in small groups and give them time to research online and find out information about the plastics codes and make notes for all the points provided.
- Then give Ss time to use their notes to prepare a poster.
- Ask various groups to present their poster to the class.

Suggested Answer Key

Plastic Codes			
Codes	***Types of plastic***	***Products***	***R***
1 PETE	*Polyethylene Terephthalat*	*drinks bottles*	✓
2 HOPE	*High-Density Polyethylene*	*shampoo bottles, milk containers*	✓
3 V	*Vinyl*	*pipes, clear food packaging*	✗
4 LOPE	*Low-Density Polyethylene*	*plastic wrap for food*	✓
5 FP	*Polypropylene*	*sauce bottles, yoghurt pots*	✓
6 PS	*Polystyrene*	*plates/cups*	✗
7 OTHER	*Other plastics*	*sunglasses, CDs*	✗

Student's Book Audioscripts

UNIT 1 – On the map

1c – Exercise 2 (p. 8)

Sarah: Excuse me, are you from around here?
Peter: Yeah, can I help you?
Sarah: I'm sorry to trouble you, but I'm completely lost. It's my first time in London and I need to meet my sister at London Zoo this afternoon. Do you know how to get there?
Peter: Yes, the zoo is inside Regent's Park, so from here it would be a good idea to get the underground to Oxford Circus. From that station you can either get a bus or stay on the underground, but change trains. Which would you prefer?
Sarah: Um, I don't really mind, which would you suggest?
Peter: The bus is slightly slower but it takes you directly to the zoo. The underground is quicker but you will have to walk for 10 minutes from the station to the zoo.
Sarah: So both journeys will take about the same time.
Peter: Yes
Sarah: OK, could you tell me both ways please?
Peter: OK – for both journeys you need to go to the nearest underground station, which is Notting Hill Gate. It's a two-minute walk along this road.
Sarah: Do I need to turn anywhere?
Peter: No, just go straight along this road and the station is on your left.
Sarah: Great! Thanks.
Peter: In the station you need to get on the Central line to Oxford Circus.
Sarah: OK – what colour line is that line on the underground map?
Peter: It's the red line. So when you get to Oxford Circus, if you want to get the bus, exit the station and walk along Regent Street for 150 metres until you get to bus stop 'RD'. It's outside the University of Westminster. Then take the C2 bus from here to London Zoo.
Sarah: Great! That sounds easy – and what about the underground?
Peter: So at Oxford Circus, do not exit. Instead change onto the Victoria line to Euston. That's the blue line.
Sarah: Blue line – got it.
Peter: Then change at Euston onto the Northern Line to Camden Town station. This is the nearest station to the zoo.
Sarah: So I'll have to walk from there?
Peter: Yes, it's about a ten-minute walk.
Sarah: Thank you very much – I'll go to Oxford Circus now and then decide on taking the bus or the underground when I get there.
Peter: Good luck and don't forget the Zoo is inside Regent's Park, so if you get lost just follow signs for there.
Sarah: You've been so helpful, thank you very much.
Peter: My pleasure. Have a nice afternoon with your sister. Goodbye.

UNIT 2 – Legends & Festivals

2b – Exercise 10 (p. 15)

The Sleeping Knights

Once upon a time, there was a blacksmith who lived in a small mountain village. One day, he was working in his shop when a strange man walked in and made him an offer. The stranger said that the blacksmith could earn a valuable reward by helping him with one special task. The blacksmith agreed, and so the stranger gave him a gold bar and asked him to make a horseshoe from it. The blacksmith did it, and once it was ready, the stranger took the blacksmith to the Koscieliska Valley.
When they arrived in the valley, they entered a small, secret cave. Inside the cave, there were many knights sleeping on the floor. They all wore suits of armour, and were holding axes, swords and spears. Their horses were sleeping next to the wall of the cave. The whole place glowed with a gold colour. The stranger pointed to one enormous horse and asked the blacksmith to replace its broken shoe with the golden one, and so he did.
"These knights began their long sleep hundreds of years ago," said the stranger, "and will wake up on the day of a great battle; one which will make the Earth shake like a leaf in the wind. On that day, they will rise and fight for Poland." The blacksmith began asking him question after question, but the stranger would say no more.
The stranger guided the blacksmith back to his village and said that he must promise never to tell anyone about the cave or the knights. The blacksmith agreed. The stranger handed him a bag of gold as payment and quickly disappeared.
However, the blacksmith was foolish, and soon he started telling everyone about the stranger and the cave. After he told the secret, his bag of gold turned into sand. The blacksmith searched again and again for the cave, but he never saw it again.

2c – Exercise 2 (p. 16)

Speaker 1
It all happened completely by chance. I was in Scotland for a hiking holiday and on my fourth day I arrived in Edinburgh. When I got off the bus, though, I discovered that I'd lost my wallet somewhere along the way, with my plane ticket home, as well as my cash card and money! It was quite a shock, I can tell you! Well, I remembered a guy I used to play football with at university was from Edinburgh, and after a couple of phone calls, I tracked him down. He offered to lend me the money to get home and invited me to stay the night at his, since it was Burns' Night. It was wonderful – the music, the poetry, the atmosphere, everything. I even tried haggis, and do you know what – it's not bad! They invited me back next year and I wouldn't miss it for the world!

Student's Book Audioscripts

Speaker 2
In the town where I live, there's a big bonfire in one of the parks on Bonfire Night every year. We were on our way there one year, when I started to feel a little hungry – especially for toasted marshmallows! We had them one year when visiting my uncle in Wales and I really loved them. But there was no point bringing them to the park to toast them, because you aren't allowed close enough to the bonfire. Anyway, when we got there, we saw a man there toasting them over a little gas stove and selling them for 25p each or something ... I don't remember exactly, but it was cheap. I ate about ten of them and that's the Bonfire Night I'll never forget!

Speaker 3
I come from a small village, and May Day was a very important celebration for us. The whole village took part and there used to be a big procession around the village with a May Queen at the head of it. Every year, a different girl from the village would be crowned May Queen, and one year, when I was nineteen, if I remember correctly, it was my turn. Now, I'm quite a shy person, and all along the route, my dad was constantly taking photos. Everywhere we went, there he was! My face was bright red in most of the pictures and I had to pretend that I didn't know him!

Speaker 4
I remember the first time my parents allowed me to stay up until midnight on New Year's Eve. We live in London near the Thames, so you always get a great view of the fireworks display they put on there. Well, my dad told me I should have a nap in the afternoon, since it would be a long wait until midnight, but of course I didn't pay any attention to him. At about 11, my eyes were closing from tiredness, so I decided to lie down on my bed for five minutes… a loud BANG from the fireworks display woke me up suddenly. I rushed outside, but I'd missed midnight and most of the fireworks. It just goes to show – when people who have experience of something tell you what you should do – listen!

Exercise 10 (p. 17)

Pat Mulligan here for my weekly podcast – What's Happening, UK? – where I take a quick look at what's going on around the UK. I was talking about the Lewes Bonfire Night celebrations last Monday, so on Friday I headed down to Lewes in Sussex to see for myself. As I told you last week, it's the biggest Bonfire Night celebration in the country and it takes place on 5th November, naturally. Five thousand local people take part and around 80,000 visitors come to watch every year!
It's all about saving the life of the king back in the early 17th century. Some people wanted to kill him and planned to blow up the Houses of Parliament while he was giving a speech there. Luckily, the king's men caught them before they blew everything up. To celebrate, we have bonfires, and that's why I was in Lewes. I got there early to find a good place to see it all. The evening began with a huge parade of locals through Lewes High Street. They were all dressed up in costumes and many people were carrying torches. There were marching bands, too, playing traditional music. Then they split into groups and each group went to a different part of the town, where they had their own bonfire set up. They all let off fireworks and then set the bonfires alight. There were seven different bonfires and fireworks displays in a town of just over 17,000 people, so you can imagine all the noise and lights. It was amazing! There were also food stalls for when spectators got hungry, with all the usual Bonfire Night food, including toffee apples and burgers. I had a delicious baked potato with cheese.
I had the time of my life at the Lewes Bonfire Night and I'm definitely going again next year! It's like nothing else I've ever seen in the UK, and it's a must for anyone who loves bonfires and fireworks.
Now, next weekend has some interesting events…

UNIT 3 – Adventures

3c – Exercise 2 (p. 24)

1
Woman: Are you going on the trip to the island next weekend?
Man: No, I don't think so.
Woman: It's very expensive, isn't it? £140 for one day!
Man: It's not unreasonable – it includes travel, lunch and dinner. Imagine how much you would pay for a plane ticket!
Woman: Good point. Travelling by ferry takes longer, but it's cheaper.
Man: Yes, but it's no good if you get seasick like me!
Woman: Oh dear. So that's the reason you're not coming.

2
Man: How was California, Katie?
Woman: Oh, it was great! But the time difference is confusing me now that I'm back in the UK. You travel a lot, don't you? Have you got any tips? Should I take a nap or something?
Man: No, you need to stay awake during the day and follow your usual routine. In the evening, don't watch TV or check your phone for an hour before you go to bed.
Woman: Right. Anything else?
Man: Yes. Make your room as dark as possible, and avoid drinks with caffeine in them, like cola or coffee. If you want a warm drink, try chamomile tea. It's calming and relaxing.

3
Man: Oh, Lucy, are you OK? What happened to your hand?
Woman: Oh, it's so silly. I was camping in the forest while I was in the USA, and one day I was lighting the campfire when I burnt myself. It was quite a bad burn and very painful.
Man: What did you do? Did you see a doctor?
Woman: Not at first. I had some cream with me, so I put that on, but it didn't help. So I ended up going to hospital because I was scared of an infection.
Man: How awful!

Student's Book Audioscripts

Voman: I know! Well, they gave me antibiotics and the edness and pain have gone. The burn still looks bad, though 's nothing like it was! The doctor said it will be all better in hree weeks!

4

nd in other news, a group of young men avoided a tragedy his morning at the Great Barrier Reef, when one of them was tung by a jellyfish. The incident happened while they were diving nd the young man in question went into shock. He would have rowned if his friends hadn't seen him and brought him back to he boat, where he quickly recovered. Jellyfish sting both tourists nd locals every year in this area, and some even die. So divers hould be extra careful, especially at this time of year.

xercise 10 (p. 25)

A Perfect Storm

was a beautiful January morning, and Emma and her guide, liver, were out husky sledding. The sky was cloudy and grey, but mma had a flask of hot chocolate in her coat pocket, and a big mile on her face.

hey had been sledding for almost two hours when they decided o take a break. Suddenly, snow started falling heavily. Before long, hey couldn't see a thing, and when they tried to move the sled, mma slipped and hurt her ankle. Emma started to panic, but liver had an idea. "We need to make a shelter in the snow," he aid, so they quickly dug a hole and climbed in.

was terrifying to listen to the storm raging around them, but their helter kept them safe, and they stayed warm by drinking hot hocolate from Emma's flask. Once the storm had finally stopped, liver took Emma to the nearest hospital and the doctors checked er ankle. Thankfully, she hadn't broken it – just twisted it.

mma felt relieved that she had been with Oliver. He had stayed alm and kept them both safe in the storm.

UNIT 4 – There's no place like home!

4c – Exercise 3 (p. 34)

ood morning, Mr Davies. This is Sarah Henderson from Star state Agents. I'm sorry I wasn't able to reach you on the hone, but I think I've found just the house you're looking for. saw it this morning and thought of you immediately! I've a eeling it's going to sell very quickly. So, if you're interested, ve should make an appointment to see it straightaway!

ou asked for somewhere near Bristol city centre and this ouse is. It's a cosy terraced property on Barony Street, number 4, to be exact. It's a nice quiet location and the centre is just 15-minute walk away. Barony Street is also on a regular bus oute into the city, which makes it very convenient.

s for the house itself, it's in excellent condition. In fact, it's ust been repainted. Downstairs there's an open-plan living oom and kitchen and upstairs are two bedrooms, a double and a single. The double has its own en-suite bathroom but there's also a separate bathroom with a bath; the owner has just fitted a walk-in shower in there, too.

There's gas-fired central heating throughout the house, and outside you'd have a mature garden both back and front.

Fortunately, there's no chain; the property is available for the buyer to move in immediately and it's going at a very good price, just £250,000. So, as I say, if you're interested, can you please get back to me as soon as possible so that we can arrange a viewing? Thank you.

UNIT 5 – Let's talk

5c – Exercise 3a (p. 42)

Speaker 1

I think textspeak is great! I use it all the time – it's much faster than using full sentences. My friends and I chat online a lot, so we're pretty fluent in it. Of course, there are some words that everyone knows, like "LOL" or "BRB", but there are others that are less common, like "PAW", which means "parents are watching". You can even make up your abbreviations and use them with your close friends. It's like a kind of secret code!

Speaker 2

As a teacher, I truly believe that textspeak is destroying the younger generation's ability to write decent English. They're terrible at spelling, and don't even get me started on their punctuation! I know things like spellcheck and predictive text are also to blame, but I think textspeak is having the biggest impact. Some of my students have even used it in their essays! Kids spend so much time on their phones these days, they don't realise that textspeak isn't appropriate for every situation.

Speaker 3

I think there are some advantages to textspeak, but that it has a time and a place. I don't like it when people say things like "LOL", rather than just laughing – we're not robots, after all! Also, if someone uses too many abbreviations it can be confusing, especially if, like me, you don't know what all of them mean. I do use simple abbreviations like "C U soon" in text messages or if I'm chatting to friends online, mainly because it saves time.

Speaker 4

I believe that textspeak is a lot more sophisticated than people give it credit for. Think about it, in a short space of time, a whole new language has been invented and is being used all over the world. Textspeak doesn't just shorten things, it can actually express feelings and make words more meaningful. This is important because, with written communication, we don't have things like body language, tone of voice and facial expressions to help us.

Student's Book Audioscripts

UNIT 6 – Challenges

6c – Exercise 3 (p. 50)

Speaker 1
I work as a nurse in a busy hospital. It's a very demanding job that often leaves me feeling exhausted. So, looking on the bright side of things is really important. If I didn't have that work value, I probably wouldn't survive in the job. And it's the same for the other nurses I work with. We all have our cups half full rather than half empty, as they say. I've been like this since my first day on the job, and I don't think my attitude will change any time soon.

Speaker 2
When I started at the company where I work now, I didn't value teamwork as much as I do now. Back then, I didn't think I needed help to complete my tasks – and I didn't want help either. I guess I was a bit arrogant – I thought the best way to do a task is to do it yourself. My boss, though, soon taught me to think otherwise. Soon, I began to realise how important it is to work as a team – using the skills of a number of different people to complete a task.

Speaker 3
I work as a sales assistant in a clothes shop. I enjoy the work, but sometimes the shop is really quiet, especially at the beginning of the week. That doesn't really suit me, because I like to be busy when I'm supposed to be working. My colleagues don't have the same problem – they happily chat to each other when there aren't any customers in the shop – but I tidy up the clothes or sweep the floors. I don't feel comfortable just sitting around doing nothing.

Speaker 4
At the company where I work, we're given a lot of trust to make important decisions on our own. It's something that the owner of the company values very highly. She wants staff members to be able to do their jobs well without having to ask their managers for advice at every step. It's something that I and all my colleagues really like. And I think it helps the company, too. When your boss trusts you, you definitely feel like working hard for her.

Speaker 5
I work in an office for an insurance company. I quite like my job, although my office manager really gets on my nerves sometimes. For one, we are given very little freedom to make decisions on our own – everything has to pass through him. But the most annoying thing is the focus he puts on punctuality. For example, he gets very cross with people when they arrive late in the morning, but then doesn't care if we don't show any effort to work well as a team.

UNIT 7 – High-tech

7c – Exercise 3 (p. 60)

1 ***F:*** What are you doing? Come on – the taxi's here and it's waiting for us!
M: Hang on! I'm just looking for a song.
F: It's always the same with you. You need to be listenin to something wherever you are, whatever you'r doing – running in the park, in the street – anywhere!

2 ***M:*** Different laptop, Tracey?
F: Yes, it is.
M: It's like the one Jake had, isn't it? You know, the on he bought online.
F: It's like it because it's the same one. He saw a bette model in an electrical shop and knew I was lookin for one so he sold me his.
M: That's Jake for you. He's never happy unless he's go the latest and the best.

3 ***F:*** Can you help me with this tablet?
M: What's wrong with it? Don't tell me it won't connec to the Wi-Fi again. It's been doing that a lot recentl Try turning it off and on again.
F: I would if I could, but it won't even turn on. I though it might be the battery, so I plugged it in and it's bee charging for over an hour.
M: Mmm, looks like we'll have to take it to be repaire then.

4 ***M:*** How are you doing with that new fitness app, Kelly It cost a fortune, didn't it?
F: It did, but I think I may have made a mistake i getting it.
M: Why's that? Is it not working well? I've heard the don't always give a correct reading.
F: I don't know about that. My problem is that ever time I look at it, I try to do another workout. To b honest, I'm exhausted, but at least I'm feeling a lc healthier.

Exercise 10b (p. 61)

A: What are you doing?
B: I'm playing Chicken Flight, that new mobile gaming app. It's really fun. It really helps pass the time, for example, when I'm travelling to work on the bus.
A: I don't really like mobile gaming apps. In my opinion, they don't look good on the phone's screen. Everything is too small and some doctors say that if you play for too long you can get headaches. I much prefer to do my gaming on my 55-inch TV at home.
B: I see what you mean, but they're not like the expensive games you have at home. For one thing, a lot of them are free. You just download them and start to play. I could play this game all day.
A: No, you couldn't. These gaming apps use up a lot of battery and if you play for too long, you might find your phone stops working halfway through the day.
B: I don't usually play that much. Anyway, it seems to me that nothing is going to change your mind – you just don't like mobile gaming apps.

A: You might be right. I'll stick to my games console and you carry on playing on your phone.

UNIT 8 – Better societies

8c – Exercises 3 & 5 (p. 68)

M: Good morning! Today on Global Issues we're going to hear from Claire Franklin, the owner of Earth, Sky, Beauty, a company that makes natural skincare products. Claire, you're pretty successful these days, but it hasn't always been so easy, has it?

F: No. I attended school and then college, and I always got good grades, but I had no idea what I wanted to do. I finished college during the economic crisis and I couldn't find work anywhere – not even in local shops. No one was hiring. On top of that, I lost my weekend job because the supermarket I worked at closed down. I found myself without work, and that was something I'd never expected.

M: So did you have to rely on your parents to help you?

F: Well, actually, I haven't seen my dad for a really long time. I live with my mum, but she struggles with depression and she's unable to work. I help look after her.

M: That's a lot of responsibility.

F: Yes, it is. I couldn't rely on Mum to pay the bills, buy and cook food, or pay the rent, so I was responsible for all that. Without a job, it was hard to make ends meet. All we had to live on were state benefits, and that's not much.

M: You must have felt under a lot of pressure.

F: I did. I felt anxious all the time. I started having trouble sleeping at night. Then I started feeling like my heart was racing, even when I was sitting still, so I went to the doctor. He told me I was suffering from stress. The doctor advised me to try therapy. I had a few sessions with a therapist, and she was brilliant. She suggested I try online learning.

M: What did you study?

F: I did several courses on how to make natural skincare products. Then I started selling my products at local markets, and finally I set up my own website. Now, I make a living from online sales.

M: That's great news, Claire! What a success story! But it sounds like you did all this yourself. Do you feel like the system let you down?

F: Well, maybe a little bit.

M: So do you think the solution is to put more funds into education?

F: Not really. Like I said earlier, I was a good student, but that didn't prepare me for life after college. I think what we need right now are job creation schemes, because there just isn't enough work for young people. I believe most people aren't unemployed because they aren't smart or talented enough, or because they don't have enough qualifications: the problem is getting access to the right jobs. I also think the government should give financial help to start-ups, to make it easier for people to open their own businesses.

M: That's an interesting idea. Well, I'm afraid that's all we've got time for now. Thanks for coming on the show today, Claire. It's been a pleasure talking to you, and best of luck with the business.

F: Thank you. It's been a pleasure to be here.

UNIT 9 – Live & Learn

9c – Exercise 3 (p. 76)

1 ***A:*** Hi, Bill. I heard you're going on a summer course to learn French in Marseilles. You must be really looking forward to it!

B: Not really. I really wish I hadn't applied, to be honest.

A: Why? Are you worried that you'll miss your family?

B: No, it's not that. I just think that I'll be the weakest student on the course. I won't be able to understand anything!

A: Oh, come on! I'm sure there'll be lots of other people who are at your level.

B: Well, I hope you're right.

2 ***A:*** Hi, Laura, do you fancy going to the cinema later?

B: I can't. I've got a paper to finish for the online Psychology course I'm doing.

A: Wow, really! But why are you doing an online course? Is it cheaper than going to classes at a local college?

B: No, it's about the same price, but I really like the fact that I can study whenever I want.

A: Oh, yes, I suppose that's important when you work nine to five every day.

3 Now, before you leave, I want to tell you all something. Don't worry, I'm not going to give you more reading before the next lecture. I just wanted to let you know that Professor Banks, our head of department, has organised for Room 3B to be used as a reading room from now on. What does that mean? Well, obviously you can study there and do your assignments, but you can also use the room to read reference books from the department library. It'll be open every day between 8 am and 7 pm.

4 ***A:*** So, Karen, what do you think about our new professor, Dr Pavlov?

B: Well, he's extremely strict, isn't he?

A: What do you mean? He doesn't let us use our phones in the lecture hall, but that's totally understandable. I actually think he's quite nice – and I love how he uses technology in the lectures.

Student's Book Audioscripts

B: You're right there, it really brings them alive – but what about his accent? I can't make out what he's saying sometimes.

A: Really? It doesn't bother me.

UNIT 10 – Green minds

10c – Exercise 3 (p. 86)

Speaker 1

I started growing my own vegetables when I moved into my new house about two years ago. To begin with, it was just a way to get some exercise, but now I have fresh food every day and I save money from not buying from the supermarkets. The other good thing about that is that I don't have all the unnecessary plastic packaging they use either.

Speaker 2

All those bills from the electricity company! It just got so annoying. They seemed to get bigger and bigger every year. At one point, I'd had enough and I decided to install solar panels. It's been very successful. They generate so much energy that I have more electricity than I need. Oh, and I don't have to pay those huge bills every month.

Speaker 3

It used to take me an hour to get to work and most of it I was stuck in traffic jams. I was sitting at the traffic lights one day, when a cyclist went past. That's the way to travel, I thought. I bought myself a bike and now I get to work in ten minutes. There are other benefits that I didn't think of, too. I feel healthier, I'm saving money and I'm not polluting the air.

Speaker 4

I used to go to the local park for a walk in the fresh air every day, but the council decided to sell it to local developers – new houses, you see. Good idea for people, but a terrible idea for all the animals that lived there and lost their natural habitats. There were birds, foxes, squirrels and I even saw a badger once. I often wonder what happened to them all.

UNIT 11 – Buying, buying, bought!

11c – Exercise 3 (p. 94)

Thank you for inviting me on *It's Your Money*, David. I know a lot of people experience difficulty returning purchases they have bought online, so today I'd like to tell listeners about our returns policy at Home For You Stores and explain to them how we take the worry and hassle out of sending something back.
First of all, it's not just about faulty goods. Home For You understands that sometimes a customer simply changes their mind a week after buying something, deciding they don't want the product after all. You can cancel your order up to 15 days after it has been delivered to you and get a full refund within 2 days.
There are three ways of returning purchased goods. Many people simply take their item back to the nearest Home Fo You store. But that's not always possible. A customer may live a long distance from a store, or others are at work during our opening hours, which are from 9 am to 8 pm Monday to Friday, closing two hours earlier on Saturday at 6 pm.
That brings me to pick-up points. Home For You has 70 o these all over the country. You can check the nearest one to you on the Pick-up Points page of our website and bring your item there. For small parcels of up to 10 kilos and nc bigger than 50 centimetres square, we offer a free collection service.
For a big, heavy items that are unsuitable for pick-up points or you cannot return to a store, we can come and collec them from your home. There is a small charge of fifteen pounds for this, which will be deducted from the refund we give you.
Whichever method you use, there are three things you wi need: your order confirmation email, your delivery receip and the payment card that you used to buy the item. And please remember that the goods you return must be in new undamaged condition.
Now, in the case of faulty goods, things are a little different ..

UNIT 12 – Health is Wealth

12a – Exercise 9 (p. 99)

I'm a university student studying Food Science, and a lot c the students on my course think that cultured meat is the future of food. I've heard about all of the pros, but I'm nc so sure it will be as successful or as positive for humanity a people think. Firstly, if people started eating a lot of culture meat, millions of people around the world would lose thei jobs, especially farmers. Farmers don't usually have universit degrees, so they would find it difficult to get other work. Alsc producing cultured meat is very expensive these days, anc despite what they might hope, I don't think scientists wi ever be able to make cultured meat affordable for ordinar people. And lastly, should we really be encouraging people to eat cultured meat anyway? We shouldn't forget that mea is not very healthy. For example, red meat contains a lot c saturated fat. By providing people with another source c meat, we are encouraging them to follow an unhealthy diet Instead, we should be encouraging people to become vegan or vegetarians. So, all in all, I really don't think cultured meat i as positive as most people think it is.

12c – Exercise 2 (p. 102)

Speaker 1

Since the school year started, I've put on quite a bit o weight, mainly because of fizzy drinks. I didn't use to drink them, but I started buying one straight after schoc each day, and drinking it on my walk home. Now, I'm not obese, but last week my doctor advised me to lose some weight. So, the first thing I did was eliminate fizzy drinks from my diet. Already, I feel more energetic, and I'm sure I'll start losing weight quite soon.

Speaker 2

A few weeks ago, I had a bit of a crisis. First, I became really stressed about my end-of-term exams, and then I had a terrible argument with my best friend. I became quite depressed, so my sister advised me to see a doctor. At first, I refused – after all, there was nothing wrong with me physically – but I decided to go in the end. And I'm so glad I did. Now, I feel much better and I'm learning ways to take care of my mental health.

Speaker 3

For some reason, I've never had a problem with my weight. It's the same with my brother – we eat quite unhealthily, but don't put on any weight. So, I've never felt the need to change my diet or start exercising – I just thought that because I was thin, I was healthy. Recently, though, I had some medical tests and got a huge shock – my doctor said I had dangerously high blood pressure! Now, I'm changing my ways, and I'm glad it's not too late!

Speaker 4

I have a really busy daily schedule. Apart from going to school and doing homework, I also have a part-time job in a café. And to make matters worse, I often stay up late watching TV. It means, I usually get just six hours of sleep each night, which I realise is really bad for me. Experts say a lack of sleep can increase the risk of heart disease and can even cause memory loss. But I find it impossible to break the habit. After a long day, I feel the need to give myself some time to relax before I go to bed.

CLIL A– PSHE

Exercise 1b (p. 108)

Road safety is the responsibility of each and every one of us. Whether we are drivers, bikers or pedestrians, we all have a duty to keep ourselves and each other safe. Today, I'd like to mention one or two of the most important points that people often forget.

What about using our mobiles when we drive? This is extremely dangerous and causes many accidents. If the police catch you, you'll get a fine – even if the car is not moving. Phoning while stuck in traffic or waiting for the traffic lights to change still counts as an offence. You have to park your vehicle and switch off your engine first!

And let's not forget about speed limits. They are there to protect us, of course, but don't think that the upper limit you see on the sign is always OK. Maybe the weather is very bad or the road is extremely busy. If that's the case, we may have to slow right down in order to be safe.

Age also plays a role in road safety. I know some of you may already drive or be thinking of taking your driving test. Unfortunately, statistics show that drivers in the youngest age bracket are more likely to crash due to lack of experience – so I'd like you to take special care!

And you may think more accidents take place on big main roads or in the heart of town, but you'd be wrong. The countryside is where drivers are more relaxed because there is less traffic; therefore, they're often less careful than they should be.

Motorbikers are in even more danger than drivers because they are less protected. That's why it's illegal not to wear your crash helmet. Of course, it also makes sense to spend some money on tough footwear and clothes that motorists can see in the dark. It could save you from a nasty injury or worse.

Have you ever seen a cyclist ride through a stop sign at a junction? Many cyclists seem to think that what applies to cars doesn't apply to them, but that's wrong. Even if there seems to be no traffic about, the law requires you to come to a full stop and check everything is clear before you move on.

And that brings me to pedestrians. A lot of accidents are caused because they are too lazy to go to a proper crossing when they want to get to the other side of the road! They just step off the pavement wherever suits them. Using a zebra crossing is by far the safest way, as motorists are obliged by law to stop the moment the pedestrian steps onto the crossing.

We should always be aware of our surroundings and pay attention to what is going on around us. So if you are going to use your phone to make or receive a call while walking, use hands-free and never try and cross the road when you are reading, or even worse, sending messages – that's really asking for trouble. If you are listening to music on the go, don't have the volume too high so you can still listen for car horns and sirens.

Now let's look at some interesting road safety facts …

Evaluations

Formative Evaluation Chart

Name of game/activity: ....

Aim of game/activity: ....

Unit: .... Course: ....

Students' names:		Mark and comments
1		
2		
3		
4		
5		
6		
7		
8		
9		
10		
11		
12		
13		
14		
15		
16		
17		
18		
19		
20		
21		
22		
23		
24		
25		

Cumulative Evaluation

Student's Self Assessment Forms

CODE			
**** Excellent	*** Very Good	** OK	* Not Very Good

Student's Self Assessment Form

UNIT 1

Go through Unit 1 and find examples of the following. Use the code to evaluate yourself.	
• use words/phrases related to map symbols	
• use words/phrases related to road signs	
• understand texts related to travel & geographical features	
• listen to and understand dialogues related to asking for/giving directions	
• research & prepare a podcast	
• ask for & give directions	
• practise intonation using discourse markers	
• research & present top tours	

Go through the corrected writing tasks. Use the code to evaluate yourself.	
• write a flyer with accurate spelling, punctuation & layout	
• write a message giving news	
• write a webpage section	

CODE			
****** Excellent**	***** Very Good**	**** OK**	*** Not Very Good**

Student's Self Assessment Form

UNIT 2

Go through Unit 2 and find examples of the following. Use the code to evaluate yourself.	
• use words/phrases related to festivities	
• use words/phrases related to types of holidays	
• use words/phrases related to UK celebrations & customs	
• understand texts related to legends & festivals	
• listen to and understand narrations related to experiences	
• narrate events	
• describe past habits	
• describe celebrations	
• narrate a story	
• describe an event	
• use stress-shift	
• research & present superstitions and/or sayings about good/bad luck	

Go through the corrected writing tasks. Use the code to evaluate yourself.	
• research & write an article about a legend	
• write a summary of a legend	
• analyse a task	
• write an email about a celebration you attended with accurate spelling, punctuation & layout	
• recommend a celebration	

CODE			
****** Excellent**	***** Very Good**	**** OK**	*** Not Very Good**

Student's Self Assessment Form

UNIT 3

Go through Unit 3 and find examples of the following. Use the code to evaluate yourself.	
• use words/phrases related to adventure activities	
• use words/phrases related to types of holidays & travel disasters	
• understand texts related to adventure activities	
• listen to and understand dialogues related to travel problems	
• describe an experience	
• express interest & shock	
• use appropriate sentence stress	

Go through the corrected writing tasks. Use the code to evaluate yourself.	
• research & write a text about an adventure activity	
• expand sentences in narratives	
• analyse a task	
• write a short story with accurate spelling, punctuation & layout	
• research and write a review about outdoor activity breaks	

CODE			
**** Excellent	*** Very Good	** OK	* Not Very Good

Student's Self Assessment Form

Values A – Public Speaking Skills A

Go through Values A – Public Speaking Skills A and find examples of the following. Use the code to evaluate yourself.	
• understand texts related to curiosity	
• describe an experience	
• use a personal anecdote in presentations	
• research & give a presentation giving advice	

CODE			
****** Excellent**	***** Very Good**	**** OK**	*** Not Very Good**

Student's Self Assessment Form

UNIT 4

Go through Unit 4 and find examples of the following. Use the code to evaluate yourself.	
• use words/phrases related to types of houses	
• use words/phrases related to accommodation	
• understand texts related to types of houses	
• compare two neighbourhoods	
• narrate a story	
• listen to and understand a voicemail about a house for sale	
• express opinion	
• express satisfaction/dissatisfaction	
• use rising/falling intonation to express feelings	
• design & present an unusual house	
• research & prepare a 2-minute video or a digital presentation about neighbourhoods	

Go through the corrected writing tasks. Use the code to evaluate yourself.	
• write an advert for a home exchange	
• use advertising language	

CODE			
**** Excellent	*** Very Good	** OK	* Not Very Good

Student's Self Assessment Form

UNIT 5

Go through Unit 5 and find examples of the following. Use the code to evaluate yourself.	
• use words/phrases related to ways to communicate	
• use words/phrases related to textspeak	
• understand texts related to communication & body language	
• describe future plans	
• listen to and understand monologues related to textspeak	
• express an opinion	
• agree/disagree & express doubt	
• express feelings	
• discuss ways to communicate	
• research & have a debate on communication	
• research & give a presentation about gestures & body language	

Go through the corrected writing tasks. Use the code to evaluate yourself.	
• analyse a task	
• use topic/supporting sentences in main body paragraphs in essays	
• write a for-and-against essay with accurate spelling, punctuation & layout	

CODE			
****** Excellent**	***** Very Good**	**** OK**	*** Not Very Good**

Student's Self Assessment Form

UNIT 6

Go through Unit 6 and find examples of the following. Use the code to evaluate yourself.	
• use words/phrases related to jobs	
• use words/phrases related to work values	
• understand texts related to work	
• describe rules	
• make deductions	
• express preferences	
• express opinion	
• listen to and understand monologues related to work values	
• congratulate	
• use reduced pronunciation in modal verbs	
• compare office etiquette	
• research & give a presentation on office etiquette	

Go through the corrected writing tasks. Use the code to evaluate yourself.	
• write a short text describing your life	
• analyse a task	
• use informal or semi-formal style in emails	
• write an email of congratulations with accurate spelling, punctuation & layout	

CODE			
**** Excellent	*** Very Good	** OK	* Not Very Good

Student's Self Assessment Form

Values B – Public Speaking Skills B

Go through Values B – Public Speaking Skills B and find examples of the following. Use the code to evaluate yourself.	
• predict content of text	
• express preference	
• understand texts related to productivity	
• research & write a text about a person	
• use questions in presentations	
• research & give an election speech	

CODE			
****** Excellent**	***** Very Good**	**** OK**	*** Not Very Good**

Student's Self Assessment Form

UNIT 7

Go through Unit 7 and find examples of the following. Use the code to evaluate yourself.	
• use words/phrases related to technology	
• use words/phrases related to apps	
• understand texts related to technology & science festivals	
• predict content of a text	
• listen to and understand monologues/dialogues related to apps	
• research & have a class debate	
• listen to & keep notes	
• describe preparations for a tech fair	
• give a report about a science fair	
• express opinion-agreement/disagreement	
• use word junctures (vowel to vowel) while speaking	
• research & have a press conference	

Go through the corrected writing tasks. Use the code to evaluate yourself.	
• write a quiz using the passive	
• use formal impersonal style	
• use formal linking words/phrases	
• analyse a task	
• write an opinion essay with accurate spelling, punctuation & layout	

CODE			
****** Excellent**	***** Very Good**	**** OK**	*** Not Very Good**

Student's Self Assessment Form

UNIT 8

Go through Unit 8 and find examples of the following. Use the code to evaluate yourself.	
• use words/phrases related to world problems	
• use words/phrases related to social problems	
• understand texts related to world problems	
• predict content of a text	
• make suggestions	
• describe situations likely/unlikely to happen	
• express wishes	
• listen to and understand an interview	
• make suggestions – agree/disagree	
• pronounce English diphthongs	
• brainstorm for ideas	
• research & present a non-profit organisation	

Go through the corrected writing tasks. Use the code to evaluate yourself.	
• write a diary entry	
• support suggestions	
• analyse a task	
• write an article suggesting solutions to a problem with accurate spelling, punctuation & layout	

CODE			
****** Excellent**	***** Very Good**	**** OK**	*** Not Very Good**

Student's Self Assessment Form

UNIT 9

Go through Unit 9 and find examples of the following. Use the code to evaluate yourself.	
• use words/phrases related to university	
• understand texts related to education	
• listen to and understand monologues/dialogues related to education	
• discuss pros & cons	
• compare types of education	
• design & present an educational AR app	
• ask for information	
• use appropriate intonation in follow-up questions	

Go through the corrected writing tasks. Use the code to evaluate yourself.	
• use formal style in emails	
• write an email asking for information with accurate spelling, punctuation & layout	
• research & write an article about an educational foundation	

CODE			
****** Excellent**	***** Very Good**	**** OK**	*** Not Very Good**

Student's Self Assessment Form

Values C – Public Speaking Skills C

Go through Values C – Public Speaking Skills C and find examples of the following. Use the code to evaluate yourself.	
• understand texts related to how to show compassion	
• express opinion	
• emphasise key moments in public speaking	
• give an award speech	

CODE			
**** Excellent	*** Very Good	** OK	* Not Very Good

Student's Self Assessment Form

UNIT 10

Go through Unit 10 and find examples of the following. Use the code to evaluate yourself.	
• use words/phrases related to environmental problems	
• use words/phrases related to carbon footprints	
• understand texts related to the environment	
• report people's questions	
• listen to and understand monologues about the environment	
• make proposals – agree/disagree	
• stress prepositions	
• research & present an eco-friendly event	

Go through the corrected writing tasks. Use the code to evaluate yourself.	
• use appropriate layout & style in proposals	
• match suggestions with reasons/examples	
• write a proposal using appropriate spelling, punctuation & layout	

CODE			
**** Excellent	*** Very Good	** OK	* Not Very Good

Student's Self Assessment Form

UNIT 11

Go through Unit 11 and find examples of the following. Use the code to evaluate yourself.	
• use words/phrases related to marketing & advertising	
• use words/phrases related to online shopping & customer complaints	
• understand texts related to shopping	
• decide on what to buy for a dinner event	
• listen to and understand an interview about how to return things bought online	
• make a complaint about a product	
• use appropriate intonation in exclamations	

Go through the corrected writing tasks. Use the code to evaluate yourself.	
• write an outline for an advert	
• use mild language in complaint forms	
• write a complaint form with accurate spelling, punctuation & layout	
• research & write an article about a popular sales period	

CODE			
**** Excellent	*** Very Good	** OK	* Not Very Good

Student's Self Assessment Form

UNIT 12

Go through Unit 12 and find examples of the following. Use the code to evaluate yourself.	
• use words/phrases related to food	
• understand texts related to healthy living	
• listen to and understand monologues related to teen health	
• express purpose, reason or result	
• express concession	
• ask for/give advice	
• use appropriate intonation in direct/indirect questions	
• have a class debate	
• research and give a presentation about foods of the future	

Go through the corrected writing tasks. Use the code to evaluate yourself.	
• use appropriate style and layout in forum entries	
• analyse a task	
• brainstorm for ideas	
• write a forum post with accurate spelling, punctuation & layout	
• research and write an article about a healthcare system	

CODE			
****** Excellent**	***** Very Good**	**** OK**	*** Not Very Good**

Student's Self Assessment Form

Values D – Public Speaking Skills D

Go through Values D – Public Speaking Skills D and find examples of the following. Use the code to evaluate yourself.	
• understand texts related to commitment	
• present a lifestyle plan	
• identify types of speech	
• use non-verbal communication in public speaking	
• give a speech giving advice using non-verbal communication	

Progress Report Cards

Progress Report Card

.... (name) can:			**Unit 1**
	very well	**OK**	**not very well**
use words/phrases related to map symbols			
use words/phrases related to road signs			
understand texts related to travel & geographical features			
listen to and understand dialogues related to asking for/giving directions			
research & prepare a podcast			
ask for & give directions			
practise intonation using discourse markers			
research & present top tours			
write a flyer with accurate spelling, punctuation & layout			
write a message giving news			
write a webpage section			

Progress Report Card

.... (name) can:			**Unit 2**
	very well	**OK**	**not very well**
use words/phrases related to festivities			
use words/phrases related to types of holidays			
use words/phrases related to UK celebrations & customs			
understand texts related to legends & festivals			
listen to and understand narrations related to experiences			
narrate events			
describe past habits			
describe celebrations			
narrate a story			
describe an event			
use stress-shift			
research & present superstitions and/or sayings about good/bad luck			
research & write an article about a legend			
write a summary of a legend			
analyse a task			
write an email about a celebration one attended with accurate spelling, punctuation & layout			
recommend a celebration			

Progress Report Card

.... (name) can:			Unit 3
	very well	OK	not very well
use words/phrases related to adventure activities			
use words/phrases related to types of holidays & travel disasters			
understand texts related to adventure activities			
listen to and understand dialogues related to travel problems			
describe an experience			
express interest & shock			
use appropriate sentence stress			
research & write a text about an adventure activity			
expand sentences in narratives			
analyse a task			
write a story with accurate spelling, punctuation & layout			
research and write a review about outdoor activity breaks			

Progress Report Card

.... (name) can:	Values A – Public Speaking Skills A		
	very well	OK	not very well
understand texts related to curiosity			
describe an experience			
use a personal anecdote in presentations			
research & give a presentation giving advice			

Progress Report Card

.... (name) can:			Unit 4
	very well	OK	not very well
use words/phrases related to types of houses			
use words/phrases related to accommodation			
understand texts related to types of houses			
compare two neighbourhoods			
narrate a story			
listen to and understand a voicemail about a house for sale			
express opinion			
express satisfaction/dissatisfaction			
use rising/falling intonation to express feelings			
design & present an unusual house			
research & prepare a 2-minute video or a digital presentation about neighbourhoods			
write an advert for a home exchange			
use advertising language			

Progress Report Card

.... (name) can:			Unit 5
	very well	OK	not very well
use words/phrases related to ways to communicate			
use words/phrases related to textspeak			
understand texts related to communication & body language			
describe future plans			
listen to and understand monologues related to textspeak			
express an opinion			
agree/disagree & express doubt			
express feelings			
discuss ways to communicate			
research & have a debate on communication			
research & give a presentation about gestures & body language			
analyse a task			
use topic/supporting sentences in main body paragraphs in essays			
write a for-and-against essay with accurate spelling, punctuation & layout			

Progress Report Card

.... (name) can:			Unit 6
	very well	OK	not very well
use words/phrases related to jobs			
use words/phrases related to work values			
understand texts related to work			
describe rules			
make deductions			
express preferences			
express opinion			
listen to and understand monologues related to work values			
congratulate			
use reduced pronunciation in modal verbs			
compare office etiquette			
research & give a presentation on office etiquette			
write a short text describing one's life			
use informal or semi-formal style in emails			
analyse a task			
write an email of congratulations with accurate spelling, punctuation & layout			

Progress Report Card

.... (name) can:	Values B – Public Speaking Skills B		
	very well	OK	not very well
predict content of text			
express preference			
understand texts related to productivity			
research & write a text about a person			
use questions in presentations			
research & give an election speech			

Progress Report Card

.... (name) can:			Unit 7
	very well	OK	not very well
use words/phrases related to technology			
use words/phrases related to apps			
understand texts related to technology & science festivals			
predict content of a text			
listen to and understand monologues/dialogues related to apps			
research & have a class debate			
listen to & keep notes			
describe preparations for a tech fair			
give a report about a science fair			
express opinion-agreement/disagreement			
use word junctures (vowel to vowel) while speaking			
research & have a press conference			
write a quiz using the passive			
use formal impersonal style			
use formal linking words/phrases			
analyse a task			
write an opinion essay with accurate spelling, punctuation & layout			

Progress Report Card

.... (name) can:			Unit 8
	very well	OK	not very well
use words/phrases related to world problems			
use words/phrases related to social problems			
understand texts related to world problems			
predict content of a text			
make suggestions			
describe situations likely/unlikely to happen			
express wishes			
listen to and understand an interview			
make suggestions – agree/disagree			
pronounce English diphthongs			
brainstorm for ideas			
research & present a non-profit organisation			
write a diary entry			
support suggestions			
analyse a task			
write an article suggesting solutions to a problem with accurate spelling, punctuation & layout			

Progress Report Card

.... (name) can:			Unit 9
	very well	OK	not very well
use words/phrases related to university			
understand texts related to education			
listen to and understand monologues/dialogues related to education			
discuss pros & cons			
compare types of education			
design & present an educational AR app			
ask for information			
use appropriate intonation in follow-up questions			
use formal style in emails			
write an email asking for information with accurate spelling, punctuation & layout			
research & write an article about an educational foundation			

Progress Report Card

.... (name) can:	**Values C – Public Speaking Skills C**		
	very well	**OK**	**not very well**
understand texts related to how to show compassion			
express opinion			
emphasise key moments in public speaking			
give an award speech			

Progress Report Card

.... (name) can:			**Unit 10**
	very well	**OK**	**not very well**
use words/phrases related to environmental problems			
use words/phrases related to carbon footprints			
understand texts related to the environment			
report people's questions			
listen to and understand monologues about the environment			
make proposals – agree/disagree			
stress prepositions			
research & present an eco-friendly event			
use appropriate layout & style in proposals			
match suggestions with reasons/examples			
write a proposal using appropriate spelling, punctuation & layout			

Progress Report Card

.... (name) can:			Unit 11
	very well	OK	not very well
use words/phrases related to marketing & advertising			
use words/phrases related to online shopping & customer complaints			
understand texts related to shopping			
decide on what to buy for a dinner event			
listen to and understand an interview about how to return things bought online			
make a complaint about a product			
use appropriate intonation in exclamations			
write an outline for an advert			
use mild language in complaint forms			
write a complaint form with accurate spelling, punctuation & layout			
research & write an article about a popular sales period			

Progress Report Card

.... (name) can:			Unit 12
	very well	OK	not very well
use words/phrases related to food			
understand texts related to healthy living			
listen to and understand a monologues related to teen health			
express purpose, reason or result			
express concession			
ask for/give advice			
use appropriate intonation in direct/indirect questions			
have a class debate			
research and give a presentation about foods of the future			
use appropriate style and layout in forum entries			
analyse a task			
brainstorm for ideas			
write a forum post with accurate spelling, punctuation & layout			
research and write an article about a healthcare system			

Progress Report Card

.... (name) can:	Values D – Public Speaking Skills D		
	very well	OK	not very well
understand texts related to commitment			
present a lifestyle plan			
identify types of speech			
use non-verbal communication in public speaking			
give a speech giving advice using non-verbal communication			

Workbook Key

Unit 1

1a – Vocabulary

1 1 canal 3 footpath 5 wood
2 railway line 4 stream 6 campsite

2 a) 1 d 2 e 3 b 4 a 5 c

b) 1 mountain range 4 epic journey
2 personal satisfaction 5 hiking trail
3 thick forest

3 1 captures 3 passed 5 range
2 is soaring 4 grabbed 6 has spent

4 1 out 3 to 5 in 7 off
2 on 4 up 6 of 8 on

5 1 route 6 peak
2 entire 7 spectacular
3 roughly 8 stretch
4 equivalent 9 complete
5 reach 10 achievement

1b – Grammar

1 1 is always taking 5 has walked
2 Does it snow 6 is getting
3 hasn't been 7 tastes
4 sounds 8 have been training

2 1 am thinking, don't think
2 does ... start, is starting
3 Are they camping, are getting
4 works, isn't working
5 Do you have, Are you having
6 are using, costs
7 are you looking, seems

3 1 have been hiking 4 has she walked
2 has been raining 5 has he been saving
3 has stolen 6 have climbed

4 1 I've ~~wanted always~~ **always wanted** to go on a walking holiday.
2 She has ~~been~~ **gone** to Ireland and won't be back for a week.
3 Have you ~~never~~ **ever** stayed in a youth hostel before?
4 I have ~~been knowing~~ **known** Ben since we were kids.
5 Do they ~~go often~~ **often go** hiking?

5 1 walk 9 am looking forward
2 So far 10 are visiting
3 have covered 11 this Sunday
4 have never walked 12 am not thinking
5 always 13 yet
6 have been trekking 14 has been cooking
7 since 15 for
8 set up 16 smells

1c – Vocabulary

1 a) 1 d 2 c 3 a 4 b

b) 1 dead end 2 speed limit

2 1 traffic 3 roundabout 5 way
2 crossroads 4 junction

3 1 traffic lights 4 junction
2 pedestrian crossing 5 roundabout
3 cycle lane

4 1 stressful 3 flight 5 attractive
2 extremely 4 curious 6 owner

Everyday English

5 1 take 3 reach 5 cross
2 go 4 turn

6 1 b 2 a 3 b

7 1 C 2 H 3 E 4 A 5 D

Reading

8 1 C 2 A 3 B 4 D 5 B 6 C

9 1 lakes 3 addicted 5 harmony
2 mirror 4 lodges 6 wonder

10 1 D 2 C 3 C 4 B

Unit 2

2a – Vocabulary

1 1 tradition 3 culture 5 stalls
2 display 4 jugglers

2 1 fireworks 3 performers 5 sculptures
2 show 4 balloon

3 1 away 3 off 5 out 7 in
2 off 4 up 6 up

4 1 Watching 2 won 3 took 4 was blowing 5 scared 6 roared 7 burst

5 1 life 2 surrounded 3 dressed 4 costumes 5 packed 6 time 7 celebrate 8 home 9 march 10 eyes

2b – Grammar

1
1 Did you attend
2 were performing
3 went
4 walked, picked, started
5 was playing, was dancing
6 started
7 was dancing, slipped, fell
8 were setting up, were practising

2
1 have just bought, went
2 took, have never visited
3 has already started, arrived, saved
4 has watched, told
5 Have you tried, had
6 Have you met, introduced

3
1 When I was a student, I ~~would~~ **used to** be in the amateur theatre group.
2 John used to get really nervous performing in front of a live audience, but now he ~~gets~~ **is** used to it.
3 Did you ~~used~~ **use** to go to Oktoberfest when you lived in Germany?
4 I ~~wouldn't~~ **didn't (use to)** like poetry until I attended a literature festival.
5 Sarah used to ~~going~~ **go** to the theatre a lot when she lived in London.
6 Jessica hasn't got ~~use~~ **used** to the hot weather in Thailand yet.

4 1 attended 2 has promoted 3 caught 4 arrived 5 was shining 6 wandered 7 bought 8 decided 9 tried 10 were eating 11 started 12 have ever been

5
1 would go to
2 were playing
3 has not worn a costume
4 you use to dress up
5 did you last take part

2c – Vocabulary

1 1 fireworks 2 procession 3 breakfast 4 toffee apples 5 bagpipes

2 1 light 2 let 3 eat 4 wear 5 hold 6 gather 7 follow 8 sing

a 2 b 4 c 1 d 3

3 1 scenic 2 interested 3 musicians 4 trendy 5 appearance 6 easily 7 exhibition 8 lucky

Everyday English

4 1 b 2 c 3 a

5 1 a 2 b 3 a

6 1 E 2 H 3 A 4 G 5 C

Reading

7 A 3 B 1 C 2 D 4

8 1 B 2 A 3 D 4 B 5 C 6 A

9 1 A 2 C 3 A 4 B

Unit 3

3a – Vocabulary

1 1 volcano 2 reef 3 abseiling 4 rainforest 5 site 6 stream

2 1 through 2 for 3 at 4 out 5 over 6 in

3 1 crystal-clear 2 habitats 3 expert 4 fully 5 pools 6 level 7 jump

4 1 descended 2 looked 3 appreciate 4 tracking 5 got 6 to explore 7 will give 8 were hiking

5 1 on 2 admit 3 experienced 4 thrilling 5 systems 6 over 7 hired 8 extraordinary 9 in 10 in 11 temperatures 12 Apparently 13 beforehand 14 anxious 15 ferocious 16 dizziness 17 came 18 exhausted 19 for

3b – Grammar

1
1 had been swimming, –
2 had ever tried, –

Workbook Key

3 had never seen, –
4 had they been sailing, the
5 had visited, the
6 had been travelling, –
7 had gone, the
8 had been watching, –

2 1 didn't know, had been, got
2 were you, was, had heard
3 Did you enjoy, was, hadn't brought
4 did you see, realised, hadn't taken

3 1 They were dirty because they had ~~walked~~ **been walking** through mud all afternoon.
2 Karen climbed up the waterfall and ~~had~~ **jumped** from the top.
3 I ~~never saw~~ **had never seen** a lion in the wild before my trip to Maasai Mara National Reserve in Kenya.
4 ~~Had you visited~~ **Did you visit** Mount Etna when you went to Sicily?
5 By the time we arrived at the river, we ~~hiked~~ **had been hiking** for 4 hours.

4 1 –, the
2 the, The, –
3 the, –
4 the, the/a, the
5 –, the
6 an, a, the, the
7 The, –
8 an, the, a
9 a, –, the
10 the, –, the

5 1 went
2 the
3 –
4 had just arrived
5 picked
6 the
7 drove
8 had already set up
9 the
10 had left
11 hired
12 a
13 The
14 began
15 was
16 stayed
17 the
18 had never seen
19 an
20 built
21 had
22 –
23 were
24 had been travelling
25 the
26 had ever been

3c – Vocabulary

1 1 agritourism
2 diving
3 cruise
4 break

2 1 stung
2 drowning
3 bit
4 got
5 twisted
6 burnt
7 fell
8 break

3 1 windy
2 relaxed
3 himself
4 Suddenly
5 surprised
6 reality

Everyday English

4 1 c 2 a 3 b

5 1 A: You'll never guess what happened.
B: Tell me all about it.
2 A: It was horrible!
B: How terrible!
3 B: And what did you do?

6 1 A 2 F 3 D 4 H 5 C

Reading

7 1 F 2 DS 3 DS 4 T 5 F 6 DS

8 1 B 2 D 3 A 4 B 5 C 6 A

9 1 B 2 B 3 D 4 A

Skills Practice A (Units 1-3)

Reading

1 1 T 2 DS 3 DS 4 F 5 F

2 1 B 2 A 3 B 4 A 5 C

3 1 D 2 B 3 C 4 B

Everyday English

4 1 g 2 b 3 e 4 a 5 f 6 h 7 c 8 d

5 1 b 2 b 3 a 4 b 5 b 6 a 7 a 8 b

6 1 F 2 D 3 E 4 B 5 C 6 H

Listening

7 1 A 2 B 3 A 4 A

8 1 C 2 A 3 B 4 E

9 1 T 2 T 3 F 4 F 5 T 6 F

Writing

10 1 green line
2 attractions
3 fridges
4 lounge area
5 washing machines
6 bunk beds
7 shower
8 French Street
9 minimarket
10 10%/ten percent

Workbook Key

1 **Suggested Answer Key**

Hi Lisa,
Good to hear from you. This sounds like a great project! My family and I attended Sant Jordi Day in Barcelona on 23rd April last year.
This traditional festival is based on the legend of Sant Jordi, or Saint George, who killed a dragon to save a princess. Legend has it that a rose bush grew where the dragon's blood spilled.
People in Barcelona celebrate the day by exchanging roses and books with their loved ones. When we arrived, first we wandered around the city's central flower market, Mercabarna-Flor and admired the beautiful roses. I also bought a couple of books from the stalls in La Rambla. The best part was the traditional sardana dancing at Plaça Sant Jaume – it was so much fun!
We all had a great time and I would definitely recommend visiting Barcelona during this celebration to anyone who loves romance, roses and books.
Speak soon,
Laura

2 **a)** A 3 B 2 C 5 D 1 E 6 F 4

b) Suggested Answer Key

It was a beautiful morning in the Serengeti National Park as Rebecca and Lisa climbed into the Jeep to start their safari.
Before setting off, their guide gave them some safety advice; the most important rule, he told them, was to stay inside the Jeep at all times. Rebecca and Lisa were having a fantastic time. They saw loads of animals, including elephants and leopards, and Rebecca took lots of pictures of the animals from a distance.
Then, a lion started approaching the Jeep. Lisa was so excited that she put her head out of the window to take a photo. Suddenly, she fell out of the window. The lion saw Lisa and started running towards her. Luckily, the guide quickly jumped out of the Jeep and helped Lisa back inside. Lisa thanked the brave guide.
Everyone was incredibly relieved that she was safe, but they thought they had had enough excitement for one day so they drove back to the hotel.

Revision A (Units 1-3)

Vocabulary

1 C, 2 C, 3 A, 4 A, 5 D, 6 A, 7 D, 8 C, 9 B, 10 A, 11 A, 12 B, 13 D, 14 B, 15 B, 16 A, 17 D, 18 D, 19 B, 20 C, 21 A, 22 A, 23 B, 24 B, 25 C

Grammar

1 B, 2 D, 3 A, 4 D, 5 D, 6 B, 7 A, 8 C, 9 C, 10 A, 11 A, 12 B, 13 C, 14 B, 15 D, 16 B, 17 A, 18 B, 19 B, 20 D, 21 B, 22 B, 23 C, 24 B, 25 B

Unit 4

4a – Vocabulary

1 1 bungalow 2 terraced house 3 detached house 4 cottage 5 mobile home 6 villa

2 1 access 2 complex 3 facilities 4 home 5 light 6 comfort 7 residents

3 1 in 2 up 3 away 4 up 5 of 6 above

4 1 level 2 uninviting 3 bumpy 4 functional 5 private 6 stunning

5 1 to express 2 stayed 3 to avoid 4 located 5 living 6 moving 7 hangs

6 1 odd 2 outside 3 enormous 4 concrete 5 lack 6 view 7 comfortable 8 house 9 furniture 10 narrow 11 soundproof 12 busy 13 dull 14 home

4b – Grammar

1 1 as, more 2 bigger, of 3 half, smaller 4 strong, strongest

2
1 My bedroom is less spacious ~~as~~ **than** my sister's bedroom.
2 This flat is even ~~as~~ **more** expensive than their house.
3 Our house has the most attractive garden ~~in~~ **of** all the houses on this street.
4 Finding somewhere affordable to live in the city is getting more and ~~most~~ **more** difficult.
5 The more beautifully you decorate the flat, ~~the quickest~~ **quicker** you'll find a tenant.
6 Your kitchen is twice ~~less~~ **as** big as mine.
7 Do you think this wardrobe is too tall to ~~fitting~~ **fit** in Tim's bedroom?
8 Your house is ~~enough stylish~~ **stylish enough** to appear in a magazine.

Workbook Key

3 1 more convenient
2 as spacious
3 smaller
4 easier
5 as expensive
6 the most attractive
7 comfortable
8 better
9 better
10 hot

4 1 There, It
2 there, It
3 It, there
4 There, it

5 1 There 2 there 3 It 4 it 5 It 6 there 7 There 8 There

6 1 is not as luxurious as
2 the least expensive flat
3 twice as much money as
4 there is a supermarket
5 more spacious than

4c – Vocabulary

1 a) 1 c 2 e 3 d 4 f 5 a 6 b

b) 1 air conditioning
2 free Wi-Fi
3 en-suite bathroom

2 1 rail
2 shower
3 basement
4 central
5 king-size
6 open
7 amenities
8 convenient

3 1 highly
2 painted
3 furnished
4 refrigerator
5 amazing
6 affordable
7 incredibly

Everyday English

4 1 b 2 c 3 a

5 1 How lovely
2 That's a big advantage
3 I'm not that impressed with it

6 1 Perfect
2 I'd prefer to have
3 Can I take a look at the room
4 I'm not sure about
5 I'll think about it

Reading

7 1 T 2 DS 3 F 4 T 5 F 6 T

8 1 C 2 D 3 A 4 B 5 C 6 B

9 1 C 2 A 3 C 4 B

Unit 5

5a – Vocabulary

1 a) 1 contact
2 messages
3 newspapers
4 gestures
5 chat
6 speech
7 TV

b) A visual communication 3, 5, 7
B verbal communication 2, 6
C non-verbal communication 1, 4

2 1 across 2 up 3 at 4 from 5 up 6 on 7 down

3 a) 1 f 2 d 3 c 4 a 5 c 6 b

b) 1 national security
2 body language
3 mind control

4 1 to send
2 to communicate
3 commit
4 interacting
5 told
6 say
7 expresses

5 1 impact
2 revolutionised
3 elements
4 touch
5 expressions
6 misunderstandings
7 breakdown
8 experts
9 part
10 worry

5b – Grammar

1 1 'll join
2 Does the bank open
3 isn't going to study
4 will help
5 Are they meeting
6 will work
7 is going to buy
8 will be

2 1 will be installing
2 will have finished
3 will be using, will have developed
4 Will you be going
5 will be having

3 1 He will call me the moment that the computer is ready.
2 Sam will reformat the hard drive before he installs the new software.
3 You can't leave the online meeting until it finishes/has finished.
4 I will help you set it up when I finish at 5.
5 It will be dark by the time they get back from the electronics fair.

Workbook Key

4 1 until, call
2 By the time, will have finished
3 is going to buy, when
4 Is the college going to send, the moment
5 will sell out, as soon as
6 after, prepare/have prepared

5 1 ~~Do you come~~ **Are you coming** to Harry's party on Friday?
2 I will text you once the event ~~will finish~~ **finishes**.
3 In the future, we ~~are communicating~~ **will be communicating** through VR technologies.
4 What time ~~will~~ **does** the video conference start?
5 I will ~~be completing~~ **have completed** the report by Friday afternoon.
6 Don't worry, I'm sure that you ~~are going to~~ **will** pass your IT exam.

6 1 as soon as it is
2 am meeting the web designer
3 robots will replace
4 are going to release
5 will have finished
6 will be having/is having

5c – Vocabulary

1 1 AFK 2 JK 3 BTW 4 ATM 5 HF 6 IDK 7 CUL 8 ASAP 9 BB

2 1 NP 2 PLZ 3 GR8 4 WB 5 BRB 6 TBH 7 L8R

3 1 reality 2 international 3 invention 4 education 5 Scientists 6 possibilities 7 endless

Everyday English

4 1 c 2 a 3 b

5 1 disagree 2 know 3 mean 4 think 5 see 6 have 7 agree

6 A 5 B 2 C 9 D 8 E 3 F 10 G 1 H 4 I 7 J 6

7 1 A 2 D 3 C 4 D 5 B 6 C 7 A

8 1 D 2 A 3 C 4 B 5 D 6 C

9 1 D 2 C 3 A 4 B

Unit 6

6a – Vocabulary

1 1 cashier 2 clerk 3 reporter 4 attendant 5 guide 6 trainer

2 1 citizens 2 fast-paced 3 management 4 deadlines 5 spice 6 spectators

3 1 blank 2 passionate 3 independent 4 artistic 5 sociable 6 inspirational

4 1 by 2 on 3 into 4 in 5 up 6 out

5 1 listings 2 suits 3 goals 4 designers 5 skills 6 code 7 squeeze 8 wonder 9 delegating 10 stressful 11 lists 12 media 13 fascinated 14 creativity 15 explore 16 steady

6b – Grammar

1 1 d 2 k 3 b 4 i 5 h 6 e 7 c 8 a 9 g 10 f 11 j 12 l

2 1 need to 2 ought to 3 don't need to 4 can 5 can't

3 1 Will you work extra hours on Monday?
2 When I was younger, I could learn new skills a lot more quickly.
3 He had to do a training course before starting his new job.
4 James is late; he might be stuck in traffic.
5 She was able to get the job although she isn't qualified.
6 You needn't have driven me to work, I could have taken the bus.

4 1 must be working 2 must have arranged 3 may write 4 can't be

5 1 don't need to submit/needn't submit
2 can get your dream job
3 are allowed to wear
4 could have got the job
5 might have left work early

Workbook Key

6c – Vocabulary

1 1 give 2 make 3 come 4 live 5 work 6 replace

2 1 punctual 2 responsible 3 creative 4 respectful 5 cooperative 6 autonomous

3 1 confused 2 responsibilities 3 adaptable 4 interesting 5 development 6 rewarding

Everyday English

4 1 interview 2 candidate 3 position 4 training

5 1 c 2 a 3 b

6 1 F 2 E 3 A 4 B 5 C

Reading

7 A 5 B 1 C 6 D 3

8 1 B 2 E 3 A 4 C

9 1 C 2 A 3 D

Skills Practice B (Units 4-6)

Reading

1 1 D 2 G 3 E 4 A 5 C

2 A 3 B 1 C 6 D 7 E 4

3 1 DS 2 F 3 F 4 DS 5 T

Everyday English

4 1 e 2 d 3 f 4 a 5 h 6 g 7 b 8 c

5 1 b 2 b 3 a 4 b 5 b 6 a 7 a 8 a

6 1 H 2 F 3 D 4 G 5 A 6 B

Listening

7 1 menswear 2 products 3 customers 4 5/five 5 sales 6 13th March

8 1 B 2 C 3 A 4 B

9 1 E 2 G 3 H 4 B 5 C

Writing

10 1 flat 2 underground station 3 dining room 4 fireplace 5 bed 6 clothes dryer 7 central heating 8 Wi-Fi 9 cable TV 10 gardening

11 Suggested Answer Key

From: Beth
To: Deborah
Subject: Congrats!
Hi Deborah,
We haven't been in touch for a while but I've just heard tha you are starting a new job as a manager at Snazzy Fashior and I wanted to congratulate you. Well done, you real deserve it. I think that you are perfect for the position.
I remember when we worked together at Shelto Department Store five years ago. You were always s hardworking and a great organiser! I was impresse by your excellent people skills and your passion fc clothes. Your work experience will definitely be an asse to your new post, and your creativity will help you com up with wonderful ideas about how to increase sales.
I imagine that your new position as manager will have its challenges. You will have to manage the staff and deal with customers' complaints. I am certain howeve that you will be able to overcome these challenges an that you will do a fantastic job.
Once again, congratulations on your new job. I wish you the best of luck.
All the best,
Beth

12 Suggested Answer Key

Many people dream of owning their own business. While being your own boss sounds great, there are also many responsibilities involved. So, what are the pros and cons of being self-employed?
In the first place, you can decide your own working hours. For instance, you can take time off when you want to spend time with your family or pursue hobbies In addition, owning your own business means that you can enjoy the rewards of your hard work by collecting all or most of your business's profits.
However, there is a lot of pressure involved when being self-employed. The success of the business is your responsibility and this requires a lot of hard work. Secondly, there is always some financial risk involved. For example, you could lose your property or savings i the business fails.
In conclusion, I believe that the advantages of owning your own business outweigh the cons. Despite the fact that there is a lot of hard work, responsibility and

risk involved, being self-employed allows people more freedom to earn money and enjoy their spare time whenever they want.

Revision B (Units 4-6)

ocabulary

1 A	6 A	11 A	16 D	21 A
2 D	7 D	12 C	17 B	22 B
3 B	8 A	13 D	18 D	23 B
4 D	9 A	14 D	19 D	24 B
5 A	10 C	15 B	20 C	25 C

rammar

1 A	6 D	11 D	16 A	21 B
2 B	7 B	12 B	17 D	22 B
3 D	8 B	13 D	18 C	23 C
4 D	9 A	14 C	19 B	24 C
5 B	10 B	15 A	20 A	25 A

Unit 7

a – Vocabulary

1 1 coffee maker 3 alarm clock
2 stationery 4 desktop computer

2 1 sensors 4 Light bulbs 7 high-speed
2 control 5 command
3 smart 6 virtual

3 1 has revolutionised 6 to alter
2 dropped 7 consist
3 track 8 to maintain
4 monitoring 9 comprise
5 dim 10 predicting

4 1 off 3 off 5 by 7 on
2 about 4 to 6 off

5 1 Things 5 offenders
2 intelligence 6 account
3 independently 7 authorities
4 automatically 8 behaviour

b – Grammar

1 1 programmed 4 hadn't been
2 made 5 will be designed
3 has been damaged 6 being repaired

2 1 are made, with
2 will have been developed, by
3 was being given, by
4 must be tested, with
5 will be provided, by
6 haven't been updated, with

3 1 I was allowed to use my brother's new digital camera.
2 We were given VR headsets by our teacher. /VR headsets were given to us by our teacher.
3 A new video game console won't be released by the company next month.
4 Has new technology been installed in the classrooms?
5 It is said that education might be revolutionised by IoT. /Education is said to be revolutionised by IoT.
6 When will my smartwatch be repaired by the technician?
7 It is claimed that humanity will be destroyed by artificial intelligence. /Humanity is claimed to be destroyed by artificial intelligence.
8 Who was the first digital computer designed by?

4 1 am having, yourself 4 have, myself
2 have had, themselves 5 herself, to drive
3 himself, get

5 1 myself, had it repaired
2 itself, is having it delivered
3 herself, having her website designed
4 yourself, have an electrician check

6 1 got her brother to install
2 made us switch off
3 upgraded her PC by herself
4 had me update

7c – Vocabulary

1 1 monitor 2 Chat 3 Stream

2 1 call 4 order 7 share
2 create 5 book
3 upload 6 browse

3 1 trainees 3 location 5 different
2 creative 4 performance

Everyday English

4 1 b 2 c 3 a

5 1 In my opinion 3 That's not true
2 It seems to me 4 You're right

6 1 E 2 A 3 G 4 C 5 B

Workbook Key

Reading

7 1 T 2 F 3 DS 4 T 5 F

8 1 devices 2 preferences 3 reception 4 database 5 assistants 6 chatbots 7 advice

9 1 D 2 B 3 A 4 C

Unit 8

8a – Vocabulary

1 1 famine 2 poverty 3 Overpopulation 4 homelessness 5 illiteracy 6 inequality

2 1 d 2 e 3 b 4 a 5 c

3 1 real 2 estimated 3 neighbouring 4 special 5 miserable 6 ordinary

4 1 out 2 in 3 to 4 apart 5 in 6 behind 7 apart

5 1 action 2 war 3 crossed 4 generate 5 fall 6 affected 7 reason 8 treat 9 relatively 10 remember

8b – Grammar

1
1 were
2 had come
3 wouldn't have thrown
4 would help
5 do
6 had given
7 lose
8 would you do

2
1 earned
2 would provide
3 would have forgotten
4 would spend
5 increases
6 will come

3
1 wishes he hadn't bullied
2 doctors had developed
3 wouldn't have found out
4 unless we all try

4 1 aren't I 2 shall we 3 haven't you 4 isn't it 5 will you 6 won't you 7 haven't they 8 aren't there

5
1 You had a fundraising event at work last week, ~~hadn't~~ **didn't** you?
2 No one left the soup kitchen feeling hungry, ~~didn't~~ **did** they?
3 Sponsor an endangered animal today, ~~do~~ **won't** you?
4 Anyone can participate in the food drive, can't ~~you~~ **they**?
5 This is a really serious social issue, isn't ~~this~~ **it**?

6
1 isn't there, would volunteer
2 could start, didn't he
3 doesn't she, hadn't accepted, would have gone
4 don't you, give, may/might/could win
5 will you/won't you, had told

8c – Vocabulary

1 1 depression 2 pick on 3 lack 4 racism 5 unemployment

2 1 high-pressure 2 overweight 3 stress 4 addiction 5 obesity

3 1 overnight 2 enable 3 permanently 4 instruction(s) 5 generosity 6 accessible

Everyday English

4 1 b 2 a 3 c

5 1 a 2 a 3 b

6 1 H 2 A 3 D 4 I 5 F 6 C 7 E

Reading

7 A 3 B 1 C 4 D 2

8 1 C 2 E 3 A 4 B

9 1 D 2 B 3 A 4 C

Workbook Key

Unit 9

a – Vocabulary

1 1 campus 2 lecture hall 3 professor 4 lecture 5 mark 6 interactive whiteboard

2 1 course 2 notes 3 reviews 4 visual 5 passive 6 concepts 7 nutritionists

3 1 on 2 at 3 off 4 out 5 to 6 over 7 on

4 1 checked 2 did 3 to meeting 4 beating 5 won't abandon 6 attend

5 1 undergraduates 2 virtual 3 creatures 4 digital 5 human 6 stimulating 7 sky 8 constellations 9 fingertips 10 chat

b – Grammar

1 1 to enroll 2 stay 3 trying 4 Finding 5 to have found 6 to talk

2 1 to collect, to pick it up 2 not going, doing 3 to sign in, have called 4 To be, talking

3
1 is thought to have been
2 means taking
3 is said to be teaching
4 is expected to be

4 1 which 2 who 3 which 4 why 5 whose 6 which

5 1 whose 2 who 3 when 4 why 5 where 6 which

6
1 Naomi, ~~that~~ **who** works in the library, writes poetry in her spare time.
2 The college ~~where~~ **which/that** Dan goes to is close to the football stadium. OR The college where Dan goes ~~to~~ is close to the football stadium.
3 The secretary to ~~who~~ **whom** I spoke didn't know where my essay was.
4 Marcus, ~~whose~~ **who** is living on campus, finishes his course in June.
5 The lecture hall was crowded with students none of ~~who~~ **whom** I recognised.
6 A lack of students is the reason ~~when~~ **why** the course was cancelled.
7 The books ~~where~~ **which/that** are in the office are for Professor Joyce.
8 All our online courses are free for anyone ~~whom~~ **who** is interested.

9c – Vocabulary

1 1 mature 2 evening 3 Study 4 Register 5 fees

2 1 c 2 e 3 d 4 b 5 a
1 official certificate
2 part-time course
3 course description

3 1 correctly 2 Staying 3 traditional 4 truly 5 suggestion 6 entertainment

Everyday English

4 1 wonder, know 2 help, ask 3 tell, hope ...

5 1 a 2 b 3 b

6 1 H 2 D 3 A 4 E 5 G 6 C

Reading

7 1 C 2 D 3 A 4 C 5 A 6 B 7 C 8 B

8
1 The college in the leaflet offers **an extensive programme of courses**.
2 Street art **is** a part of the Art History course.
3 It is said that **everyone has a story** to tell.
4 **Cherry Phelps** leads the Creative Writing course.
5 The Economics course **includes** history.
6 Dr Barbieri has won a number of awards for her **TV show**.

9 1 A 2 D 3 C 4 B

Skills Practice C (Units 7-9)

Reading

1 1 G 2 F 3 C 4 A 5 E

2 1 professor 2 chatbot 3 mental 4 session 5 communicate 6 personality

3 1 B 2 A 3 C 4 B

Workbook Key

Everyday English

4 1 f 2 h 3 c 4 e 5 b 6 g 7 a 8 d

5 1 a 2 a 3 b 4 b 5 b 6 b 7 a 8 a

6 1 F 2 A 3 H 4 D 5 B 6 E

Listening

7 1 T 2 F 3 T 4 F 5 F 6 T

8 1 A 2 A 3 C 4 B

9 1 A 2 B 3 C 4 B

Writing

10
1 summer creative writing course
2 what types of writing will be covered
3 if poetry will be included
4 I started on the 29th of July
5 I am attending my cousin's wedding on the 28th
6 to pay in cash
7 I don't possess a credit card

11 Suggested Answer Key

Solving the problems of the homeless

Homelessness in Hamilton is a major problem.

Unfortunately, there is a great number of people in our city who have no home or a job and, as a result, they cannot afford the basics in life. This is mainly caused by rising unemployment rates and the high cost of rent in the city. So, what can we do about this serious issue?

One possible solution is to provide more affordable housing. For example, the city could build basic flats with very low rents. In this way, people who have a low income would be able to keep their homes.

Another useful suggestion is to lower unemployment. This can be done by helping people start their own businesses. This means that more people will find work and earn enough money to pay for their rent.

In conclusion, providing more affordable housing and decreasing the unemployment rates are both good ways to solve the problem of homelessness in Hamilton. I believe that, by taking responsibility and acting sensibly, we can definitely improve the situation.

12 a)
1 takes years to learn vocabulary, less time to study other subjects
2 not remember unless used regularly, makes hours of learning waste of time
3 can work as translator, tour guide, etc, can apply for jobs in foreign country
4 less confusion with food, getting around, etc, can make friends with locals

b) Suggested Answer Key

Nowadays, speaking foreign languages is considere extremely beneficial. So, more and more student study one or more foreign languages at school. I my opinion, learning foreign languages at secondar school is important for all students for a number c reasons.

First of all, learning a foreign language improves yo job prospects. For example, you could work as translator or a tour guide. It also increases your futur opportunities because you can apply for jobs abroad Moreover, knowing a foreign language is useful fc travelling. It is easier to order food and get aroun a new place if you can speak the language. I addition, you can also make friends with the locals On the other hand, learning a foreign languag requires a lot of time. You need to study har because it can take years to learn the vocabular for instance. This also means you might have les time to study other subjects.

All in all, I think that all students should learn foreign language in secondary school. Even thoug it takes a lot of time, the benefits of speaking foreig languages – such as better job prospects an travelling abroad – make it worthwhile.

Revision C (Units 7-9)

Vocabulary

1 D	6 C	11 C	16 B	21 A
2 C	7 C	12 D	17 A	22 C
3 A	8 B	13 C	18 B	23 C
4 A	9 B	14 C	19 B	24 A
5 C	10 B	15 A	20 C	25 B

Grammar

1 C	6 D	11 C	16 D	21 C
2 A	7 C	12 B	17 D	22 C
3 C	8 A	13 D	18 C	23 B
4 A	9 C	14 D	19 C	24 B
5 D	10 D	15 B	20 A	25 B

Unit 10

10a – Vocabulary

1 1 rain 2 change 3 growth 4 species 5 pollution 6 warming 7 production

2 1 bottles 2 jars 3 menus 4 boxes 5 bags 6 grounds 7 cans 8 phones

3 1 for 2 down 3 off 4 under 5 up 6 at 7 on 8 in

4 1 vital 2 natural 3 rotting 4 deep 5 purifying 6 deadly 7 lonely

5 1 push 2 mess 3 reefs 4 wander 5 scavengers 6 bacteria 7 seabed 8 signal 9 infections 10 acids

0b – Grammar

1
1 said, she, had, immediately
2 told, had been, that
3 me, could, my
4 were, following
5 said, had, before

2 1 a 2 a 3 b 4 a

3
1 He ~~told~~ **said** a few words about his job at the wildlife park.
2 The biologist ordered us ~~to not~~ **not to** go near the turtles.
3 Julie says that plastic waste ~~didn't~~ **doesn't** pollute the ocean.
4 Mr Crawley asked where ~~was~~ the new recycling plant **was**.
5 They said it ~~had to~~ **must** be awful for the animals to live in such terrible conditions.

4
1 Anna told me (that) I didn't need to take anything with me to the park clean-up that day.
2 Dave asked Julie if/whether she had tried organic vegetables before.
3 Rob said (that) he couldn't come to the talk on global warming the following Sunday.
4 Beth asked if/whether/I/we could help her carry those bags to the recycling centre the following day/the day after.
5 Alex says (that) he wants to become a marine biologist.

5
1 denied throwing waste
2 insisted on me/my trying his
3 encouraged Sam to finish
4 threatened to call the police
5 instructed us not to throw

6 "Thank you all for volunteering to plant trees tomorrow. Wear old clothes and bring gloves as it will be messy work. You should bring a hat, because it may be very hot and sunny. You don't need to/needn't bring anything else."
"Are you going to provide any food for the volunteers?"
"There will be plenty of sandwiches and water for everyone."

10c – Vocabulary

1 **a)** 1 c 2 e 3 d 4 a 5 b

b) 1 reusable cup 2 organic food 3 public transport

2 1 carbon 2 Compost 3 waste 4 detergent 5 dioxide 6 paperless 7 carpool 8 local 9 friendly 10 energy-efficient

3 1 suggested 2 Introducing 3 dramatically 4 latest 5 exactly 6 explanations

Everyday English

4
1 that would be a great idea
2 I'm not so sure about that
3 I'm sorry, but I don't agree

5 1 b 2 a 3 b

6 1 I 2 C 3 F 4 E 5 A 6 D 7 G 8 B

Reading

7 1 be 2 well 3 in 4 is 5 by 6 at 7 make 8 able 9 to 10 or

8 1 DS 2 F 3 F 4 T 5 DS 6 T

9 1 C 2 D 3 A 4 A

Unit 11

11a – Vocabulary

1 1 commercial 2 display 3 hoarding 4 research 5 slogan 6 marketing

2 1 agency 2 effective 3 of 4 customers 5 associated

Workbook Key

3 a) 1 b 2 d 3 e 4 a 5 c

b) 1 prime time 2 human mind 3 common sense

4 1 after 2 on 3 from 4 back 5 on 6 for 7 in

5 1 will encourage 2 to grab 3 has created 4 rushed 5 spot 6 to experience 7 supports

6 1 trolleys 2 experience 3 audience 4 products 5 annoying 6 sneaky 7 call 8 for

11b – Grammar

1 1 either 2 every 3 whole 4 is 5 None 6 nor 7 each 8 all

2 1 every 2 Both 3 neither 4 either 5 another 6 other

3
1 both Sam and Amy act
2 neither humour nor
3 every time
4 no other shopping trolley
5 his whole

4 1 anything 2 little 3 bar 4 nobody 5 couple 6 slice 7 too much 8 lot of 9 somewhere 10 no

5
1 There's nothing like a ~~tin~~ **can** of cola on a boiling hot day!
2 Can I have ~~any~~ **some** more chocolate cake, please?
3 How ~~many~~ **much** milk have we got left in the fridge?
4 I can't find the crisps I saw on TV ~~everywhere~~ **anywhere**.
5 Don't eat too ~~much~~ **many** sweets – they're bad for your teeth.
6 On its opening day, the store had hundreds **of** customers.
7 Do you have a ~~little~~ **few** cherry tomatoes for the salad?
8 Everyone ~~are~~ **is** buying healthy snacks these days.

6 1 anyone, few 2 packet, much 3 Nobody, lots 4 Everyone, many

11c – Vocabulary

1 1 cracked 2 missing 3 weak 4 torn 5 dead 6 broken

2
1 cracked camera lens
2 damaged handle
3 damaged smartphone
4 scratched smartwatch

3 1 annoying 2 faulty 3 unpacked 4 advertisement 5 replacement 6 complaint

Everyday English

4 1 b 2 c 3 a

5 1 b 2 a 3 a

6 1 D 2 F 3 C 4 H 5 A

Reading

7 A 2 B 4 C 3 D 1

8
1 Advertisers want us to think that 'you' refers to **each one of us directly**.
2 Using 'you' in an ad makes consumers **more** likely to believe it.
3 Advertisements also use **adjectives** to describe various products.
4 The word 'fresh' means **more than** one thing to consumers.
5 Celebrities **are** paid lots of money to appear in TV commercials.
6 Hyaluronic acid is a type of acid the human body produces to **help repair damaged** cells.

9 1 A 2 C 3 D 4 B

Unit 12

12a – Vocabulary

1 1 pasta 2 soft 3 lean 4 poultry 5 wholegrain 6 lentils 7 oily 8 dark 9 dairy

2 1 build 2 give 3 organs 4 absorb 5 system 6 affect 7 down 8 options

3 a) 1 d 2 e 3 b 4 a 5

b) 1 major breakthrough
2 soil pollution
3 global warming

4 1 on 3 off 5 in 7 off
2 of 4 out 6 about 8 in

5 1 rise 5 pesticides 9 produce
2 processed 6 healthy 10 affordable
3 cultured 7 vegan
4 fertilisers 8 farming

2b – Grammar

1 1 though 6 Despite
2 due to 7 such a
3 with a view to 8 Since
4 much 9 As a result
5 so as not to 10 so

2 1 In spite **of** the fact that I asked him not to, Robert gave up going to the gym.
2 ~~However~~ **Although** she's only been doing it for a while, Jill is great at coming up with vegan recipes.
3 They eat ~~such~~ **so** badly that they always feel tired and sick.
4 Look after your body when you're young ~~avoiding~~ **to avoid** running into health problems later.
5 Josh explained to Theo that his poor diet was the reason ~~for~~ **why** he was gaining weight.
6 I always carry fruit and nuts with me in case I ~~will~~ need a healthy snack on the go.

3 1 Now that you're here, why not come for a jog with me?
2 He's been eating less, yet he hasn't lost any weight.
3 Running hurts my knees. Therefore, swimming is a better option. / Running hurts my knees and therefore swimming is a better option.
4 Eat carbohydrates so as not to run out of energy.
5 Trevor went to the doctor for a check-up.
6 He wrote down the recipe so that he wouldn't forget it.
7 Take some fruit with you in case you get hungry.

4 1 absolutely 3 quite 5 really
2 much 4 extremely

5 1 B 2 A 3 B 4 D 5 C

6 1 on the other hand, 4 due to the fact that
2 as a consequence of 5 far more fruit than
3 order that they

12c – Vocabulary

1 1 Apply 3 Floss
2 Exercise 4 Eliminate

2 1 Maintain 4 consume 7 sleep
2 cardio 5 servings 8 limit
3 balanced 6 mental

3 1 active 3 quickly 5 naturally
2 professionally 4 flexibility 6 aching

Everyday English

4 1 b 2 c 3 a

5 1 a 2 a 3 b

6 1 C 2 D 3 G 4 B 5 E 6 H

Reading

7 1 from 5 which/that 9 and
2 way 6 in 10 more
3 for 7 as
4 take 8 age

8 1 Turmeric is most famous for its **bright yellow colour**.
2 Turmeric **contains** a powerful chemical that reduces swelling.
3 Greece is **one Mediterranean** country where people commonly consume olive oil.
4 Olive oil contains fatty acids which **prevent** heart disease.
5 Cilantro **is a source of** natural vitamins.
6 Ginger has **a wide variety of** medicinal uses.
7 Açaí berries are **native** to South America.
8 Eating Açaí berries can **treat skin conditions**.

9 1 B 2 D 3 C 4 B

Skills Practice D (Units 10-12)

Reading

1 A 7 B 2 C 4 D 6 E 1

2 1 F 2 T 3 DS 4 T 5 DS

3 1 B 2 C 3 A 4 D

Everyday English

4 1 g 3 h 5 e 7 b
2 f 4 d 6 a 8 c

Workbook Key

5 1 b 2 a 3 b 4 a 5 b 6 a 7 a 8 a

6 1 G 2 D 3 E 4 F 5 H 6 A

Listening

7 1 ankle 2 sports science 3 film director 4 150 5 strength 6 pool

8 1 A 2 D 3 E 4 C

9 1 B 2 A 3 A 4 C

Writing

10 1 e-reader 2 delivery 3 screen 4 dropped 5 replacement 6 credit card

11 Suggested Answer Key

To: Jennifer Brown, Manager, Crawford Insurance
From: Peter Sinclair, Team Leader, Crawford Insurance
Subject: How to promote healthy living among staff

Introduction
As discussed during the staff meeting on 26/08/2020, I am writing this proposal to set out the ways in which Crawford Insurance can promote healthy living among its staff.
Knowledge is Power
It would be a good idea if health experts gave talks to the staff. For instance, doctors could talk about the physical and mental benefits of healthy living. Doing this would encourage staff to lead healthier lifestyles.
Eating Well
The company should also encourage staff to eat healthier snacks. For example, putting a fruit bowl with free fruit on every floor could reduce the number of employees buying unhealthy snacks from vending machines or fast-food restaurants.
Staying Active
It is important to encourage employees to get moving during the day. We could do this by giving staff the option of standing desks and encouraging more face-to-face communication.
Conclusion
I believe that Crawford Insurance should provide its staff with talks from health experts, encourage them to consume healthier snacks during the day and offer them more opportunities to move around the office. With these recommendations, we will effectively promote healthy living among our staff.

12 a) 1 b 2 a 3 c

b) Suggested Answer Key

Eco-Friendly Travel
Hi guys! In this forum, I've read a lot of posts about amazing trips, but I've never come across a post about eco-friendly travel. So, here are some tips about how to be a more eco-friendly traveller.
First, don't overuse resources. Just because you're staying in a hotel doesn't mean you should leave the lights on when you go out or keep the tap running while you're brushing your teeth. Save water and electricity just as you would do at home. Secondly, don't hire a car as this causes air pollution. Instead, walk or take public transport to get around; it's cheaper and less stressful than driving. You could even hire a bike – it's a great way to explore a new city!
Lastly, protect the local wildlife. One way you can do this is to avoid buying souvenirs made from endangered species. For example, you shouldn't buy ivory souvenirs which are made from elephant tusks.
So, there you have it. Follow these simple tips to protect the planet while you travel. Do you have any more eco-friendly travel tips? Post your comments below!

Revision D (Units 10-12)

Vocabulary

1 B	6 C	11 C	16 C	21 C
2 B	7 D	12 C	17 B	22 D
3 D	8 A	13 A	18 C	23 A
4 C	9 B	14 C	19 A	24 A
5 D	10 A	15 B	20 C	25 D

Grammar

1 A	6 C	11 C	16 B	21 D
2 D	7 C	12 D	17 A	22 B
3 C	8 A	13 C	18 D	23 D
4 B	9 C	14 A	19 C	24 C
5 D	10 B	15 B	20 C	25 A

Workbook Audioscripts

Skills Practice A

xercise 7 p. 18

ecording 1
ow, some local news. Two men were rescued in Hook Forest ıis morning after they got lost while on a hike. The two men adn't packed a compass or a paper map – instead, they tarted their hike using maps on their phones. During the ike, though, both men fell into a stream, destroying their hones. Unable to find a way out, the men had to spend ıe night in the forest. They managed to light a fire in the ıorning that a rescue team spotted from a helicopter. Both ıen were healthy, but went to Summerville Hospital for ɔme tests. "We will definitely prepare better the next time," ne man said to reporters.

ecording 2
: Did you go to the traditional music festival at the weekend? I didn't see you there.
: Yeah, I was there. It wasn't very enjoyable, was it? The music was far too loud.
: I didn't mind that – maybe you were too close to the stage. I was disappointed by the entrance fee, though. £15 was too much for a one-day festival.
: Yes, that was a bit of a shock. And to make matters worse, a lot of the performances were really short.
: Why do you think that? Most bands played around five songs or so.
: Really? Maybe I wasn't paying attention.

ecording 3
: Hi, Lisa. Why are you walking like that? Did something happen to you on your holiday in Spain?
: Yes, I was jogging on a beach near my hotel when I twisted my ankle.
: Oh, no! Did you have to go to hospital there?
: Well, at first, I wanted to, because I was sure I had broken it. But then another tourist on the beach came over to me – she was a doctor from Italy, actually. She took a look at my ankle and said that it just needed some rest.
: That's good. Going to hospital abroad can be really expensive.
: Yes, I've heard that, too.

ecording 4
: Stan, are you interested in going to a festival in Ypres tomorrow? It's a two-hour drive from here, but it looks really interesting.
: What's it about?
: It's called the Festival of the Cats! It honours the cats who protected the city from diseases in the past by catching rats and mice. I'm not sure what happens exactly, but I think it'll be fun.
: Hmm, I suppose there'll be a parade or something. I think we should check it out!

Exercise 8 p. 18

Speaker 1
Last summer, I went on a diving holiday in Jamaica. For the first few days, I had the time of my life. I dived for a few hours in the afternoons, and enjoyed the local culture in the evenings. One day, though, I hit my head on the boat while jumping into the water. I had stupidly dived when the boat was still moving – something the instructor had warned us not to do. Anyway, I immediately knew I had a problem and was rushed to hospital. Luckily, it wasn't very serious, but I had to spend the rest of my holiday in my hotel room resting.

Speaker 2
When my wife and I decided to go on a hiking holiday in Sweden, I had mixed feelings. On the one hand, I did want to visit Sweden and experience the local culture, but I wasn't looking forward to spending all of our time there in the countryside. Anyway, while hiking in Sarek National Park, I got an infection in my foot. It didn't help that I ignored it for a few days – I didn't think it needed treatment. But in the end, I had to spend two nights there in hospital. So, it was probably our first and last hiking holiday!

Speaker 3
Last year, I travelled to New Zealand for an adventure holiday, and one of the activities I did was a bungee jump. I felt really nervous before the jump. I had never done anything so extreme in my life. In the end, though, nothing bad happened – I followed the guide's safety advice and had a great time. Then, on the day before my flight back home, I twisted my ankle on a pavement in Wellington, the capital city. It was a pity, because I had wanted to enjoy some of the city's culture before I left.

Speaker 4
A few years ago, while I was on a beach holiday in Greece, I broke my arm. I had only myself to blame – I was climbing a tree to pick some oranges and fell. Anyway, I had to spend a day in hospital – and it was actually a great experience. Before, I had never been interested in the culture of the places I visited. I just travelled for the good weather. But in the hospital, from talking to other patients, I learned so much about the country – I even tried Greek food for the first time! Now, I go back to Greece every summer – and not just for the sun!

Exercise 9 p. 18

A: Hello, I wonder if you could help me? I arrived from Spain last night and it's my first time here, so I'm a bit lost.
B: Welcome to Dublin! How can I help?
A: Well, I'm mainly here to see the St Patrick's Day parade, but I don't know where it takes place.

B: Oh, it's in the city centre. It starts at Parnell Square at the top of O'Connell Street, and ends close to St Stephen's Green, a public park in the city. Basically, it passes along most of the main streets in the centre, so you can't miss it.

A: And could you tell me how to get into the centre? I hired a car at the airport ...

B: Oh, I wouldn't drive into the centre today. You'll never find parking! Around 750,000 people gather to watch the parade, so it's really busy! Just take public transport.

A: Is there a bus stop near here?

B: Yes, but it'll be quicker for you to take the LUAS – that's the name of the tram system here. There's a stop just two minutes down the road called Bride's Glen. It's on the green line, so you can take it directly into the city and get off at O'Connell Upper – you don't have to change lines or anything.

A: And one more thing. When does the parade start?

B: At noon, and it lasts for around three hours. But if I were you, I'd arrive before that, at around 11, or you won't find a space to see the parade pass. And another tip: bring some water and a snack before you choose your spot. Nobody will save it for you if you leave!

A: I see. Well, I'd better go now, then. Thanks for all your help!

B: No problem at all. Enjoy the parade!

Exercise 12a p. 19

I'll never forget the time I went on a safari with my friend Lisa in the Serengeti National Park in Tanzania. It was a beautiful morning as we got into the Jeep to start our adventure. We were part of a group with three other people, and there was also our guide, who gave us some safety advice before we started. The number one rule, he said, was to always stay inside the Jeep. At first, we were really enjoying ourselves. We saw a lot of animals from a distance, like elephants, leopards and buffalo, and I took lots of pictures. Then came the moment we had all been waiting for: a lion started walking slowly towards our parked Jeep. Lisa, who was really excited, grabbed her camera and stuck her head far out of the window to get a good photo. Then, though, the Jeep started moving and Lisa fell out! At first, we were all terrified, because the lion was just around 100 metres away. Then it started running towards Lisa! Quickly, the guide stopped the Jeep, got out and picked Lisa up. They rushed back inside the Jeep and we drove away, with the lion just metres behind us. We all felt relieved that Lisa was OK. After she got her breath back, she thanked the guide for his bravery, and we all agreed that we had had enough excitement for one day. So, the guide drove us back to our hotel. Surprisingly, Lisa wasn't nervous about getting back in the Jeep the next day, but she made very sure not to go close to the windows!

Skills Practice B

Exercise 7 p. 36

Good morning, listeners. My name's Sarah Andrews ar I'm the CEO and founder of Snazzy Fashions. Today, want to announce a job opening in our Hereford branc We're looking for a new floor manager, specifically for ou menswear department, though the person might have t fill in in our womenswear and sportswear departments necessary. This is a full-time position with a generous salar Your responsibilities will include managing staff, decidir how products should be displayed, and handling custome who have complaints. You must have worked in a clothe shop for at least five years, either as a sales assistant or manager, and you must be fluent in English. We're especial looking for someone who is cooperative, so that they ca work well with senior management. Also, being creative w be an advantage, as you will have a lot of freedom to fir ways to grow sales. We will accept applications by email on Please send your email of application with an attached C to jobs@snazzyfashion.com. We will not accept applicatior after the 13th of March, as we hope to have found someor to start working in the position on the 27th of the sam month.

Exercise 8 p. 36

Recording 1

A: Have you heard of Vivline, Paul? It's a new video chattir app for smartphones.

B: No, I haven't. Is it any good?

A: I think it's great. I installed it yesterday, and it's bee working brilliantly. The picture is always clear, and it easy to use, too.

B: Sounds great. I'm not very keen on video chattin though. I prefer just sending texts.

A: OK, I understand. My brother's the same. He's a b camera shy, so he's a texter, too.

Recording 2

A: So, what do you think? I'm in two minds, to be honest like the flat itself, but the rent is a bit too high.

B: I wouldn't say that. I think we could afford it easily. It exactly what we've been looking for. It'll give us th extra space that we wanted.

A: OK, I'm with you there, but are you not worried about th neighbourhood? I mean, it has a lot of street crime.

B: I know it has a bad name, but it's improved a lot recent I don't think it's anything to worry about.

Recording 3

Could I have everyone's attention for a second? As we a know, some businesspeople from Japan will visit us tomorro for a meeting. We've been preparing presentations for th meeting for a long time, but we should also think about boo anguage. When we first meet the Japanese, we should bow ur heads rather than shake hands, and please take your me with this gesture. Also, about eye contact, do not stare t anyone, and please do not look at the translator when you ave something to say to one of the businesspeople. This vould be very rude. Apart from that, just use your common ense and act naturally.

ecording 4

.: Lisa, how was the interview? Did you get the job?

: I don't know yet. The interviewer will call me tomorrow. I'm not very hopeful, though.

.: Why not?

: I'm sure the person who had the interview before me got it. When she left, the interviewer was far more friendly to her than he was to me.

.: Maybe he just behaved like that because they know each other. It doesn't mean she's got the job.

: Well, I hope you're right, anyway.

xercise 9 p. 36

peaker 1

ast month, I moved out of the flat I had been living in or six years, and moved into a bungalow in the same eighbourhood. It's slightly closer to my office, but that's not ne reason why I chose it – I just needed somewhere with nore space for all my possessions. But, after living here for few weeks, I kind of wish I had stayed put. The problem is ne garden at the front. I hadn't realised it would need so nuch care. Now, I spend most of my weekends gardening, nd I don't really enjoy it.

peaker 2

was really disappointed when my landlord told me to move ut of the flat I was renting. He decided to sell it, so I had no hoice but to leave. It was a large flat with an office, so it was erfect for working from home. Anyway, thankfully, he gave ne a lot of time to find another place, and I finally chose a ownhouse in the suburbs. At first, I wasn't sure, because ne neighbourhood doesn't have a good name, but after a nonth here, I have no regrets. Sometimes, a change can be or the better!

peaker 3

ast year, I had some money problems, so I decided to move nto a smaller flat with cheaper rent. The flat where I used o live was really spacious, and I had filled it with lots of urniture and decorations. So, when I moved, I had to give a ot of stuff away. And that experience was really eye-opening. At first, I hated losing some of my favourite possessions, but radually I realised that I never really needed them! Now, in ny new flat, I have a simpler and happier life, with far fewer ossessions. I've even changed jobs, because I realised my ld job was giving me too much stress.

Speaker 4

A few years ago, I moved out of my mum's home and into a small flat. She didn't force me to leave – but I had started my first job at the time, so I could finally afford to pay rent. And even though the flat was in a poor part of the city, I was really looking forward to living independently. One thing I regret, though, was hiring a moving company. Somehow, a box of my favourite books went missing. I was really upset, because they were kind of special to me – and I still don't know what happened.

Speaker 5

I was quite sad to leave the studio flat where I used to live. It had been my home ever since I left university, and over the course of six years, I had put a lot of work into it, making it look exactly as I wanted. But it's good in a way that my current job forced me to move city – the area where that flat was had become quite dangerous. Once, someone broke into the flat and stole some of my valuable possessions! So, I suppose I'm better off in a new flat in a new city.

Skills Practice C

Exercise 7 p. 54

A: Hi, Vanessa. Do you have any plans for this evening? A few of us in the Sales Department are planning to eat out at that new pizza restaurant in Oak Street at around eight.

B: Oh, I'd love to join you, Greg, but I'm busy this evening. I've decided to do an evening course in life coaching, and my first class is today! I saw an advertisement for it online yesterday and registered straight away, right at the last minute!

A: Oh, that's exciting. But what's a life coach exactly? It's a bit like a psychologist, isn't it?

B: Well, in a way. Basically, life coaches help people to reach their goals. So, a person who hires a life coach might want to succeed at work, have better relationships, or lose weight … something like that.

A: Oh, I see. So, it's not really about mental health, then?

B: Not really, though setting yourself goals and trying to achieve them is a good way to find happiness anyway, I think.

A: Yes, that's true for me at least. I play tennis, and I love practising and seeing myself improve over time. It gives me a great buzz! Anyway, how often will you have classes?

B: Just two times a week, at Clifton College in Market Square. And if everything goes to plan, I'll have a certificate in life coaching in six months. Then, I'll be able to start working online!

A: Oh, I hope that doesn't mean you'll be leaving the office?

Workbook Audioscripts

B: No, of course not. But I'm thinking of buying a flat, you see, so I really need to increase my income. So, after I've finished the course, my plan is to take on one or two clients. I'll have to contact them daily, but I can do that in the evenings. I don't think it'll take up a lot of my time.

A: Well, that sounds like a good plan. Good luck with it, Vanessa!

Exercise 8 p. 54

Recording 1

A: Well, it seems like the kids had a great time at the Science Museum. All of the interactive exhibits were kid-friendly, so they never got bored.

B: That's true. I wonder how much they really learned, though. I mean, the exhibits were fun, but I don't think they did a good job at actually teaching the kids anything.

A: You've got a point. Even I couldn't understand what some of them were about. But at least none of them were dangerous.

B: I wouldn't say that. Ned nearly fell off that giant hamster wheel. To be honest, I'd prefer not to go there again.

Recording 2

A: What's wrong, Ted? You look a bit down.

B: I'm just feeling a bit stressed these days. I have a lot of reports to finish at work this week, plus I'm meeting my girlfriend's parents for the first time this weekend, too.

A: Oh, well, you should take care of yourself. Long-term stress can lead to serious health problems and it can be bad for your relationships, too.

B: Yes, I know. I've been thinking about getting professional help, but I don't know any psychologists around here.

A: Hmm, me neither. Maybe your doctor could point you in the right direction, though.

Recording 3

Now class, I have a treat for you. This week we've been learning about the Moon, and today we're going to experience what it feels like to walk on its surface! That's right, I have two VR headsets here and everyone will get five minutes to experience a moonwalk! First, I want you to move some desks to make a large space in the centre of the room, because we have to be careful not to injure ourselves while using them. Also, please tell me if you feel dizzy while using the devices, as this could be dangerous. OK, let's get started.

Recording 4

A: Have you decided what you want to study next year, Sarah?

B: Yes, I've already applied to study Medicine at Newcastle University.

A: Oh, are you sure that was the best choice? I mean, you'll need really good marks in your final exams to get a place in Medicine.

B: I know that, Bob, and being realistic, I probably won't d well enough – but I'm going to try anyway.

A: What's your second choice, then?

B: French Literature at Newcastle, too. And I'd be perfect happy to study that ... I just want to dream a little abou becoming a doctor, though!

Exercise 9 p. 54

A: Welcome back to the show. I'm joined in the studi now by Kendra Logan. Kendra is a History student a Keele University, but she spends her free time runnir a smartphone app she created called EthicalShoppe Kendra, how did you get the idea for this app?

B: Well, this app aims to help stop child labour. I came u with the idea while I was backpacking through Southea Asia last year. In one city in Cambodia, I witnessed long line of children walking into a clothes factory. I late learned that they worked there 12 hours a day. It wa very upsetting, so, when I returned to England, I decide to make this app.

A: I see. So, what does the app do exactly?

B: Well, basically, it's a shopping app for clothes. I don't ow my own online shop, though. Instead, this app connect with the online shops of clothes companies that hav proven that they have no link to child labour. So, after yo download the app, you can browse through thousanc of ethically-produced clothing items from more than on hundred online shops, all in one app.

A: What a wonderful idea! And has the app been a success

B: Yes, we think so. Right now, we're in the top one hundre clothes shopping apps worldwide, and we have ove 100,000 regular users. Plus more and more ethic companies are contacting us, asking us to display the products. I think the success of our app shows tha customers care about child labour, so, hopefully, mor companies will take notice of this and cut all links wit this terrible practice.

A: And is the app free to download?

B: Yes, of course. I don't earn anything from the app, an the programmers that maintain the app work for fre We do receive some money from the companies tha pay us to display their products, but all this mone goes to charities to help fight child labour. Since th app is becoming bigger and bigger, we might have t change this model, and hire some programmers, bu for now, we're very proud that the app is run entirely b volunteers.

A: Well, Kendra, it's been interesting talking to you. Thank for joining us.

B: My pleasure.

Workbook Audioscripts

Skills Practice D

Exercise 7 p. 72

A: Now, we have a very special guest in the studio, fitness trainer for the stars Brad Donovan. Brad, did you always want to become a fitness trainer?

B: Not exactly. Growing up, I was a talented football player, and I even had a chance to become a professional. But when I was 18, I suffered a terrible ankle injury, which destroyed those dreams. So, I had to rethink my future, and eventually, I decided to become a fitness trainer.

A: So, did you do any courses before you got started?

B: I know some fitness trainers who've got jobs in gyms without any qualifications, but before I started, I did a one-year course in sports science, and I found it really useful. Also, since then, I've done some smaller courses in physiotherapy and nutrition.

A: And how did you become a fitness trainer for the rich and famous?

B: Well, ten years ago, I was working in a gym in London, and one day I did a training session with the personal assistant of a famous film director. I guess she liked the work-out, because that evening I got a call to come to train her boss! After that, he recommended me to an actor, and the rest is history ...

A: So, what's it like training celebrities?

B: Well, they're usually really self-motivated. Working out isn't a hobby for them – they want to look good in front of the cameras, so they treat it like it's a part of their job. Most other clients, at least those who aren't athletes, don't want to work out for more than 90 minutes, but with celebrities I usually do a 150-minute session. They take it very seriously.

A: And what are the negatives of being a fitness trainer for celebrities?

B: Well, in my job there's no such thing as an easy day. Most times I do a training session, I work out with the client. And since many of my clients are actors who want to get fit for action films, they need to do a lot of strength training. Imagine doing that a few different times in one day ... it's exhausting!

A: And I can't let you leave without you giving us an interesting story about one of your celebrity clients!

B: Well, I can't give you a name, but a few years ago I got a call from an actor asking me to train him for a sports film. So, I turned up at his house – and there he was lying on a floating bed in his pool eating ice cream! I knew I had a lot of work to do when I saw that!

A: Brad, thanks for speaking to us!

B: My pleasure!

Exercise 8 p. 72

Speaker 1

I usually just buy from the same four or five online shops – well-known companies that I can trust. But last month, I made the mistake of buying from a shop I'd never heard of before. I really wanted a video game they were selling, and I hadn't been able to find it elsewhere. Anyway, the game arrived quite quickly, but when I opened the package, I was really disappointed. It was the correct game, but not for the games console I owned. Luckily, the seller replied to my emails, and even though he wasn't very apologetic, I managed to get my money back.

Speaker 2

Last year, I bought a designer watch from an online shop to wear to my sister's wedding. The delivery wasn't a problem – thankfully, it arrived before the big day – and everyone at the wedding was impressed. The next day, though, the watch stopped working. I immediately called the company and angrily demanded a refund. Then, though, as I was still on the phone, I caught a glimpse of the back of the watch. 'Not waterproof' it read in capital letters. There was nothing I could do but apologise and hang up. I had worn it in the shower that morning, so I only had myself to blame.

Speaker 3

Around two months ago, I broke my smartphone, and decided to buy a new one online. So, I placed the order, paying a little extra for express delivery. After all no one wants to be without a phone for a long time. But after it arrived, I was shocked to see that the phone wasn't in its original packaging – as if it was second-hand! When I contacted the seller, she told me I shouldn't be worrying – that they sent all their phones that way! It was all very strange, so I sent it back, and eventually got a refund.

Speaker 4

I buy a lot of books online and I've rarely had any problems. One time, though, I bought a rare book from an online shop based in the USA. It took over a month for the book to be delivered, which I had expected, because I had told the seller to send it by ordinary post. The problem was, after the book arrived, I noticed several pages were badly torn. Any of the emails I sent the seller, though, were completely ignored. And to make matters worse, the phone number listed on the site didn't work at all! Naturally, it was the last time I shopped from that site.

Exercise 9 p. 72

A: Welcome back to the Environment Show. I'm joined now by the fashion journalist Heather Rhodes. Heather has just released a book about the clothes industry and the environment. Heather, why did you decide to write this book?

Workbook Audioscripts

B: Thanks for having me, Charlie. I first got the idea for this book around a year ago. One evening, I was watching the news – there was some footage of a march for action against climate change. Anyway, one thing I noticed was the clothes a lot of the people taking part were wearing – popular sports brands, which I know for a fact are not at all eco-friendly. I was shocked that environmentalists could care so little about the carbon footprint of their clothes.

A: I see. Can you tell us about the carbon footprint of the clothes industry in general?

B: Considering all of the different stages involved in making and selling clothes, the industry produces around 10% of the world's carbon emissions. This is more than the airline and shipping industries combined – though in the news we hear much more about how harmful these industries are to the environment. Also, clothes pollute our oceans with microfibres. These are tiny pieces of plastic that are released by synthetic clothes when we wash them.

A: That's shocking. And it doesn't help that people buy a lot of clothes these days, does it?

B: You're right. It's partly the fashion industry's fault. Fashion blogs and magazines are always telling us what clothes are in or out of fashion, so some people feel the need to buy new clothes all the time – just to be stylish. But even people who don't follow fashion trends still buy a lot of clothes. Nowadays, there's a lot of low-cost clothes shops where you can buy cheap clothes made from cheap materials. These clothes don't last long, but because they're so cheap, it doesn't bother us – we just go clothes shopping again! But this attitude is terrible for the environment.

A: So, Heather, what can we as consumers do to help?

B: Well, we can recycle clothes by donating them to charity, or support clothes brands that are eco-friendly. My main message to your listeners today, though, is simply to buy fewer clothes. Amazingly, in some developed countries, 40% of the clothes people buy are never worn! Instead, let's ignore the fashion industry a bit, and avoid changing our wardrobe every year. And if you need to go clothes shopping, concentrate on buying clothes made from strong materials, so that they last a long time.

A: I think that piece of advice would save people a lot of money, too! Thanks a lot, Heather, for coming in.

B: My pleasure, Charlie.

Grammar Book Key

Unit 1

+ -s	captures, gives, completes, holds
-ss, -sh, -ch, -x, -o, + -es	dresses, does, fixes, crashes
vowel + -y + -s	plays, enjoys, buys, delays
consonant + -~~y~~ → -ies	tries, empties, cries, flies

+ *-ing*	seeing, sleeping, snowing
-~~ie~~ → -y + *-ing*	lying, dying
-~~e~~ → *-ing*	writing, taking, shining, living
double consonant + *-ing*	planning, stopping, getting

3
2 a (present simple)
3 h (present continuous)
4 e (present simple)
5 b (present simple)
6 g (present continuous)
7 d (present simple)
8 c (present simple)

4
2 scores (present simple for narration)
3 Does the AT pass (present simple for a permanent state)
4 isn't Sam wearing (present continuous for an action happening around the time of speaking)
5 ends (present simple for a schedule)
6 is always talking (present continuous to express annoyance)
7 does it take (present simple for a general truth)
8 am waiting (present continuous for an action happening now)

5
2 are you constantly asking
3 always have
4 are visiting
5 does it open
6 'm checking
7 don't suit
8 never get up
9 usually buys
10 's coming
11 's getting
12 rains

6
2 is seeing (continuous form = is meeting)
3 hates (stative verb expressing feelings/emotions)
4 does that tent cost (stative verb – no continuous form)
5 am enjoying (continuous form – specific preference)
6 don't fit (stative verb = aren't the right size)
7 don't want (stative verb expressing feelings/ emotions)
8 doesn't taste (stative verb = doesn't have a particular flavour)
9 is appearing (continuous form = is performing)
10 is Zoe smelling (continuous form = is sniffing)
11 doesn't include (stative verb – no continuous form)
12 Do you have (stative verb = own, possess)

7
2 a are looking — b looks
3 a is appearing — b appears
4 a is thinking — b thinks
5 a is feeling — b feels
6 a see — b is seeing

8
1 is thinking
2 is being, doesn't seem
3 is looking, is tasting
4 Do you want, contains
5 tastes, don't agree

9
2 Sam is always talking about hie expensive hiking equipment!
3 Drivers must never go over the speed limit.
4 I often do the cooking when we go camping.

10
2 Petra occasionally goes water skiing on the lake.
3 I can usually put up my tent quickly.
4 Layla has never been late for work.
5 I rarely/seldom see my college friends nowadays.
6 Oliver and Cody are always very friendly.
7 The Joneses sometimes have a picnic in the park.

11
2 h (present perfect continuous)
3 e (present perfect)
4 c (present perfect)
5 g (present perfect continuous)
6 f (present perfect)
7 d (present perfect)
8 i (present perfect continuous)
9 a (present perfect)

12
2 for
3 ever
4 yet
5 before
6 never
7 just
8 since
9 already
10 recently

13
2 gone to
3 been to
4 been in
5 gone to

Grammar Book Key

14 2 he's been hiking (an action that started in the past and lasted for some time, and whose results are visible in the present)
3 haven't booked (an action which happened at an unstated time in the past)
4 has visited (an action which happened at an unstated time in the past)
5 have been waiting (emphasis on the duration of an action which started in the past and continues up to the present)
6 has just arrived (a recently completed action)
7 have moved (a personal experience)
8 has been ringing (emphasis on the duration of an action which started in the past and continues to the present)

15 2 have already passed
3 has been talking
4 Have Val and Sean been camping
5 haven't put
6 have those boots been hurting
7 Have you read
8 Have you been running

16 2 have just heard, has been telling
3 Has Rob phoned, has been trying
4 Have you spoken, haven't seen
5 Have you brought, have been giving
6 have been complaining, haven't done

17 2 'm staying
3 haven't written
4 've been thinking
5 runs
6 goes
7 've already taken
8 've made
9 've been
10 love
11 is always complaining
12 've never felt
13 'm getting
14 's told
15 've been looking
16 's just stopped

18 2 b 3 a 4 b 5 a 6 a 7 b 8 a

19 2 has been hiking since
3 has been in
4 has never been to
5 have not seen Harry for
6 am always getting

Unit 2

1 1 took (an action happening at a specific, already known, time in the past)
2 did you book (an action that happened at an implied time in the past); went, picked, paid (actions that happened one after the other in the past)
3 cooked (an action that happened at a stated time in the past); was making, followed (an action which happened at a specific time in the past, implied)
4 Did you spend, had (past habits)
5 Did you see (an action that happened at a stated time in the past); was watching, went (an action in progress when another action interrupted it)
6 was playing (an action in progress at a stated time in the past)
7 took (a past action which won't take place again)

2 2 didn't win
3 was falling, was blowing
4 wasn't gathering
5 were you talking
6 enjoyed
7 Did Jack drive

3 2 Did you hear about the festival on the radio? I did, was listening, mentioned
3 Was Frank working yesterday morning? he was, didn't see
4 Were James and Lily studying yesterday at noon? they weren't, were watching
5 Did the parade start at 10 am last Sunday? it didn't, was pouring, delayed

4 2 arrived
3 was walking
4 ran into
5 were marching
6 were playing
7 were performing
8 was taking
9 noticed
10 explained
11 started
12 explored
13 bought

5 2 've only lived
3 've taken part
4 've spent
5 had
6 haven't reserved
7 did it start
8 has celebrated
9 began
10 didn't let off
11 've offered

6 2 A 3 C 4 A 5 A 6 C 7 B 8 B 9 A 10 C

7 2 used to/would
3 used to
4 used to/would
5 used to/would
6 used to

8 2 is used to
3 will get/gets used to
4 got used to
5 is getting used to
6 am not used to

9 2 C 3 A 4 B 5 B 6 B 7 A 8 C

Grammar Book Key

0 2 visited
3 invited
4 found out
5 was shining
6 were wearing
7 were trying
8 came out
9 'm not used to
10 was shivering

1 2 When I woke up, the wind was blowing and the rain was pouring down.
3 We lit a bonfire last night.
4 On Saturday, I painted some decorations green for the St Patrick's Day parade.
5 While Kim was marching in the parade, her sister was taking photos of her.
6 Janet hasn't got used to living/isn't used to living on her own yet.
7 When he was a baby, my younger brother hated/ used to hate the loud noises on Bonfire Night.
8 When I moved to Mexico, I got used to eating the spicy local food after a couple of months.
9 Jack has had a dog his whole life so he is used to taking care of a pet.
10 Were you sleeping when I called you?

2 2 went to Ireland in
3 used to play
4 ever get used to living
5 were having/eating
6 is used to performing
7 used to be
8 would not spend
9 got used to waking up
10 didn't use to celebrate
11 would bake cakes
12 moved to Krakow a year

Unit 3

1 2 a (past perfect continuous)
3 c (past perfect)
4 b (past perfect)

2 2 e 3 a 4 c 5 b

3 2 had already put
3 Had John finished
4 had been saving
5 had they been walking
6 hadn't flown

4 2 boarded (actions that happened one after the other in the past)
3 been driving (an action that lasted for some time in the past and whose result was visible in the past)
4 had been training (emphasis on the duration of an action which started and finished in the past, before another action or stated time in the past)
5 had forgotten (an action which finished in the past and whose result was visible at a later point in the past)
6 bit (an action which happened at a stated time in the past)

5 2 had booked
3 had heard
4 had been waiting
5 had been jumping
6 had slipped
7 had warned
8 had been chatting

6 2 b 3 a 4 b 5 b

7 2 had finished, wandered (First action: had finished)
3 took, had said (First action: had said)
4 had booked, surprised (First action: had booked)
5 had already learnt, tried (First action: had learnt)

8 2 went
3 had been feeling
4 looked
5 were descending
6 hadn't expected
7 preferred
8 pointed out
9 was tying
10 didn't see
11 lifted
12 had flown
13 had
14 had been recording
15 captured

9 2 A 3 C 4 B 5 A

10 2 got used to
3 used to diving
4 were trekking through
5 had been waiting for
6 went hiking a year ago
7 used to visit Ireland

11 1 the, the
2 The, –, the
3 the, some
4 The, the
5 –, –, –, –
6 the
7 the, the, the
8 a, the, –, –
9 The, –
10 the
11 The, –
12 the, –

12 3 the
4 The
5 –
6 The
7 –
8 –
9 a
10 The
11 an
12 the
13 –
14 the
15 the
16 the
17 –
18 –

13 2 an, a
3 a, the
4 –, –
5 –, the, the, the
6 –, –, –
7 the, The, –

Grammar Book Key

14 3 ✗ ~~had listened~~ listened
4 ✗ ~~got used to jump~~ used to jump
5 ✗ ~~an waterproof jacket~~ a waterproof jacket
6 ✓
7 ✗ ~~would hate~~ used to hate
8 ✗ ~~the Mount Nyiragongo~~ Mount Nyiragongo
9 ✓
10 ✓

15 2 A 3 A 4 A 5 C 6 C 7 B 8 B

Revision A (Units 1-3)

1
1 don't like, are you going, is having
2 has Tara known, have been
3 does the plane arrive, is running
4 Has Jessie finished, has been working
5 is leaving, don't want
6 is Betty's singing getting, has been practising

2
1 didn't drop
2 had lost
3 had you been driving
4 had dried up
5 had been studying
6 was doing
7 wasn't raining
8 did Mike visit

3
1 attended
2 used to love
3 am used
4 didn't use to be
5 grew up
6 weren't used to
7 get used to
8 is used to cooking

4
1 isn't going
2 Do you prefer
3 had just reached
4 was trying
5 didn't go
6 Have you finished
7 have been waiting
8 hadn't been working

5
1 The, –, a, the
2 a, the, the, –
3 –, –, the, a
4 –, the, an
5 The, the, the, the
6 –, the, –, –

6 1 A 2 C 3 B 4 C 5 A 6 C 7 D 8 A 9 D 10 C

7
1 I'm getting used to ~~work~~ **working** night shifts at the hotel.
2 Joan had ~~eaten never~~ **never eaten** a tastier meal in his life.
3 Ian has ~~been~~ **gone** to Adam's house but he'll be back before noon.
4 Liam ~~would~~ **used to** be much fitter when he was at university.
5 Our train hasn't left ~~already~~ **yet**.
6 My cousin has ~~being~~ **been** having quite a lot of trouble with her degree lately.
7 Sean asked the old man whether he had met ~~the~~ **President Kennedy**.
8 The coat you've just put on ~~is belonging~~ **belongs** to me, Jonathan.

8
1 has never been
2 are you being
3 had already finished
4 did not use to play
5 has been exercising fo
6 hasn't been home sinc
7 does not have
8 had been raining

Unit 4

1
2 busy, busier
3 more expensive, the most expensive
4 strong, the strongest
5 good, better
6 lovelier/more lovely, the loveliest/the most lovely
7 little, the least
8 thinner, the thinnest
9 sensible, the most sensible
10 quieter, the quietest

2
2 more slowly, the most slowly
3 harder, the hardest
4 better, the best
5 more seriously, the most seriously
6 farther/further, the farthest/the furthest
7 later, the latest
8 faster, the fastest
9 less, the least
10 more, the most

3
2 a lot
3 by far
4 very
5 even
6 slightly
7 much
8 far

4
1 closer
2 popular, the most commonly
3 the most luxurious, the cheapest
4 the worst, less attractive
5 sooner, more quickly
6 noisier, less

5
2 busy
3 better
4 more peacefully
5 more slowly
6 bigger
7 the most enormous
8 the most amazing
9 the most
10 The nearest
11 farther/further
12 faster
13 best

6 2 a 3 b 4 a 5 b 6 b 7 a 8 a 9 a 10 b

7 2 modern
3 the least affordable
4 worse, worse
5 more slowly, longer
6 nicely
7 big
8 small
9 comfortable
10 further/farther, further/farther
11 the best, better
12 enjoyable

8 2 There
3 It
4 It
5 There
6 There
7 There, It
8 It

9 2 there
3 there
4 there
5 It
6 there
7 It

0 2 by far the most comfortable
3 there is a big fireplace
4 the most eco-friendly
5 cook better than
6 as/so attractive as
7 the most picturesque of
8 it is raining
9 leave the less traffic
10 are more and

Unit 5

1 2 g (future simple)
3 d (present continuous)
4 a (present simple)
5 f (going to)
6 c (going to)
7 b (future simple)

1 2 g (future simple)
3 d (present continuous)
4 a (present simple)
5 f (going to)
6 c (going to)
7 b (future simple)

2 2 'll buy
3 isn't going to attend
4 Will you show
5 won't understand
6 's going to shut down
7 Is Adam going to participate

3 2 are going to start (intention)
3 will emojis replace (prediction based on what we believe)
4 'll message (on-the-spot decision)
5 comes out (timetable)
6 will keep (hope)
7 won't reply (threat)
8 'll be (action that will definitely happen)
9 will become (prediction based on what we believe)
10 Will you send (polite request)

4 2 aren't going to win
3 won't buy
4 will be
5 're meeting
6 does the seminar start
7 won't forgive
8 's going to rain
9 isn't having
10 doesn't start

5 ... My plane ~~is going to leave~~ **leaves** at 4 am on Monday.
... I want to study there and my preferred university ~~will hold~~ **is holding** interviews on Saturday 24th May. I've made all the arrangements and I ~~will stay~~ **am going to stay** with a family while I'm there. ... I'm afraid I ~~am going to get~~ **will get** confused and do ... Perhaps I ~~am looking up~~ **will look up** some information online about ...
I hope I ~~am having~~ **will have** some free time too. The weather forecast predicts it ~~is~~ **is going to be** sunny all week ...

6 2 will be taking
3 won't be attending
4 Will you be driving
5 won't be giving
6 will be communicating
7 Will you be watching, will be working
8 won't be coming

7 2 Will Celia have met Mr Lee by 12?
Yes, she will.
3 Will Celia have eaten lunch by 1:00?
No, she won't. She will have eaten lunch by 2:00.
4 Will Celia have completed the report by 3:00?
Yes, she will.
5 Will Celia have emailed all new clients by 2:30?
No, she won't. She will have emailed all new clients by 4:00.
6 Will Celia have finished the teleconference by 5:00?
No, she won't. She will have finished the teleconference by 6:00.

8 2 won't be meeting
3 won't have prepared
4 Will you have revised
5 will have stopped
6 Will you be working
7 won't be having
8 will be travelling

Grammar Book Key

9
2 will have graduated
3 won't have received
4 Will you be reading
5 won't be teaching
6 won't be using
7 will be giving
8 Will Frank have downloaded

10
2 will be buying, will have bought
3 will be installing, will have installed
4 will have written, will be writing
5 will be preparing, will have prepared
6 will have arranged, will be arranging

11
2 after
3 before
4 As soon as
5 once

12
2 while
3 whenever
4 just as
5 after
6 by the time

13
2 find out
3 are doing
4 turned
5 will the shop deliver

14
2 after, read/have read
3 before, moved
4 as soon as, started
5 Whenever, listens

15
2 C 3 C 4 A 5 B 6 C 7 B 8 A 9 B 10 A 11 B

16
2 is going to take
3 will be
4 will be having/are going to have
5 will send
6 will be launching
7 will have finished
8 will be coming/is coming/is going to come

17
2 is going to call
3 is holding a
4 will not have replied
5 will be giving
6 soon as I go

Unit 6

1
2 i 3 g 4 a 5 f 6 j 7 b 8 e 9 c 10 h

2
2 have to
3 needn't have done
4 had to
5 Were you able to
6 Could, may
7 mustn't
8 might

3
2 need
3 shouldn't
4 don't have to
5 mustn't
6 needs
7 has to
8 ought to

4
2 can't
3 can
4 can
5 shouldn't
6 should

5
2 may
3 mustn't
4 can
5 can't
6 can
7 must

6
2 might
3 Shall
4 can
5 could
6 could
7 Would
8 Can

7
2 couldn't
3 needn't
4 mustn't
5 Would
6 may
7 can
8 must

8
2 didn't need to sit
3 didn't need to go
4 needn't have spent
5 needn't have got
6 didn't need to stay
7 needn't have hired
8 didn't need to reply

9
2 C 3 B 4 B 5 A 6 C 7 A

10
2 must
3 may have told
4 could be
5 might
6 couldn't have said

11
2 may/might/could
3 must
4 can't
5 must
6 can't
7 may/might/could
8 may/might/could

12
2 have turned
3 be sleeping
4 have been doing
5 be working
6 apply
7 have been gossiping
8 have changed
9 move
10 have seen

13
2 have been telling the truth
3 have a part time job
4 have been travelling to York yesterday morning
5 have asked for a pay rise
6 have been thinking about quitting before they fired him
7 go back to her old job
8 be closing down

4 2 Paula may/might/could not have done well in the interview.
3 He can't have renewed his work visa yet.
4 They must be looking for a new art director.
5 Sharon may/might/could have been trying to solve the problem on her own.
6 They must give her a bonus for her hard work.
7 His application may/might/could have got lost in the post.
8 Jenna can't have lied on her CV.

5 2 a 3 a 4 b 5 b

6 2 was able to (ability on a specific occasion in the past)
3 needn't (absence of necessity)
4 must (positive logical assumption)
5 had to (necessity in the past)
6 didn't have to (absence of necessity in the past)
7 would (request)
8 Can (request)
9 might (possibility)
10 can (general possibility)

7 2 can't
3 may/might/could
4 can't
5 Could/Would/Can
6 mustn't/can't
7 didn't have/need to

8 2 You should/ought to be more responsible in your work.
3 Can I/Shall I/Would you like me to drop you off at the airport on my way to work?
4 Amanda doesn't have to/doesn't need to/needn't wear a uniform at the bank.
5 He had to report to work at 7:00 am when he worked at a nursing home.
6 Carol wasn't able to/couldn't find the missing files.
7 Can/May/Could I start work an hour later on Friday?
8 Brad couldn't miss the meeting.

9 2 A 3 B 4 B 5 A 6 A

10 2 B 3 A 4 C 5 A 6 B 7 A 8 B

11 2 A 3 A 4 C 5 B 6 A 7 C 8 A

12 2 was not able to meet
3 can't have been paying
4 mustn't/must not enter
5 might be presenting

Revision B (Units 1-6)

1 1 looks
2 has Peter been avoiding
3 has just moved in
4 are staying
5 seldom comes
6 doesn't share
7 is not getting
8 doesn't depart
9 have you been
10 am I seeing

2 A 1 hadn't been working
2 heard
3 came
4 raced
5 had crashed
6 were exchanging

B 1 invented
2 had been working
3 was sitting
4 heard
5 had ever heard

3 1 better
2 larger
3 more spacious
4 the biggest
5 farther/further
6 more quickly
7 soon
8 more brilliant

4 1 b 2 a 3 a 4 b 5 b 6 a 7 a 8 a

5 1 is going to love
2 leaves
3 Will you make
4 will have finished
5 is introducing
6 be exercising

6 1 won't come
2 will be working
3 won't be
4 won't have completed
5 Will you have eaten
6 will have worked

7 1 gets
2 will hike
3 started
4 will you come
5 Will you cut
6 went

8 1 needn't
2 should
3 can't
4 Would
5 don't have to
6 could
7 can
8 Shall

9 1 I will be having/doing a
2 as soon as I get
3 is going to
4 are not allowed to play
5 will have opened
6 not so inspirational as

Grammar Book Key

Unit 7

1
2 being asked
3 will have been replaced
4 was bought
5 is being installed
6 to be sold
7 had been repaired
8 was being used
9 have been developed
10 be refilled
11 are launched
12 will be announced

2
2 a with — b by
3 a with — b by
4 a by — b with
5 a by — b with

3
2 I've been invited to the new smartphone launch at the TechCentre so I'm going (to go) there.
3 My laptop is being repaired at the shop at the moment and I want to do some research online.
4 Where is this tablet sold?
5 It should be used by all schools.
6 It needs to be repaired.
7 I hope it will be delivered to me on Monday as they said.

4
2 A documentary about the Internet of Things is being filmed by some IT students.
3 The Internet will have been reconnected by noon.
4 Online passwords need to be changed regularly.
5 Who was this application developed by?
6 We are not allowed to use our phones in class.
7 Dan was seen copying the file onto his USB stick by Alex.
8 Our IT project must be handed in by Friday.

5
2 f What is a chatbot designed to do?
A chatbot is designed to mimic humans.
3 b When was the World Science Festival founded?
The World Science Festival was founded in 2008.
4 a Who was the TV invented by?
The TV was invented by Baird, Farnsworth and Jenkins.
5 d How many emails are exchanged every day?
About 300 billion emails are exchanged every day.
6 e Where was the Internet created?
The Internet was created in the USA.

6
2 George will be given a company phone by Brian.
A company phone will be given to George by Brian.
3 Mum is being taught Internet slang by my brother.
Internet slang is being taught to Mum by my brother.
4 Our school has been offered ten new laptops by a local company.
Ten new laptops have been offered to our school by a local company.
5 The technician must be paid fifty pounds by Jennife
Fifty pounds must be paid to the technician by Jennifer.
6 I was read the report on digital marketing by Sue.
The report on digital marketing was read to me by Sue.

7
2 being forced
3 has just been made
4 is being spent
5 have been/are registered
6 be used
7 will be/is charged

8
2 It is believed that he is developing a new app.
He is believed to be developing a new app.
3 It is reported that the new software is useful.
The new software is reported to be useful.
4 It is expected that he will launch the new app soo
He is expected to launch the new app soon.
5 It is considered that he is an expert developer.
He is considered to be an expert developer.
6 It is known that a virus deleted the files.
A virus is known to have deleted the files.
7 It is understood that he has created a new comput system.
He is understood to have created a new compute system.
8 It is said that he is writing a book about the IoT.
He is said to be writing a book about the IoT.

9
2 Steve was using the tablet all morning.
3 I saw the technician controlling the robotic arm.
4 Which company designed this phone?
5 The IT programmer will have completed the app b the end of the week.
6 Sarah updates the cooking blog every week.
7 Everyone will use shopping apps in the future.

10
2 are having
3 had
4 has ... had
5 have
6 have
7 will have
8 was having

11
2 b
3 a
4 a
5 b

12
2 has already had her report published.
3 will have their robots built in Japan.
4 must have my laptop fixed by Wednesday.
5 doesn't like having things on her desk rearranged.
6 are having our wireless speakers repaired.
7 had my new tablet delivered yesterday.
8 had/got her phone stolen (by a pickpocket).

Grammar Book Key

3 2 had a meeting set up
3 will have some research done
4 have it tested
5 to have the app approved
6 have had all my apps accepted

4 2 Greg is having voice-activated lights fitted in his flat.
3 They had/got their camera shop broken into last night.
4 Sam wants to have the computer files organised.
5 She had had an e-shop created.
6 He had been having his house renovated for months.

5 2 Will Bruce have Jason connect his Wi-Fi?
3 Lee got Philip to download a fitness app.
4 Tim made me buy him an e-reader.
5 Adam will have the computer shop deliver his new hard drive on Wednesday.
6 Mary got Mark to lend her his MP3 player.
7 Will you make the shop give you a refund?
8 Roger had his grandson show him how to send a text message.

6 2 herself
3 himself
4 itself
5 herself
6 ourselves

7 2 d (emphatic)
3 e (reflexive)
4 g (reflexive)
5 h (emphatic)
6 a (reflexive)
7 f (reflexive)
8 c (reflexive)

8 2 taught himself how to create apps
3 herself emailed the inventor
4 designed this laptop case myself
5 behaved themselves
6 herself caused the problem

9 2 hurt myself
3 burnt himself
4 relax
5 was concentrating
6 introduced herself

0 2 itself
3 themselves
4 ourselves
5 himself

1 3 ✗ ~~cut by herself~~ cut herself
4 ✓
5 ✗ ~~will be gave~~ will be given
6 ✓
7 ✗ ~~It is believe~~ It is believed
8 ✓

22 2 had been fixed
3 to have been caused
4 am not allowed to
5 had to be completed
6 got his computer system upgraded
7 is expected to be launched
8 being told

Unit 8

1 2 if
3 Unless
4 When
5 Unless
6 if
7 Unless
8 when

2 2 d (2nd conditional)
3 b (1st conditional)
4 e (2nd conditional)
5 a (0 conditional)
6 h (3rd conditional)
7 c (1st conditional)
8 f (3rd conditional)

3 2 would have paid
3 go
4 wouldn't have known
5 will continue
6 would help
7 carry on
8 would have felt

4 2 will need
3 employ
4 not have started
5 wouldn't have met
6 are sometimes given
7 didn't do
8 would have tried
9 won't be punished
10 hadn't been staring

5 1 sells
2 were, would take
3 hadn't reminded, would have forgotten
4 use, save
5 get, affects

6 2 If I make a list of my chores, I won't forget them.
3 If I had called Amy, she would have come.
4 If there are any problems, I tell the coordinator.
5 If Jo's car hadn't broken down, she wouldn't have been late.
6 If we had enough money, we would renovate the building.

7 2 had read
3 close
4 will suffer
5 might not have overcome
6 don't get
7 joined
8 cuts down on

8 2 fills in
3 had had
4 would have learnt
5 were
6 would try
7 turns
8 gets
9 will introduce
10 didn't live
11 would need

Grammar Book Key

9 2 I wish I had some food for him.
3 I wish there was/were an animal shelter nearby.
4 I wish people would stop abandoning their pets.
5 I wish someone would give him a home soon.

10 2 I wish they'd given me enough/more warning.
3 I wish I'd had time to look for another job.
4 I wish I hadn't spent all my savings on a new car.
5 I wish I hadn't taken this job.

11 2 knew
3 wouldn't use
4 could send
5 wouldn't argue
6 hadn't refused
7 would turn down
8 wasn't/weren't leaving

12 2 hadn't ignored
3 could find
4 wouldn't bully
5 had
6 weren't studying
7 weren't used
8 had paid
9 hadn't put on
10 wouldn't always complain

13 2 I wish/If only Lucy wouldn't make fun of other people.
3 I wish/If only I was/were confident enough to become a teacher.
4 I wish/If only there were eco-friendly buses in my town.
5 I wish/If only I had taken part in the protest about racism.
6 I wish/If only you wouldn't make nasty comments about your brother's weight.
7 I wish/If only the drought would end.
8 I wish/If only I hadn't dropped out of secondary school.

14 2 I wish my friends had paid their bank loan.
If my friends had paid their bank loan, they wouldn't have lost their home.
3 I wish I had a job with an NGO.
If I had a job with an NGO, I would work in refugee camps.
4 I wish I hadn't been addicted to junk food when I was a teenager.
If I hadn't been addicted to junk food when I was a teenager, I wouldn't have been overweight.
5 I wish Harry didn't live on the streets.
If Harry didn't live on the streets, he could get a job and rent a flat.
6 I wish there was/were a bottle bank in my town.
If there was/were a bottle bank in my town, I could recycle empty bottles.
7 I wish some owners wouldn't abuse their pets.
If owners abuse their pets, they should be put in prison.
8 I wish Ally had dealt with her stress.
If Ally had dealt with her stress, it wouldn't have seriously affected her health.
9 I wish junk food didn't cost so little.
If junk food didn't cost so little, people wouldn't be able to afford to eat it very often.
10 I wish video games weren't highly addictive.
If video games weren't highly addictive, I could sto playing them.

15 2 g 3 i 4 h 5 f 6 b 7 j 8 d 9 a 10 e

16 2 didn't he
3 aren't I
4 did she
5 don't you
6 will you
7 isn't it
8 shall we
9 do they
10 will/won't you
11 haven't you
12 will he

17 2 will have finished, won't you
3 volunteer, shall we
4 had already met, hadn't she
5 am not doing, am I
6 don't travel, do they
7 didn't know, did he
8 reported, isn't it

18 2 shall we
3 am I
4 aren't they
5 do they
6 didn't you
7 won't she
8 have you
9 will you
10 did he

19 2 wouldn't leave
3 will you
4 would do
5 had talked
6 get
7 shall we
8 hasn't she
9 Unless
10 could put

20 2 Unless we get more money, the soup kitchen w have to close.
3 I wish I could spend more time at the animal shelte
4 Let's set up a helpline for gaming addiction, sha we?
5 Millions of people around the world wouldr become ill every day if they had clean drinking wate
6 If only all companies paid female staff fairly.
7 If you go to the obesity seminar next week, I'll com with you.
8 I wish I hadn't ignored the advice my doctor gave m

Grammar Book Key

9 This is the best way to help areas affected by the famine, isn't it?
10 Help me fill in this form, will/won't you?

1 2 B 3 A 4 A 5 B 6 B 7 B 8 C 9 B 10 A

2 2 were you, I would
3 wish I'd had
4 he had done something
5 don't take action
6 only Jack had asked
7 only you would
8 wouldn't have fallen through
9 had been able to
10 he were confident
11 had some money
12 we don't spread the

Unit 9

1 2 to submit 3 to leave 4 to tell 5 to install 6 use 7 to do 8 to argue 9 submit 10 to watch

2 2 to realise 3 to share 4 perform 5 return 6 to walk 7 take

3 2 solve
3 concentrating
4 to scan
5 getting
6 researching
7 to do
8 to receive
9 studying
10 Reading
11 damaging/having damaged
12 work

4 2 revising 3 lying 4 practising 5 try 6 to play 7 doing 8 change

5 2 watching, having seen
3 to have been teaching
4 be submitted
5 to have been erased
6 being named

6 2 starring
3 to say
4 passing up/having passed up
5 restarting
6 to concentrate
7 writing
8 to buy
9 telling
10 knowing

7 2 To begin 3 be 4 to attend 5 checking 6 to see 7 to fit 8 studying 9 working 10 make 11 to do 12 to find out

8 2 a 3 b 4 b 5 a 6 a 7 a 8 a

9 2 B 3 C 4 C 5 B 6 C

10 2 looking forward to starting
3 has difficulty (in) learning
4 to have been studying
5 being lied to
6 to be working

11 2 b, where
3 h, whose
4 d, why
5 e, whose
6 g, whom
7 a, which/that
8 c, where

12 2 where, b
3 when, b
4 which, b
5 who, a
6 whose, b
7 which, b

13 2 Last month, when it celebrated its 30th anniversary, the museum announced a series of new exhibitions. /The museum announced a series of new exhibitions last month, when it celebrated its 30th anniversary.
3 The museum has a special exhibition where you can learn about the new technology used in education.
4 At this exhibition you can see new apps whose purpose is to make learning easier.
5 During the exhibition, you have the chance to meet people who are leading experts in technology.
6 At the museum, there will be a special place where you can use AR-enabled textbooks.
7 Another reason why I'd like to go is that they will also be giving away free gifts.

14 2 who/that D (cannot be omitted – no commas)
3 which ND (cannot be omitted – comma after 'museum' and after 'free')
4 where D (cannot be omitted – no commas)
5 which D (can be omitted – no commas)
6 why D (can be omitted – no commas)
7 when D (can be omitted – no commas)
8 whose D (cannot be omitted – no commas)
9 who ND (cannot be omitted – comma after 'Jane' and after 'friend')
10 where ND (cannot be omitted – comma after 'Brisbane' and after 'lives')

Grammar Book Key

15 2 Friday is the day which we're taking a school trip on.
Friday is the day we're taking a school trip on.
Friday is the day when we're taking a school trip.
3 That's the university which she teaches at.
That's the university she teaches at.
That's the university where she teaches.
4 I can't find the paper which I wrote down your phone number on.
I can't find the paper I wrote down your phone number on.
I can't find the paper where I wrote down your phone number.
5 That's the classroom which we do ICT in.
That's the classroom we do ICT in.
That's the classroom where we do ICT.

16 2 both of whom
3 none of which
4 half of whom
5 some of whom
6 most of which

17 2 Lynn goes to a school in London where they use interactive whiteboards.
3 I have a sister whose name is Christina.
4 There is a mistake in this sentence which/that you need to correct.
5 Our school has a science lab where/in which we do science experiments.
6 The reason why he missed class yesterday was that he was ill.
7 Mr Sinclair is a Science teacher who/that gives very interesting lessons.
8 He'll never forget the day when/on which he won an award for his ICT project.

18 2 when
3 where
4 whose
5 why
6 which/that
7 where
8 who/that

19 2 ~~getting~~ to get
3 ~~start~~ starting
4 ~~to jog~~ jogging
5 ~~when~~ which
6 ~~who~~ whom
7 ~~being~~ to be
8 ~~to argue~~ arguing
9 ~~that~~ which
10 ~~which~~ who/that
11 ~~to be~~ being

20 2 A
3 B
4 A
5 B
6 C
7 B
8 A

21 2 he prefers walking to catching
3 only to be informed
4 you mind repeating
5 remember having paid
6 would rather have bought
7 who is my cousin
8 are not allowed to check
9 reason why she was
10 who I waved at
11 is no point (in) spending
12 whose aunt is

Revision C (Units 1-9)

1 1 has gone, Do you want
2 used to travel, stopped
3 had been surfing
4 aren't going to find
5 's been living, isn't used to
6 arrive, will have finished
7 was jogging, saw
8 had grown
9 Do you have, 'm putting
10 'll be sitting, 'll be

2 1 the most sweetly
2 harder, more
3 worse
4 better, the most beautiful
5 as tall, heavier
6 healthier, healthier
7 less
8 farther/further

3 1 You needn't have bought me a gift, but thank you.
2 We must report this to the manager.
3 We had to pay excess baggage because our suitcase was too heavy.
4 Shall I help you set up your email account?
5 He can't have quit his job.
6 May I leave my bike on your driveway?

4 1 is believed to have stolen her ideas
2 will the charity event be organised by
3 is said that she's doing a good job
4 has been given a pay rise by Mr Smithers
5 will have been finished by noon
6 was offered £1,000

5 1 is having a burglar alarm installed
2 has had three bones broken
3 are not having/are not going to have our house painted
4 have my computer upgraded

5 did you have your hair cut
6 are/will be having the air conditioning serviced

6
1 Would you stop
2 will have
3 floods
4 would have called
5 won't stay
6 hadn't found
7 helped
8 comes

7
1 I hadn't crashed my car
2 I could go on holiday
3 you wouldn't make all that noise
4 I had prepared well for my driving test
5 my oldest friend wasn't/weren't moving away
6 I didn't get dizzy on theme park rides

8
1 being told
2 to pay
3 to be feeling
4 to have met
5 getting
6 have given
7 opening
8 to be made

9
1 Ian's moving back to Bolton, where he was born.
2 No one wants to go to Cornwall on holiday again, which I think is a shame.
3 There's the professor who teaches Ancient Egyptian Studies.
4 Joanne is one of my colleagues whose fashion sense I really admire.
5 June 9th was the day when our son first walked.
6 This is the recipe that I use to make bread.

10
1 Are you enjoying ~~yourselves~~ **yourself**, Adam?
2 How can I get to ~~the~~ Hyde Park?
3 I can't ~~to~~ concentrate with all this noise.
4 Don't laugh, ~~won't~~ **will** you?
5 Would you like **a** cup of tea?
6 He hasn't got a boat, ~~does~~ **has** he?
7 Tom ~~itself~~ **himself** told me what happened.
8 Let's go for a walk, ~~will~~ **shall** we?

11
1 was given a promotion by
2 had woken up
3 wish I had called
4 are having the grass cut
5 must have been playing

Unit 10

1 2 said 3 speaks 4 talk 5 told

2 2 said 3 tell 4 told 5 said

3
2 say
3 Speak
4 said
5 told
6 Ask
7 talking

4
2 he, my
3 she, her
4 she, her
5 their, them
6 he, she, their

5
2 didn't know – "I don't know to recycle used batteries."
3 would – "I will lend you some (gloves)."
4 had run – "We have run out (of LED light bulbs)."/ 'They/The LED light bulbs have run out."
5 was going – "I'm going to the library."
6 hadn't read – "I haven't read it yet."

6
2 Lily said (that) I wouldn't have to do the dishes that night.
3 Jim said to his son (that) he would be able to drive him to school the following/next day / the day after.
4 I told Ann (that) she could leave her bike there.
5 I said (that) Lee must have worked late the previous day/the day before.
6 Jacob said to Mariah (that) they wouldn't have to bring lunch with them to the clean-up the following week.
7 Owen said to Emma (that) he might become a vegan.

7
2 Olga said (that) she wouldn't have known about the tree planting day if Mike hadn't told her. (tense does not change – type 3 conditional)
3 Christa said (that) she was thinking about joining Greenpeace. (tense changes – the introductory verb is in a past tense; out-of-date reporting)
4 The zookeeper said that butterflies help/helped the environment by pollinating flowers. (tense changes or remains the same – law of nature)
5 Jon said (that) if he had more free time he would make a bee home for his garden. (tense does not change – type 2 conditional)
6 Andrew said to me that giraffes lived in trees. (tense changes – we consider what the speaker said to be untrue)

8
2 Janet asked Timothy where the nearest recycling centre was.
3 Paul wanted to know how many people had signed up for the beach clean-up day.
4 Celia asked her roommate if/whether he/she would help her sort out the recyclables.
5 Patrick enquired who was organising the environmental awareness event that year.
6 Kate wondered if/whether teabags went in the compost bin or the paper recycling bin.
7 Brian asked them if/whether they had been picking up litter all morning.

Grammar Book Key

8 Timothy asked his teacher if/whether he should print out the flyers for the following month's park clean-up.
9 Louis asked me if/whether I saw/had seen any elephants at the sanctuary in Thailand.

9 2 Ben asked how long she had been working on her current project.
3 Ben wanted to know if/whether she had ever thought about doing a TV series about her work.
4 Ben wondered if/whether she was planning to write another book soon.
5 Ben asked what she thought the biggest threat to the environment was.
6 Ben enquired if/whether in her opinion people would finally manage to save all those endangered species from extinction.

10 2 Greg suggested watching the nature documentary.
3 The teacher ordered everyone to sit down.
4 The police officer commanded the man to pick up his litter immediately.
5 She begged him to help her.
6 She ordered her daughter to turn off the TV and go to bed immediately.
7 My sister suggested that we (should) buy organic fruits and vegetables from then on.
8 Joe asked Sandra to show him how to make a birdhouse.
9 The judge commanded everybody to be quiet in the courtroom.
10 My housemate asked me to get some LED light bulbs from the shop.

11 2 She suggested going over the safety tips.
3 She asked them to use a litter picking stick.
4 She told them to put the litter in the black bin bags.
5 She told them not to go beyond the park limits.
6 She asked them to take photos so that they could post them on their social media pages.
7 She suggested that they (should) put on sunscreen and wear their hats at all times.
8 She told them to meet her back there at three o'clock.

12 2 him to move his car away from the ambulance zone
3 losing/having lost Ben's keys
4 how he could save/to save money on electricity
5 Adam to add the food scraps to the compost bin and close the lid
6 that it was a fantastic garden
7 Cynthia that the carpool left at 8:30 from West Street
8 Alison and her family to spend the weekend at their summer house

13 2 Adam encouraged his uncle to sign up for the charity race.
3 He insisted on me/my asking around before deciding which solar panels I would have installed
4 Dave wondered which greengrocer's in his area sold organic vegetables.
5 Andrew suggested to Donna that she should see a doctor about her headaches.
6 Eve claimed to have given/that she had given a talk on the environment at an international conference the month before/the previous month.
7 Dinah explained to Sandra how to turn a plastic bottle into a plant pot.

14 2 warned 3 suggested 4 admitted 5 informed 6 explained 7 complained

15 2 suggested getting something to eat then
3 boasted that she had collected/boasted about collecting/having collected the most bags of rubbish
4 Brad offered to help carry Ivy's bags
5 reminded them to put their bags next to the gate

16 2 Helen boasted that she made/about making the best vegan dishes in town.
3 Andrew apologised to Maria for borrowing her camera without asking (her).
4 The park warden ordered/told us not to give/forbade us to give the ducks any bread.
5 Phil refused to discuss what happened/had happened.
6 The hotel guest demanded to change rooms immediately.

17 2 threatened not to give 3 allowed us to plant 4 about being 5 begged me to let him 6 urged Ted to read his 7 agreed to install

Unit 11

1 2 whole 3 every other 4 both 5 either

2 2 another 3 each other 4 all 5 none 6 whole

3 2 None of the bath products we want are on sale in this cosmetics shop.
3 Both the shopping centre and the high street shops currently have sales on.
4 The whole shop is filled with customers.
5 Neither the bookshop nor the supermarket accepts returns without a receipt.
6 Every one of us shops at the winter sales.

Grammar Book Key

4 2 both of 3 neither of 4 another 5 whole 6 All 7 every 8 either

5 2 C 3 B 4 B 5 A 6 C 7 A 8 C

6 2 a little 3 too many 4 hardly any 5 any 6 some

7 2 several 3 plenty 4 a couple of 5 a bit of

8 2 many 3 lots of 4 a few 5 much 6 any 7 both 8 few

9 2 many 3 much 4 plenty 5 no 6 little

0 2 bowl 3 glass 4 packet 5 piece 6 slices 7 jar 8 bars

1 2 any 3 some 4 every 5 no 6 any 7 no 8 any 9 some 10 every

2
1 some
2 none
3 everyone/everybody, somewhere
4 anywhere, no
5 no one/nobody
6 something

3 2 B 3 B 4 C 5 B 6 A 7 C 8 B 9 A 10 B

4
2 ~~each~~ every
3 ~~so~~ such
4 ~~much~~ many
5 ~~so~~ such
6 ~~every~~ each
7 ~~all~~ both
8 ~~some~~ any
9 ~~nothing~~ anything
10 ~~How~~ What

5
2 wasn't anyone who
3 were very few
4 aren't enough
5 with a lot of
6 not eat anything
7 living somewhere where
8 hasn't got much/doesn't have much

Unit 12

1 2 though 3 Still/However 4 In spite 5 However/Still 6 Even though 7 despite

2
2 too much sugar is bad for our health, we still consume a lot of it
3 many health benefits, running can be bad for your knees
4 Kim is a vegan, her whole family eats meat
5 Mark is allergic to dairy products, he ate a piece of cheesecake
6 warning labels on energy drinks, children still drink too many of them

3 2 in order 3 to prevent it 4 could 5 have 6 so that 7 with a view to 8 so as not to get

4
2 Mark's taken up cooking lessons with a view to becoming a better cook.
3 The restaurant has created a new menu to offer vegetarians more choices.
4 The school has a qualified nurse in case students get sick.
5 She takes short breaks from sitting at her desk to avoid getting backache.

5 2 so 3 such an 4 so 5 such 6 such 7 so 8 So 9 such a 10 such 11 such an 12 such a

6
2 Lucy's dentist was on holiday and consequently she couldn't see him.
3 There were such a lot of vegetarian options on the menu that Celia couldn't decide what to order.
4 Mark developed an allergy to nuts so he stopped eating them.
5 So few people turned up to the yoga class that the instructor cancelled it.
6 Bill hurt his ankle and therefore he was unable to take part in the race.

7 2 Now that 3 The reason for 4 because 5 on account of 6 as 7 since 8 for

8 2 Now that 3 due to 4 The reason for 5 since

Grammar Book Key

9 2 Pesticides should be banned for they cause soil and water pollution.
3 The reason why I get up at 6:00 am is that I want to have time for jogging before I go to work.
4 Due to the extra interest in yoga classes, there will be another one on Tuesdays.
5 The reason for my trip to Asia/The reason for me/my going to Asia was to research traditional Chinese medicine.
6 I don't eat meat due to the fact that animal farming contributes to global warming.
7 We cancelled our hike because of the rain.
8 Since Christina feels very stressed, she doesn't sleep well at night./Christina doesn't sleep well at night since she feels very stressed.
9 I started cycling to work as I wanted to get more exercise./As I wanted to get more exercise, I started cycling to work.
10 Now that Brandon has hurt his arm, he can't play tennis as well as he used to./Brandon can't play tennis as well as he used to now that he has hurt his arm.

10 2 a 3 b 4 b 5 a 6 b

11 2 consequently
3 in order to
4 due to the fact that
5 Despite
6 so as not to
7 while
8 so that

12 2 Paul has so much work that he'll stay late at the office.
3 Poultry is high in protein whereas it's low in fat.
4 Sam had to go to hospital on his holiday because of getting food poisoning.
5 We booked our tickets a month in advance in order not to miss the show.
6 I pack my own lunch for work so that I will spend less money.
7 Our local hospital has a lot of good doctors. Nevertheless, it has a shortage of nursing staff.
8 Susan started going to the local gym twice a week since she wanted to do some weight training.

13 2 because of
3 much
4 Yet
5 so many
6 prevent
7 as
8 absolutely

14 2 B 3 C 4 A 5 B 6 C 7 C 8 B

15 2 in case he got
3 in spite of being
4 in order to
5 on account of his
6 so little space
7 and as a consequence
8 due to his
9 the reason for
10 such interesting information that
11 to avoid going
12 with a view to inviting

Revision D (Units 1-12)

1 1 plays
2 went
3 think
4 won't be having
5 will fail
6 used to
7 gonc
8 Was it raining
9 hadn't left
10 is giving

2 1 the most expensive
2 further / farther
3 the most quickly
4 healthier
5 the worst

3 1 might
2 didn't have to
3 was able to
4 Would
5 must

4 1 is having it repaired
2 all the tickets had been sold
3 it has been postponed
4 is having her nails done
5 have it checked
6 will have been delivered

5 1 have climbed
2 running
3 to be performing
4 living
5 to test

6 1 had
2 gets
3 hadn't spent
4 hadn't studied
5 wouldn't be
6 finish
7 could
8 won

7 1 Iris said (that) she was thinking about moving house the following/next year.
2 My daughter begged me to let her adopt the pupp
3 Paul informed/told me (that) he wouldn't have enough time to cook dinner that night.
4 Frank offered to bring some food over.
5 The café owner asked the customers if they had their own coffee cups.

Grammar Book Key

6 Judith accused the man of stealing/having stolen her bag.
7 Tina asked me where I had bought my shoes.
8 Carlton refused to share details of the meeting with us.

8 1 C 2 A 3 B 4 A 5 B 6 C 7 C 8 B 9 C 10 C

9
1 All flights were delayed due to fog.
2 The town let off fireworks for Independence Day.
3 Despite the fact that Louis hates chess/Despite Louis' hatred for chess/Despite Louis hating chess, Charlotte made him play with her.
4 The river was full of rubbish so we couldn't go fishing.
5 It was such an expensive smartphone that I decided not to buy it.
6 Danny opened the windows to let in some fresh air.
7 Nora recycles since she cares about the environment./Since Nora cares about the environment, she recycles.
8 Although Simon doesn't like the theatre, he went to see a play. /Simon went to see a play although he doesn't like the theatre.

0
1 have never been completed
2 seemed to have hurt
3 in order not to upset
4 wish I had not failed/wish I had passed
5 on account of

Word Formation

1 1 amazing 2 scenic 3 beautiful 4 migration 5 comfortable 6 impressive 7 lucky 8 sailor

2 1 creatively 2 convertible 3 occupant 4 easily 5 basis 6 craftsmanship 7 original 8 awareness

3 1 friendly 2 truly 3 shocked 4 basic 5 typical 6 accidental 7 introduction 8 carefully

4 1 industrial 2 information 3 analysis 4 actions 5 normally 6 endless

5 1 angrily 2 Hopefully 3 sympathetically 4 reasonably 5 strangely 6 publicly 7 truly

6 1 beautician 2 guitarist 3 participants 4 historian 5 designer 6 interviewee 7 director 8 artist 9 cyclists 10 residents

7 1 distance 2 silence 3 Jealousy 4 coverage 5 inquiries 6 fitness 7 security 8 development

8 1 dissatisfied 2 unlikely 3 irregular 4 inconvenient 5 illiterate 6 impossible 7 insecure 8 dishonest 9 disapproving 10 immoral

9 1 deactivate 2 illogical 3 uninstall 4 inability 5 impatient 6 disadvantage

10 1 majestic 2 attractive 3 excellent 4 decorative 5 classical 6 charming 7 luxurious 8 active

11 1 wonderful 2 friendliness 3 welcoming 4 famous 5 performances 6 talented

12 1 hiking 2 marvellous 3 fascinating 4 archaeological 5 lovely 6 speechless 7 natural 8 adventurous 9 transatlantic 10 bitterly

13 1 traditional 2 annually 3 healthy 4 tasty 5 colourful 6 absolutely 7 authenticity 8 misunderstood 9 unforgettable 10 enthusiastic

14 1 promotion 2 musician 3 subconscious 4 cooperation 5 advantageous 6 potentially

15 1 students 2 semicircle 3 confusion 4 violent 5 ensure 6 safety 7 retrace 8 return 9 outrun 10 embarrassed

16 1 Illustrator 2 writer(s) 3 trainee 4 novelist 5 electrician 6 owner

17 1 hugely 2 busily 3 intention 4 forgetful 5 enable 6 living

Grammar Book Key

18 1 visualise 2 dimensional 3 various 4 interact 5 statistical 6 creative

19 1 undercooked 2 preview 3 triangle 4 non-alcoholic 5 unicycle 6 overheats 7 monolingual 8 neighbourhood 9 originate 10 bimonthly 11 arrival 12 refreshments 13 conclusion 14 foolish

Phrasal verbs

1 1 out 2 up 3 off 4 out 5 off/up 6 up 7 off 8 off

2 1 off 2 into 3 up 4 away 5 up 6 away 7 out 8 off

3 1 back 2 out for 3 around 4 over 5 through 6 back 7 out for 8 over/through

4 1 on 2 in 3 away 4 up 5 into 6 on 7 up 8 in

5 1 up 2 down 3 from 4 out 5 on 6 down 7 out 8 from

6 1 up 2 in 3 up 4 out 5 in/out 6 in 7 up 8 in/out

7 1 by 2 off 3 out 4 off 5 off 6 out 7 by 8 off

8 1 out 2 behind 3 in with 4 through 5 behind 6 apart 7 in with 8 apart

9 1 up on 2 off 3 out 4 out 5 up on 6 in 7 in 8 out

10 1 off 2 out 3 off 4 for 5 off 6 up 7 for 8 up

11 1 after 2 for 3 after 4 in 5 back 6 off 7 for 8 for

12 1 off 2 out for 3 off 4 in 5 down on 6 down on 7 off 8 off

Revision: Phrasal verbs

1 1 C 2 D 3 B 4 B 5 A 6 D 7 A 8 D 9 A 10 C

2 1 off 2 away 3 back 4 on 5 up 6 in 7 in with 8 in 9 up 10 off

3 1 out 2 into 3 over 4 into 5 out 6 out 7 out 8 through 9 off 10 out

Key word transformation

1 spite of being
2 each (one) of the
3 agreed to walk my
4 suggests building a/suggests that we build a
5 were you, I would hire
6 was painted with
7 you like me to put
8 not have prepared
9 more you study, the better
10 is no point in/us/our attending
11 Julian played football was when
12 came to an
13 has not travelled abroad since
14 did not use to like
15 had never been on/had never had
16 as big as
17 as soon as I read
18 might be talking
19 got his car scratched
20 had not fallen out with
21 whose car was
22 promised to return my/promised she would return my
23 did not pay much
24 cut down on
25 as not to
26 both of which/but both of them
27 accused Ben of leaving/having left
28 was a relief to
29 was not raining, we would
30 on his own
31 to be filled in
32 can't have been making
33 more and more families
34 did not stop complaining

Grammar Book Key

5 has not been hiking since
6 not been to Naples for
7 rarely goes
8 were having a meeting when
9 had been looking for
0 is by far the kindest
1 will be flying to
2 did not need to
3 reported to have been hanging
4 wishes she had accepted
5 where (we want) to go
6 denied calling Mary the night
7 were few people
8 news was so exciting that
9 despite the fact that
0 how many guests you are
1 I should wash
2 not necessary to water
3 wish I could take
4 like being given
5 until I have
6 not spicy enough
7 keep up the good
8 he would go
9 far is it from
0 has been snowing for
1 get used to living
2 had been driving for
3 the least interesting of
4 will have started
5 was not able to fix
6 be allowed to make
7 you would not interrupt/would stop interrupting
8 who/that drive carefully
9 wondered why Allan had quit
0 park the car anywhere you
1 in case it gets
2 call you back
3 who I share secrets with
4 looking forward to presenting
5 unless you exercise every
6 must have written
7 are still having/eating
8 have lived in London for
9 were blown away
0 had cleaned our flat by
1 cook as well as
2 ought to be
3 as a consequence he
4 with a view to volunteering

85 not tell anyone
86 had more/enough people, we would
87 to get his office decorated
88 must be delivered
89 am seeing my dentist
90 the fastest you can

Prepositions of Place/ Movement/Time

1

1	C	4	C	7	B	10	A	13	A	16	B
2	A	5	C	8	B	11	B	14	C		
3	B	6	A	9	C	12	A	15	B		

2

1	–, at	8	in, on
2	in, –	9	at, –, at, in
3	in, –	10	on, at
4	on, at	11	–
5	at, on	12	in, on
6	in, –	13	–, on
7	in, at	14	in, at, –

Verbs/Adjectives/Nouns with Prepositions

1

1	on	6	to	11	of	16	for
2	in	7	by	12	in	17	in
3	to	8	with	13	in	18	on
4	in	9	in	14	over	19	with
5	of	10	in	15	for	20	on

2

1	at	6	about	11	about	16	with
2	of	7	to	12	out	17	in
3	across	8	by	13	for	18	to
4	on	9	by	14	to	19	in
5	from	10	on	15	on	20	as

3

1	A	4	C	7	B	10	B	13	A
2	B	5	C	8	C	11	B	14	B
3	A	6	A	9	A	12	C		

4

1 on, by, by
2 to, to, about
3 between, to, on
4 in, in, of
5 by, for, in
6 for, to, under
7 with, on, of
8 with, within, with

Grammar Book Key

Revision

1

1 on	10 of	19 of
2 out of	11 at	20 to
3 of	12 on	21 from
4 of	13 by	22 on
5 from	14 on	23 about
6 with	15 into	24 of
7 about	16 with	25 of
8 at	17 into	
9 in	18 at	

2

1 by	4 for	7 on
2 at	5 to	8 under
3 from	6 in	

3

1 b	3 h	5 g	7 e	9 i
2 f	4 a	6 c	8 j	10 d

4

1 on	5 in	9 with
2 to	6 of	10 about
3 of	7 for	11 in
4 on	8 of	

5

1 of/about	4 for	7 to
2 at	5 with	8 at
3 as	6 for	

6

1 B	4 C	7 A	10 C	13 C
2 A	5 A	8 A	11 B	14 C
3 B	6 C	9 B	12 A	15 C

Progress Test A (Units 1-3)

1 B	7 C	13 A	19 B
2 C	8 D	14 A	20 A
3 C	9 D	15 A	
4 B	10 D	16 C	
5 D	11 B	17 B	
6 C	12 A	18 B	

Progress Test B (Units 4-6)

1 A	6 D	11 B	16 B
2 D	7 A	12 C	17 A
3 B	8 C	13 A	18 A
4 C	9 C	14 C	19 C
5 C	10 D	15 D	20 D

Progress Test C (Units 1-6)

1 C	6 B	11 A	16 D
2 B	7 C	12 C	17 B
3 D	8 D	13 A	18 C
4 A	9 A	14 D	19 B
5 D	10 B	15 D	20 C

Progress Test D (Units 7-9)

1 D	6 A	11 A	16 C
2 B	7 B	12 A	17 D
3 C	8 D	13 D	18 C
4 C	9 C	14 B	19 A
5 B	10 C	15 B	20 A

Progress Test E (Units 10-12)

1 A	6 C	11 D	16 B
2 A	7 C	12 B	17 A
3 D	8 B	13 D	18 D
4 B	9 A	14 C	19 D
5 C	10 A	15 D	20 A

Progress Test F (Units 1-12)

1 B	6 B	11 A	16 B
2 A	7 B	12 D	17 C
3 B	8 D	13 C	18 C
4 C	9 A	14 A	19 B
5 A	10 B	15 B	20 B